Debating Human Rights

Debating
Human
Rights

Daniel P. L. Chong

LYNNE
RIENNER
PUBLISHERS

BOULDER
LONDON

Published in the United States of America in 2014 by
Lynne Rienner Publishers, Inc.
1800 30th Street, Boulder, Colorado 80301
www.rienner.com

and in the United Kingdom by
Lynne Rienner Publishers, Inc.
Gray's Inn House, 127 Clerkenwell Road, London EC1 5 DB

Library of Congress Cataloging-in-Publication Data
Chong, Daniel P. L.
Debating human rights / Daniel P. L. Chong.
    pages cm
Includes bibliographical references and index.
ISBN 978-1-62637-046-3 (hc : alk. paper)
ISBN 978-1-62637-047-0 (pb : alk. paper)
    1. Human rights—History. 2. Human rights—Philosophy.
3. Civil rights. I. Title.
JC571.C5534 2014
323—dc23

                                                    2013043448

British Cataloguing in Publication Data
A Cataloguing in Publication record for this book
is available from the British Library.

Printed and bound in the United States of America

The paper used in this publication meets the requirements
of the American National Standard for Permanence of
Paper for Printed Library Materials Z39.48-1992.

5   4   3

Contents

Acknowledgments

This book would not have been possible without the participation of my undergraduate students at Rollins College. Many of the debates featured in the book began as an activity for my International Human Rights course, in which students had to choose a side and defend it to the best of their ability. Over the years, my students have approached this assignment with enthusiasm and professionalism. They researched the issues thoroughly, argued their positions passionately, and treated their opponents with respect. Some of the research that they conducted laid the groundwork for the arguments in the pages that follow. Although there are too many students to name individually, the energy that they brought to their debates inspired me to write this book, and I am grateful to them.

I have also been inspired by my students at both Rollins College and American University who have committed much of their time outside the classroom to promoting human rights. Whether the issue was better wages for people working in their residence halls or empowerment for people suffering halfway across the planet, these students have shown empathy, optimism, and dedication in their own human rights activism. As the faculty adviser for the Amnesty International student club at Rollins College, I have had the pleasure of working alongside many young people whose leadership and charisma have made their campus, and the world around them, a better place. I am particularly indebted to the student leaders who have carried forward the vision of Amnesty International on campus, including Ted Scott, Bubba Scott, Danielle Gal, Kathy Allan, Justin Mitchell, Airam Dato-On, Ashley

Jones, Kelsey Uhl, Rebecca Hamilton, Melissa McGuire-Maniau, and Roxy Szal. It is my hope that this book will encourage other students to develop strong opinions about these critical issues and take action to defend their most cherished values.

I am grateful to the Office of Community Engagement and the dean of arts and sciences at Rollins College for providing funding for the research, writing, and editing of the manuscript in its various stages. In particular, I want to acknowledge Micki Meyer for her central role in co-curricular activities at Rollins College involving responsible citizenship. I also want to thank the members of the Department of Political Science for their input and support as I developed the book. I benefited tremendously from the research and editing that two student assistants provided. At the beginning of the writing process, Amy Uhl helped me to formulate the ideas behind several chapters and conducted some of the initial research. As the book was nearing completion, Shelby McGuire assisted with proofreading, editing, and indexing. Amy and Shelby were reliable, competent, and truly a joy to work with.

I am deeply appreciative of the advice and support that I have received from Lynne Rienner and all of the staff at Lynne Rienner Publishers. Lynne's encouragement and constructive criticism have undoubtedly improved the format, flow, and content. I am also grateful to the anonymous reviewers for their thoughtful and detailed comments. Many of their recommendations have been incorporated into the book.

Finally, I am eternally thankful for my wife, Amy, and our two children, Tyler and Owen, who showed patience and understanding as I was working on this project. Although I love my vocation, there is nothing on Earth that I love more than my family.

—*Daniel P. L. Chong*

Introduction

The test of a first-rate intelligence is the ability to hold two opposing ideas in the mind at the same time.

         —F. Scott Fitzgerald, *The Crack-Up*

Human rights are based on the idea that every single person on the planet deserves to be treated with dignity and respect. It is truly a profound idea that has changed the course of human history over the past century. Struggles to achieve dignity and equality have spread dramatically across the globe, sometimes meeting failure, and at other times achieving resounding success. When we think of human rights, we think of the inspiring movements for freedom led by people such as Mahatma Gandhi, Martin Luther King Jr., and Nelson Mandela.

Today, human rights have become the "lingua franca of global moral thought";[1] in other words, they now provide the most common global standard by which to judge right from wrong in political life. Human rights help to define how wars are fought, how states are built, how economic policies are made, and which leaders are considered legitimate. If you have ever witnessed mistreatment and unnecessary suffering and said to yourself, "No human being should ever endure this," then you have claimed a human right.

Yet human rights have also been the source of hugely controversial debates and have led to wars and political conflicts. Who exactly should have rights, and what rights are they entitled to? Are rights applicable within certain cultures and not others? Can states afford to protect human rights, even when it might be harmful to their own self-interests? If the attempt to protect

1

some rights threatens other rights, how do we balance these concerns? These are some of the many debates addressed in this book.

Critical Thinking

The goal of this book is to encourage the reader to think critically about international human rights. Critical thinking involves the willingness to challenge conventional wisdom, to question one's preexisting assumptions, and to develop opinions about controversial issues. It does not mean cynically disagreeing with every received idea, but it does require evaluating the quality of the evidence and the arguments behind a position. Critical thinkers read a text (like this book) and assume that the author is relating his or her own perspective of the truth, not that the text itself is the objective truth. Authors' perspectives may be partly right and partly wrong, and it is up to the reader to decide for him- or herself.

Why is critical thinking about human rights so important? First, because critical thinking can help us to overcome the cognitive biases that we often employ when we approach new ideas. A cognitive bias is a trap that our minds tend to slip into, distorting our view of reality in predictable ways. Biases prevent us from seeing the world as it really is, or from seeing the world from someone else's perspective. Psychologists have identified a number of common cognitive biases, but I encourage the reader to reflect on a particular few while reading this book. For example, the egocentric bias is our tendency to believe that our own ideas and behaviors are superior to those of others. As the humorist Garrison Keillor famously satirizes about the people of the fictional town of Lake Wobegon, "All the children are above average." In debates about human rights, we tend to believe that our side is always the right side. Through the within-group bias, we extend this egocentric belief to the particular groups we belong to; for example, our family, our ethnic group, our religion, and our country. Through the confirmation bias, we tend to hold on to existing beliefs about the superiority of our group's ideas and behaviors, despite evidence to the contrary. We ignore or reinterpret contradictory evidence, while focusing our attention and memory on evidence that confirms our preexisting beliefs. In other words, we tend to overlook evidence that our own ideas about human rights may be incorrect, or that our own country's actions might be violating the rights of others. Critical thinking allows us to reflect upon our own personal biases and deliberately open ourselves up to different perspectives.

Second, critical thinking is important because the conventional wisdom on human rights may be wrong. Most human rights activists believe (or at least say publicly) that there is a strong international consensus that accepts human rights; that this consensus is manifested in a clear set of international laws; and that failure to enforce the law represents a lack of political will by states and other actors. In other words, political actors know the right thing to do; they simply do not want to do it. That, however, is not the assumption that guides this book. The book is grounded, instead, in the notion that political actors sometimes fail to uphold human rights standards not only because they lack the motivation or self-interest to comply, but also because they have competing ideas about which rights are important and how those rights should best be implemented. In other words, political actors justify their behavior by referencing a competing idea or value. If this assumption is correct, then understanding the different perspectives that animate human rights debates will be central to better realizing human rights in practice, because we will know how political actors justify human rights violations. It is not simply a matter of political will, but of competing ideas.

Third, critical thinking also involves divergent thinking, or the ability to generate new ideas by considering multiple perspectives simultaneously. When presented with competing ideas, critical thinkers do not merely reject or accept one set of ideas in its entirety; rather, they are able to see the strengths and weaknesses in both perspectives, and to see how each perspective might be improved. This can lead to a more creative combination of opposing arguments, a new synthesis of ideas. Thus, at a time when human rights are violated daily across the globe, and solutions do not seem obvious, critical thinking has the potential to identify new solutions to our most pressing problems.

The Structure of the Book

This book is structured in a way that outlines some of the most critical debates in the field. Instead of presenting a series of facts about human rights to be memorized, each chapter details two opposing arguments on a particular topic. In each of these debates, I present the point of view from one side in the debate, and then I present its opposite. Each chapter therefore contains shifts in point of view, making the strongest arguments possible from the perspective of each opposing side in the debate. It is up to the reader to judge the strengths and weaknesses of each argument. The reader should be careful not to dismiss the arguments as "mere opinions." The arguments are more than opinions; they are making theoretical and empirical claims about how the world really works. In some cases, the arguments debate the empirical facts themselves (for example, whether torture produces useful intelligence); in other cases, the arguments marshal different sets of facts to bolster their stance, or interpret the same set of facts in different ways. Practiced critical thinkers are able to discern the fine line between facts, interpretations of facts, and opinions. Through this process, we can not only learn new facts about the role of human rights in the world today, but also learn to develop and defend our own opinions about the resulting controversies.

Note

1. Michael Ignatieff, *Human Rights as Politics and Idolatry* (Princeton: Princeton University Press, 2001), p. 53.

1

The History and Philosophy of Human Rights

December 10, 1948, was a special day in the history of human rights. On that day, world leaders came together in the United Nations General Assembly to adopt the **Universal Declaration of Human Rights (UDHR)*** (see Figure 1.1). It was the first time in history that representatives of the major countries of the world publicly attested to the fact that all people deserve a set of rights based solely on their inherent dignity as human beings. This day is commemorated annually as Human Rights Day. Social movements, from antipoverty campaigners in Albania to democracy activists in Zimbabwe, now frame their actions as struggles to achieve human rights.

There were many precursors to our modern system of universal human rights. One of the earliest written constitutions, the **Code of Hammurabi** (1772 B.C.E.), granted a handful of rights to residents of Babylon. These included the presumption of innocence for those accused of crimes, and the right to present evidence before a judge. It was perhaps the first time that a king's subjects were considered to possess rights, rather than merely duties to society and the monarch. However, the Code of Hammurabi did not recognize human rights principles such as equal citizenship or the **rule of law**, and the level of punishment for crimes often depended on the offender's social status. Similarly, of the 282 legal obligations imposed by the code, only one regulated government officials, and none applied to King Hammurabi himself.[1] Indeed, monarchs continued to claim authority to rule based on

_____

*Terms in boldface are defined in the Glossary, which begins on p. 247.

5

Figure 1.1 The Universal Declaration of Human Rights

Article 1: Universal equality
Article 2: Nondiscrimination
Article 3: Life and personal security
Article 4: Freedom from slavery
Article 5: Freedom from torture
Articles 6–11: Equal protection and due process under the law
Article 12: Privacy
Articles 13–14: Freedom of movement, and freedom from persecution
Article 15: Nationality
Article 16: Marriage
Article 17: Property
Article 18: Belief and religion
Article 19: Speech and expression
Article 20: Peaceful assembly
Article 21: Participatory government and voting
Article 22: Social security
Article 23: Unions and fair working conditions
Article 24: Rest and leisure
Article 25: Food, housing, and medical care
Article 26: Education
Article 27: Cultural participation
Article 28: An international order in which the above rights can be achieved

---

divine appointment, and so the distinction between religious and secular authority was yet to be established. In effect the king remained above the law and immune from its constraints.

This limited set of rights was expanded upon with the development of the first democracies in ancient Greece and Rome. Citizens of Greek city-states and throughout the Roman Empire were given the right to express their opinions, vote directly for legislation, and be tried by a jury of their peers. However, as was customary at the time, the rights of citizenship were limited to men who had completed military service, thus excluding women, children, slaves, and anyone who had broken certain laws.[2]

> **Think Again**
>
> Do you think that everyone should be entitled to all of the rights listed in the Universal Declaration of Human Rights? Are there any other rights that you would add to this list? How does the UDHR compare to the Bill of Rights in the US Constitution?

When King John of England was forced by his aristocracy to sign the **Magna Carta** in 1215, it represented another important step in the development of human rights. The Magna Carta proclaimed that all citizens (excluding serfs) accused of a crime must be tried according to the "law of the land." This formed the basis for concepts such as the rule of law (i.e., that rulers themselves are held accountable to the law) and **habeas corpus** (i.e., that defendants have a right to challenge their detention in a court of law). Although these rights still only applied to an elite group of citizens of a particular state, the Magna Carta remains a template for some of the constitutional rights that citizens in many countries enjoy today.

Thus the historical development of human rights has been a process of gradual expansion, starting from a limited set of rights for a limited group of subjects and eventually leading to a broader set of universally applicable rights. The seventeenth-century Enlightenment in the West provided a major impetus for this expansion, as philosophers began to assert that humans shared a common moral foundation outside of any religious affiliation or national citizenship. Whereas religious texts occasionally referred to all people as "children of God," centuries of religious conflict made it clear that this phrase typically applied only to fellow members of the faith. And while other philosophers such as Confucius, Plato, and Socrates believed in common human characteristics and universalist ethics,[3] it was the Enlightenment that defined humanity as possessing inherent, "natural" rights.[4] According to Enlightenment philosophers, these rights could be justified by abstract rationality rather than religious authority or government decree.

It was during the Enlightenment that democratic revolutions sprang up in England, France, and the United States, leading to constitutional protections of basic rights in the English Bill of Rights (1689), the French Declaration of the Rights of Man (1788), and the US Constitution (1789). A broad set of **civil and political rights**, including due process, political participation, and religious freedom, was incorporated into these national constitutions. Over the course of the next century, and through arduous and sometimes violent struggles, these same rights were extended to people who held no property, former slaves, women, and other groups. Similar struggles allowed workers in these Western societies to acquire several labor rights, such as safe working conditions, limited working hours, and the right to form unions.

Yet it was not until the latter half of the twentieth century that international institutions were created with the intention of applying these rights on a truly global scale. In response to the devastation of World War II and the Holocaust, the states of the world created the United Nations and increasingly committed themselves to a set of international laws and norms that would apply to all humans, regardless of national citizenship. Starting from the principles outlined in the UDHR, states negotiated dozens of treaties over the ensuing decades (see Figure 1.2) in which they promised to hold each other accountable for protection of civil and political rights, protection of civilians during wartime, and for most states, protection of **economic, social, and cultural rights** as well. The term "human rights" became a rallying cry for nations freeing themselves from colonial domination in the 1960s and 1970s, and for idealistic activists joining new transnational **nongovernmental organizations (NGOs)** such as **Amnesty International**.[5]

Just as human rights were expanding in breadth and scope in the middle of the twentieth century, however, they were also becoming a source of huge ideological battles. The global consensus that led to the signing of the UDHR in 1948 soon revealed itself to be thin and short-lived. The United Nations General Assembly unanimously adopted the UDHR with forty-eight states voting in favor, zero opposing, and eight abstaining. However, beneath the surface, tensions simmered over which rights should be included, and over the proper foundations for rights. Six of the eight states that abstained from voting for the UDHR belonged to the Soviet bloc of communist

---

Figure 1.2 Major International Human Rights Treaties

Treaty Name	Date Signed	State Parties
Convention on the Prevention and Punishment of the Crime of Genocide	1948	142
International Convention on the Elimination of All Forms of Racial Discrimination (ICERD)	1966	175
International Covenant on Civil and Political Rights (ICCPR)	1966	167
International Covenant on Economic, Social, and Cultural Rights (ICESCR)	1966	161
International Convention on the Suppression and Punishment of the Crime of Apartheid	1973	107
Convention on the Elimination of All Forms of Discrimination Against Women (CEDAW)	1979	187
Convention Against Torture and Other Cruel, Inhuman, or Degrading Treatment or Punishment (CAT)	1984	154
Convention on the Rights of the Child (CRC)	1989	193
Rome Statute of the International Criminal Court	1998	119
Convention on the Rights of Persons with Disabilities (CRPD)	2006	110

Note: For current information on which states have ratified each treaty, see the United Nations Treaty Collection, http://treaties.un.org/pages/Treaties.aspx?id=4.

countries, which claimed philosophically that rights could be granted only by the state, and not inherently acquired by virtue of being human. Saudi Arabia abstained because of its belief that Articles 16 and 18 violated the laws and principles of most Muslim countries. South Africa abstained because a number of rights conflicted with its apartheid system of racial segregation.[6]

In the late 1940s, an even deeper fissure opened up between the Soviet bloc (the "East") and the United States and its allies (the "West"). Disagreements over human rights became one of the central battlegrounds in the global Cold War over the next half-century. The East-West dispute over human rights was not just a rhetorical debate played out at UN summits; it was a motivation for proxy wars and military confrontations that killed millions of people during this period. While the West argued that it was civil and political rights (generally, UDHR Articles 3–21) that should be the state's primary responsibility, the East countered that it was economic, social, and cultural rights (UDHR Articles 22–27) that should be the state's primary responsibility. Indeed, it was not merely a difference in emphasis. Each side argued that their enemy's set of rights was ultimately invalid; in other words, that they were not really human rights at all. States of the West celebrated their (often inconsistent) protection of civil and political rights, while states of the East proclaimed their (often repressive) support for economic, social, and cultural rights. These arguments are further explored in Chapter 12.

The drafters of the UDHR initially hoped that their declaration would lead to a single, comprehensive international treaty to protect all human rights. However, as a result of the Cold War divide, international human rights law split into two separate treaties in 1966, the **International Covenant on Civil and Political Rights (ICCPR)** and the **International Covenant on Economic, Social, and Cultural Rights (ICESCR)**. While nearly all states signed both treaties, it was clear that the Soviet Union had no intention to comply with the ICCPR, and the United States had no intention to enforce the ICESCR.[7] While human rights activists in NGOs and the United Nations were defining rights as indivisible, in practice these rights became both divided and politically divisive. Even as dozens of new states emerged in the 1960s and 1970s through the process of decolonization, this failed to resolve the debate. Many of the new states (the global "South") were afflicted with extreme poverty and identified themselves with the Marxist ideas of the Soviet Union. They tended to advocate for the international protection of economic, social, and cultural rights, which the United States strongly opposed. Thus, a North-South divide over human rights was layered onto the existing East-West split.[8]

Since the dissolution of the Soviet Union and the end of the Cold War, the debate over what rights should be the primary responsibility of the state—civil and political rights, or economic, social, and cultural rights—has become less divisive. Today, only a handful of states continue to deny the legitimacy of either category of rights. Many states have moved closer to the idea of a universal set of human rights by writing both categories of rights into their national constitutions. Part 2 of this book focuses on the debates surrounding the definition and implementation of civil and political rights, while Part 3 focuses on debates surrounding economic, social, and cultural rights.

How Are Human Rights Enforced?

Even as our notions of human rights have become increasingly global in recent decades, the mechanisms for their implementation remain primarily at the national level. The most common way that human rights are protected is for governments to incorporate them into their national constitutions, through a bill of rights that becomes the law of the land. For states that truly respect the rule of law, all citizens, including political leaders, are then held accountable to the law through a well-functioning and independent judiciary. In these cases, when human rights violations are committed, victims can seek a remedy by having violators prosecuted and their rights restored. This is referred to as the domestic enforcement of human rights. Citizens throughout the world have formed grassroots movements to hold their own governments politically and legally accountable to these standards.

Clearly, not all states respect the rule of law, so some human rights enforcement must be international. Still, the primary enforcers of human rights across national borders are states, which are the only actors with significant coercive power to force compliance with the law. States can attempt to influence the protection of human rights in other states in a variety of ways, from engaging in quiet diplomacy with human rights abusers, to imposing economic and financial sanctions, to intervening with military force. Yet states often incorporate human rights into their foreign policies in ways that are inconsistent, self-serving, or hypocritical. Chapter 2 discusses the question of whether states' foreign policies can truly be driven by a concern for human rights.

Over the past half-century, states have banded together to create a large number of regional and global institutions to help implement human rights. However, the only global institution with substantial coercive enforcement capacity for human rights is the **United Nations Security Council**, which is controlled by the five states that won World War II. These five states—the

United States, Russia, China, France, and the United Kingdom—can individually veto any proposal within the UN Security Council that does not meet their interests. This is because, in an anarchic world system, states jealously guard their sovereignty—that is, their ability to act independently without outside interference. Even the **International Criminal Court (ICC)**, founded in 2002 to prosecute individuals who commit gross violations of human rights almost anywhere in the world, depends on the cooperation of national governments to arrest and extradite defendants to the court.

Coercive enforcement is important, but it is not the only pathway to implementing human rights. The United Nations has served as an important forum for the promotion of human rights, as states have negotiated and signed dozens of human rights treaties under UN auspices. Even when these treaties are not enforced, they can serve a norm-setting function, clarifying the standards of expected behavior for everyone. Many of the **intergovernmental organizations (IGOs)** established by states have the primary role of monitoring, investigating, and reporting on human rights violations in particular areas. For example, there are several UN committees that can receive individual complaints of human rights violations, send human rights experts to various countries to investigate claims, and pass resolutions to publicly condemn violators. Regional organizations, such as the Organization of American States and the European Union, also contain similar kinds of accountability mechanisms among their members. This has provided some social pressure for states to abide by human rights standards. Even when they know that there is no threat of coercive enforcement, they may fear the loss of reputation from being condemned by a particular UN committee. This pressure can be amplified by **transnational advocacy networks**, which can bring the power of mass protests and shine a media spotlight directly on human rights abusers.[9]

Thus the primary mechanism of enforcement for international human rights is still through national constitutions, legislatures, and courts. However, today there exists a wide range of NGOs, social movements, and regional and international institutions that can help define, advocate, monitor, and otherwise protect human rights.[10] For the first time in human history, human rights have become one of the central defining features of national and international politics. These enforcement mechanisms are far from perfect or consistent. States, private actors, and international organizations still ignore or actively violate a wide set of human rights. The debates in Part 1 of this book examine the effectiveness of our current mechanisms for protecting human rights across the globe.

In sum, the history of human rights has been a rocky road, slowly evolving toward the greater protection of a wider range of rights for a larger population of humans. Each step along the path has been met by major set-backs and counter-movements, such as the Napoleonic era that followed the French Revolution, or the dictatorships that sprang from decolonization, or the Cold War rivalries that hamstrung the United Nations.[11] Yet the overall trajectory remains clear. Human rights began as a limited set of privileges voluntarily bestowed by a king upon an elite class of his own subjects. The scope of human rights has expanded to include political participation, religious freedom, freedom from slavery, economic and social rights, sexual identity, and more. Whereas originally it was only male aristocrats in particular national jurisdictions who possessed rights, the concept of rights has evolved to include former slaves, women, and human beings across all societies. Whereas human rights were once only written into Western societies' constitutions, today virtually all states have some legal protections for human rights.

Defining Human Rights

Our modern understanding of human rights represents a certain level of consensus about what human rights are. According to the UDHR and the international treaties that followed, human rights are universal, inalienable, and indivisible. Human rights are **universal** in the sense that all humans deserve them equally, simply by virtue of being human, and not because of citizenship within a particular state. Human rights are **inalienable** in the sense that individuals acquire them at birth and cannot lose them by any act that they commit during their lifetime. We cannot earn rights; we simply have them. All human rights are also perceived as **indivisible**, in that all of the rights laid out in the UDHR are equally justified because they are necessary to uphold human dignity.[12] There is no human right that can be privileged over any other human right.

Claims for human rights are also commonly understood as both legal and moral claims. Human rights are often written into law and protected within judicial systems, but even when they are not, they still represent valid moral claims that people deserve rights based on their humanity. Most commonly, people have demanded these legal and moral claims from their own governments, but increasingly from other actors as well, including other states, private corporations, and international organizations. The individual making these claims is called a "rights bearer," and the recipient of the claim is called a "duty holder." Fundamentally, claims for human rights are claims that all individuals must be treated with at least a minimal respect for human dignity. As such, they do not attempt to prescribe a maximalist vision of the "good life" or provide a recipe for a utopian society. Rather, they set a minimal threshold of common decency that no actor is allowed to violate. Because of this absolute threshold, human rights are therefore believed to trump all other considerations when judging the legitimacy of a policy or action. In other words, human rights can never be sacrificed to achieve other political or economic goals.

Of course, if this consensus about human rights represented the whole story, then this book would be very short. In fact, just as the history of human rights has witnessed the ebb and flow of competing ideas, all of the characteristics of human rights detailed here are similarly disputed. While the universal enforcement of equal rights remains a goal for advocates, the "partisan interpretations and applications" of human rights will continue.[13]

Philosophical Sources of Human Rights

One of these controversies involves the philosophical justification for human rights. Why do we think that humans deserve rights in the first place? Why do they belong to all humans, and for that matter, only to humans? If the definition of "human" has evolved throughout history to include new groups and categories, are there other populations (for example, fetuses or animals) who deserve the same set of rights? Identifying the source of rights represents one of the key debates in the historical development of human rights.

Although there are many possible sources and justifications for human rights, **essentialism** claims that humans are born with inherent dignity, and that this dignity is essential to what it means to be human. To take away people's basic dignity, whether by violating their physical security, their economic livelihood, or their ability to speak freely, is to deny them the core of their humanity. Because rights can be inferred from the very definition of being human, rights are an inherent and essential characteristic that all humans share, regardless of what community or state they belong to, and regardless of anything they might have done to "earn" these rights.

Where does this dignity come from? For Jewish, Christian, and Muslim theologians, it is the result of being created in God's image.[14] This religious doctrine undergirds the widespread belief that the inherent dignity that forms the basis of rights is a God-given feature of being human. As the US Declaration of Independence famously states, "We hold these truths to be self-evident, that all men are created equal, that they are endowed by their Creator with certain inalienable rights." According to religious texts, the Creator endowed humans with unique qualities that separate us from the animals, including the ability to reason and to freely decide how we want to live. The core of these qualities is the human soul; in other words, the individual identity that never changes in a person from birth to death (and in some religions, continues after death), even though a person's other traits may change over time. Because God endowed all humans with a soul, and because the soul gives rise to the ability to freely choose our destiny, all humans have rights. Rights are the tools we use to ensure that our choices are truly free.

Of course, not everyone believes in a God, so there are also secular justifications for inherent and essential human rights. This is provided by the theories of **natural law**, the **social contract**, and other ideas popularized by the liberal philosophers of the Enlightenment. According to the ancient Roman statesman Cicero (106–43 B.C.E.), innate rights arise from the law of nature, which is a set of universal rules that can be discovered through reason alone.[15] Setting aside questions about the existence of God, natural law philosophers argue that rights are an inherent element of human nature, since humans are the only creatures capable of rational thought and free choice. This idea was reinforced by the French rationalist René Descartes (1596–1650), who posited that through reason itself, it could be proven that humans possess both a material body and a nonmaterial mind. In this philosophy, known as dualism, the mind is analogous to the religious "soul"; in other words, it is the locus of human individuality that gives us our dignity and justifies our rights.

According to essentialists, if rights are a foundational characteristic of human nature, they exist prior to any social interaction or government decree. In other words, government rulers do not give us rights; rights belong to us by virtue of our status as human beings. Philosophers such as Jean Bodin (1529–1596), Hugo Grotius (1583–1645), and Immanuel Kant (1724–1804) applied this concept directly to political rule, arguing that sovereignty does not belong to leaders, but to individual people. As such, rulers should be held accountable to the same set of laws that they enforce upon their own citizens, and those laws cannot violate citizens' natural rights. Individuals cannot be sacrificed as a means to achieving the interests of the state; rather, people must be treated as ends in themselves. Fulfilling people's natural rights is the raison d'être of the state itself. These liberal Enlightenment ideas set the foundation for both modern democracy and international law, the latter of which (at least in theory) applies universal rules to all leaders across all cultures. Indeed, as Grotius claimed, even though people live in many different cultures, natural law dictates that we all belong to the same human society, and therefore we should all be subject to the same rules.

John Locke (1632–1704) further developed this notion with the theory of the social contract. Locke argued that freethinking individuals with natural rights would rationally choose to form a society in which the government's primary duty is to protect those rights. The state's role is therefore as an impartial judge and rule-enforcer, allowing people to exercise their individual rights without having to rely on themselves for their own security. Because rational people would voluntarily choose this arrangement, then the social contract is a description of the natural order of society, rather than a specific agreement at a specific moment in time. The legitimacy of a government is therefore dependent on how well it protects the natural rights of its people, contrary to the antiquated notion that people's rights depend on the decrees of their rulers.

In sum, essentialists argue that human rights are inherent and inalienable, shared by humans equally, because humans share characteristics that make us unique among all other creatures. While theologians might locate these characteristics in the soul, and Enlightenment philosophers would locate them in rationality, humans are the only creatures who are endowed with self-consciousness, the ability to reflect upon the meaning of life, and the freedom to make moral choices. Because this freedom is central to human dignity, it represents a basic human need, and when this freedom is restricted, it causes a uniquely human form of suffering. Although other living creatures have basic physical needs, which may lead to certain kinds of rights that would prevent them from undue suffering, humans are the only creatures with these higher-order needs that lead to the full spectrum of rights.

On the other hand, **non-essentialism** claims that human rights are not an essential or inherent characteristic of being human, because there are no provable or observable features that all humans share that would somehow distinguish our species as being uniquely deserving of rights. Theologians and philosophers may assert that we have a nonmaterial soul, or a mind, or a universal sense of rationality, but this is merely an unfounded assertion, not a proven claim. However, this does not mean that humans do not have any rights. It simply means that we have precisely the rights that we ourselves create, rather than any rights given to us by nature or God. All people may or may not deserve the same rights, because it is up to us, within our own societies, to define the rights we want to have.

Religious doctrines such as the "image of God" can be helpful in encouraging people to treat each other with respect and dignity, but there is actually very little support in religious texts for our modern understanding of human rights. Most religious texts emphasize religious duties instead of rights, and those duties are owed primarily to God rather than to fellow humans. Indeed, some of the rules that God has ostensibly commanded have been quite antagonistic to human rights, such as acceptance of slavery, postwar slaughter of infidels, and subjugation of women, to name just three. Most religious traditions seem far more concerned with the eternal salvation of the soul through adherence to the guidelines of a particular faith, than with the kind of earthly protections that human rights promise for people of all faiths. Many faiths even seem to celebrate the (voluntary or involuntary) sacrifice of personal freedoms in order to fulfill religious duties.

According to non-essentialists, the existence of the soul, and therefore the existence of any inherent human dignity, is an article of faith rather than a proposition of reason. Where is the soul, and how do we know that every human has a soul? It is a label invented to preemptively settle the mysteries of human existence without really solving those mysteries. The same can be said for arguments about natural law, Descartes's nonmaterial mind, and universal rationality. As skeptics such as David Hume (1711–1776) noted, these are untestable and unobservable assertions that do not provide adequate justification for human rights.

Clearly, not all Enlightenment thinkers believed in natural law, rationality, and human equality. Conservatives such as Edmund Burke (1729–1797) believed that the notion of human equality, at least insofar as it applied to the political and economic spheres, was a "monstrous fiction."[16] In other words, humans are naturally endowed with different levels of intelligence, capabilities, motivations, and personality traits. Any attempt to impose political or social equality upon all of humanity would therefore be unnatural and ultimately counterproductive. Thomas Hobbes (1588–1679) used a similar line of reasoning in his own explanation of the social contract. Unlike Locke, Hobbes argued that life would be "nasty, brutish, and short" in the state of nature, because humans with unequal capabilities would inevitably fight over scarce resources. As a result, people entering into a hypothetical social contract would naturally be willing to give up some of their rights in order to have an all-powerful state protect their security. The main purpose of the state is not to provide freedom, but to provide order, which may require the repression of some rights.

Even among Enlightenment philosophers who agreed with the notion of human equality, many were not necessarily led to adopt a belief in inherent rights. For example, utilitarians such as Jeremy Bentham (1748–1832) suggested that actions should be judged according to their consequences, not by the morality of the actor's intentions. As a result, the most rational society would try to achieve the maximum amount of utility, or well-being, for the greatest number of people.[17] Although some societies would determine that the granting of rights accomplished this goal, other societies might find that some individual rights would need to be sacrificed in order to achieve the greater good. This principle can be seen in many current societies, as when a country needs to displace people from their traditional homelands in order to build development projects that benefit the entire country.

According to non-essentialists, rights are not a necessary or inherent feature of belonging to the human species. Instead, rights are just one of several possible strategies that a society could use to achieve its common aspirations. Because societies literally "construct" rights, this perspective is often called **social constructivism**. Social constructivists acknowledge that there are different ways to create rights. Some rights are implicit and unspoken norms; in other words, they are moral principles that are taken for granted because we accept their legitimacy. For example, although many centuries ago it was not uncommon for the victors in war to kill their enemy's adult males, and enslave their enemy's women and children as the spoils of war, today this practice is implicitly unacceptable. Some of these implicit norms, or common social understandings of what is morally acceptable, can eventually become more concrete laws that are enacted and enforced by governments. Indeed, according to **legal positivism**, these laws that are agreed on by governments are the only things that can endow us with rights. As Bentham stated, "From real laws come real rights, but from imaginary law, from the 'law of nature,' come imaginary rights." This led Bentham to conclude that the mystical idea of inherent rights amounted to nothing more than "nonsense on stilts."[18] Thus, for legal positivists, the notion of the social contract is not some kind of hypothetical situation used to determine what people would naturally or rationally choose. Social contracts are actual, legal agreements through which people grant each other rights if they so choose.

> **Think Again**
>
> Do you think that humans deserve a greater set of rights than animals? If so, on what basis do you believe this?

Thus, if human rights are constructed by societies, they cannot be essential and inherent to the human species. We have exactly those rights that we are able to acquire, either through implicit social norms or positive law. This perspective does not rule out the possibility of having universal rights, but universality would have to be achieved through an actual consensus among societies, rather than simply asserted as fact. Indeed, a certain level of consensus has already been achieved by most states around the globe, as demonstrated throughout this chapter.

What are the political implications for this debate of the philosophical sources of human rights? Because human rights have gained strength over time primarily through the expanding belief in inherent rights, there is a legitimate fear that discarding essentialism would lead to the weakening of human rights protections around the globe. Political and military leaders have a range of motives and goals for their actions, some of which run counter to the defense of human rights, and so abandoning a belief in inherent rights can open up new justifications for violating rights in the name of the "greater good" or national sovereignty. Leaders invariably have some kind of justification for their actions, however hypocritical or manipulative, so perhaps an appeal to a set of ahistorical, universal moral principles is the best way to limit their violations. If human hands have constructed the entire edifice of human rights, then there is a fear that those same hands can just as easily destroy it. All of the rights that we take for granted today, such as the prohibition against torture or slavery, would be perpetually open for reconsideration.

Likewise, if we accept social constructivism as an approach to human rights, we must also accept the plausibility of **cultural relativism**. If rights are granted by specific societies rather than inherently human, then it is clear that different societies might endow their peoples with different sets of rights. For example, many Islamic-majority states enforce women's rights quite differently than do Western states, as seen in the debate on female circumcision in Chapter 11. Leaders such as Singapore's Lee Kuan Yew and Malaysia's Mahathir Mohamad have claimed that the "Asian values" of collectivism, social duty, and economic welfare are inconsistent with Western values of individualism and political rights. These leaders have applied the cultural relativist argument to claim that Western democracy is neither appropriate nor necessary for Asian cultures. According to cultural relativism, there is no universal basis to judge any human rights practices across cultures; indeed, in this sense, there are no human rights at all. Societies can only be judged according to the standards that they have explicitly adopted (or that some self-appointed representative has proclaimed for them), and rights only exist within specific political boundaries. If this position were accepted, it would represent not only a decline or weakening of certain rights, but a repudiation of the entire notion of human rights.

Perhaps it is not so damaging to weaken the notion of human rights after all. Political leaders may want to discard human rights, not because of hypocrisy or self-serving manipulation, but because there are other worthy goals to achieve that are limited by the human rights framework. If human rights are merely one pathway that humans have built toward achieving individual happiness, or social harmony, or utopia, then perhaps there are better pathways available. Since human rights are legal entitlements and political claims that are largely enforced by existing governments, then this is a fairly gradualist and reformist pathway toward well-being. Alternative approaches to happiness abound, ranging from revolutionary Marxist visions of utopia, to the extreme individualism of Ayn Rand's objectivism, to the religious doctrines already covered. Who is to say that human rights are the best way to frame our desire to achieve happiness?

Therefore, it is clear that discarding the belief in essentialism has the potential to weaken the enforcement of human rights in lieu of other interests and ethical frameworks. However, the belief in social constructivism could also lead to the strengthening and expansion of human rights, rather than their decline. In fact, history has shown exactly such an evolution in the global human rights system. Even if rights are created by societies, it is increasingly evident that all humans may belong to a single society, given the now truly global nature of such things as travel, communication, economic trade, epidemics, environmental concerns, and law enforcement. Increasingly, this global society has agreed on a set of rights that will protect our most vulnerable citizens and provide for the most happiness possible. This set of rights has been expanding over time, and the mechanisms for their enforcement have been deepening.

Those who assert that human rights are universal will inevitably meet with dissent from those who believe that a particular rights claim should not apply in a particular situation. When this disagreement appears, how should the human rights activist respond? Essentialists can only respond by asserting the rationality and truthfulness of their claim based on unprovable appeals to metaphysics or theology: "We *know* we have these rights." This is a fundamentally imperialist approach that ultimately invites even more dissent and backlash. Social constructivists, on the other hand, would respond to this disagreement by asking the question, "What rights do we both *expect*?" Through this process of mutual accommodation and consensus building, a stronger foundation for universal human rights might ultimately be constructed.

In this view, instead of threatening the human rights system, discarding the notion of inherent rights opens up new possibilities for that system to evolve further. Now that our human society has finally begun to grant rights to women, children, and racial minorities, whom else are we still neglecting to count as fully human? Is it time to create equal rights for sexual minorities, or unborn children? For that matter, if humans are not uniquely endowed with rights by God, is it time for us to realize that animals are also living creatures that suffer and (to some extent) aspire to happiness, and therefore deserve the protection of their rights as well?[19] These are some of the most current struggles for "new" rights that are occurring around the globe, and the expansion of rights seems to be the direction that the "arc of history" is pointing toward, as Martin Luther King Jr. so famously described. Of course, essentialists could adapt themselves to this expansion of rights by claiming, "These rights were inherent all along; we simply didn't recognize them." However, since social constructivists embrace the idea that new norms are created and lost all the time, they are able to explain this evolutionary change more easily.

Ultimately, we cannot be certain about where rights originate from, or to whom they apply. We can only be sure that having rights is far better than being denied rights. Debates such as this are what make the politics of human rights so fascinating. Are all of the rights listed in the UDHR equally important, or are some rights more fundamental to protecting human dignity than others? When different rights conflict with each other (for example, when the freedom to practice a religion may result in discriminatory treatment of women), how should these conflicts be resolved? If rights are universal, but most enforcement mechanisms are national, who should have the authority to stop violations that cross national borders? If the enforcement of some rights requires the violation of others (for example, when war may be necessary to protect a population from genocide), how should we evaluate these trade-offs? These are the questions being asked at the forefront of contemporary human rights practice, and there are no easy answers. Although some have proclaimed an "end of history" and the settling of such debates,[20] this proclamation seems premature in the long struggle for human rights.

Notes

1. See "Code of Hammurabi," http://www.commonlaw.com/Hammurabi.html, accessed January 31, 2012.

2. See Richard A. Bauman, *Human Rights in Ancient Rome* (London: Routledge, 1999).

3. Micheline Ishay, *The History of Human Rights: From Ancient Times to the Globalization Era* (Berkeley: University of California Press, 2004), p. 23.

4. Moira Rayner, "History of Universal Human Rights—Up to WW2," December 3, 2005, http://www.universalrights.net/main/histof.htm.

5. Samuel Moyn, "Human Rights in History," *The Nation,* August 30–September 6, 2010, pp. 31–37. Indeed, Moyn claims that the worldwide expansion of human rights was a result of the social movements of the 1970s, much more than of the international institutions of the 1940s.

6. Johannes Morsink, *The Universal Declaration of Human Rights: Origins, Drafting, and Intent* (Philadelphia: University of Pennsylvania Press, 1999), p. 21–26.

7. Indeed, in order for a state to become legally obligated to comply with a treaty, it must ratify the treaty in its own legislature. While the United States did sign the ICESCR in 1979, its Senate has never ratified it, and no US administration has ever pushed for its ratification. See Amnesty International, "Economic, Social, and Cultural Rights: Questions and Answers," 1998, http://www.amnestyusa.org/pdfs/escr_qa.pdf, p. 6.

8. Some would reasonably argue that many countries in Europe and elsewhere actively supported economic, social, and cultural rights from the beginning, at least in their domestic policies. However, since the United States was the most powerful and vocal representative of the West during this time, its opposition to economic, social, and cultural rights was the clearest signal of the West's lack of support for these rights in its foreign policies. See Daniel Whelan and Jack Donnelly, "The Reality of Western Support for Economic and Social Rights: A Reply to Susan L. Kang," *Human Rights Quarterly* 31, no. 4 (2009): 1030–1054.

9. See Margaret E. Keck and Kathryn Sikkink, *Activists Beyond Borders: Advocacy Networks in International Politics* (Ithaca: Cornell University Press, 1998).

10. See, for example, Aryeh Neier, *The International Human Rights Movement: A History* (Princeton: Princeton University Press, 2013).

11. Ishay, *The History of Human Rights,* p. 4.

12. See Daniel Whelan, *Indivisible Human Rights: A History* (Philadelphia: University of Pennsylvania Press, 2010).

13. Moyn, "Human Rights in History," p. 37.

14. See Michael Haas, *International Human Rights: A Comprehensive Introduction* (London: Routledge, 2008), p. 11.

15. Ibid., p. 17.

16. See, for example, Edmund Burke, *Reflections on the Revolution in France* (1791), cited in Fordham University, *Modern History Sourcebook,* http://www.fordham.edu/halsall/mod/1791burke.asp, accessed February 16, 2012.

17. Although utilitarians vary in how they define the term *utility,* they typically use it to refer to material things or states of life that humans have good reason to value.

18. Philip Schofield, "Jeremy Bentham's 'Nonsense on Stilts,'" *Utilitas* 15 (2003): 1.

19. See Peter Singer, *Animal Liberation* (London: Pimlico, 1975).

20. Francis Fukuyama, *The End of History and the Last Man* (New York: Free Press, 1992).

Part 1

The Global Human Rights System

2

When Should States Protect Human Rights?

Human rights have evolved from their beginnings as general ethical or religious principles into an expanding web of international treaties and institutions. In the past half-century, we have witnessed the emergence of dozens of new rights and thousands of new organizations created for their protection. A partial list of these new groups would include

- Local **community-based organizations**, which typically undertake the struggle for rights and provide services locally.
- More formalized nongovernmental organizations, which provide services and undertake legal and political advocacy at the local, national, and international levels.
- National judiciaries and ombudsmen, which primarily monitor and enforce human rights within the state, but occasionally pass judgment on human rights violations abroad.
- Regional political and legal institutions, such as the Organization of American States, the Inter-American Court of Human Rights, the European Union, and the European Court of Human Rights.
- International legal institutions, such as the International Criminal Court.
- Intergovernmental organizations, such as the agencies, treaty bodies, working groups, and committees that operate under the auspices of the United Nations.

Despite this tremendous expansion of the global human rights system, we cannot view these developments as successful unless and until they

25

result in greater protections for people's actual rights in action. Are more people around the globe able to overcome the barriers to meeting their basic needs, and express themselves freely? Are these new actors (and some old ones) effective in deterring violations of human rights, and holding perpetrators accountable? Even though the language of human rights has become the most common moral language that diplomats speak, some analysts remain skeptical about its effectiveness, decrying the "proliferation of the endless normativity of human rights standards."[1] In this view, the global human rights system might be characterized by too much moral posturing and not enough action.

The chapters in Part 1 outline the debate over whether the global human rights system is (or can be) built in a way that effectively protects people. To begin, this chapter focuses on states, because for the past few centuries states have been the primary political unit in the world. Looking at a political map of the globe, the most obvious feature is that we have carved the world into more than 190 distinct and autonomous states, each with its own territory and population. States have the ability to collect taxes, maintain armies, enforce laws, and garner their people's allegiance, all of which give states tremendous power to either violate or protect human rights. Because states serve so many political and economic functions, there are myriad ways that states can affect human rights, both domestically and in their foreign policies. Domestically, states can incorporate human rights into their national constitutions and use the power of the police and judiciary to enforce those rights. Indeed, this is probably the most common way that human rights are enforced around the world. At the same time, governments can actively violate their citizens' rights by, for example, depriving them of property, restricting their ability to participate in the political process, or imprisoning them without due process. Governments can also fail to fulfill their obligation to create the conditions whereby people can meet their basic needs in a secure environment. Internationally, states can choose whether to incorporate human rights into their foreign aid, immigration, trade, environmental, diplomatic, and military policies. Human rights considerations may play a role in determining when states go to war, how they fight wars, and what they do in the aftermath of war. States must also decide whether, and how, they will support international institutions designed to protect human rights, such as the United Nations and the International Criminal Court. A state's own courts may even choose to prosecute foreign citizens for human rights violations that are committed outside of that state's jurisdiction. In sum, states have extremely wide-ranging impacts on human rights.

Since most states hold a "monopoly on the legitimate use of violence" within their territories,[2] and have significant influence outside their borders, the next question that arises is whether states really care about using this power to protect human rights. In other words, do human rights play a central role in states' policymaking domestically and internationally, or do states mostly follow other interests that supersede or even contradict human rights? Once again, scholars disagree about the answer to this question. The opposing positions in this debate are drawn from the major theories of international relations: **realism**, **liberalism**, and **constructivism**. In short, realists believe that states are fundamentally unconcerned about human rights, particularly for noncitizens, while liberalists and constructivists believe that human rights can play a determining role in states' policymaking.

The implications for this debate are profound. If states are unconcerned with human rights in some fundamental sense, then the future for human rights may be bleak. In this case, the only effective way to protect rights in the long term may be to transform the nature of the state system itself—for example, by ceding more power to the United Nations or undermining the state from within. If, conversely, states can be relied on to protect human rights, then existing state institutions could potentially be reformed, pressured, and redirected toward the further enforcement of those rights.

Argument 1
States protect human rights only when it is convenient or in their self-interest.

From this perspective, human rights are not a determining factor in states' policymaking. This is not because individual persons, such as political and military leaders, are lacking in education, compassion, or a moral conscience. Rather, it is because of the nature of political leadership, states, and the international system. Individual people can be motivated to respect others' rights, but states must prioritize their own national interests if they want to survive and prosper.

The argument here is drawn from the theory of political realism, which is committed to understanding the world not as we want it to be, but as it really is. For realists, the primary purpose of the state is to provide order and stability within its territory. In the state of nature, without a government to provide order, people would constantly fight over limited resources, because their security would always be threatened by people around them. A modern illustration of this situation can be seen in Somalia, which did not have a well-functioning central government in the 1990s, and thus was ravaged by warlords, pirates, Islamic militants, and foreign invaders. In order to avoid this kind of "wild west" scenario, people willingly cede authority (and some personal freedoms) to a government that can provide them with security and order. The security provided by the state is the foundation for social harmony, economic development, and the rule of law.

It is not that states are opposed to human rights, but rather that they have prevailing concerns that override the protection of rights. Some states have established order by granting their citizens an extensive list of individual rights (e.g., the Western democracies); and to the extent that these rights do not threaten the fundamental purpose of the state, then it might still be possible for states to protect human rights. However, other states have established order under an authoritarian style of government, perhaps because their citizens respect a charismatic leader who is able to repress dissent (e.g., North Korea under Kim Jong Il), or because the authoritarian government is effective in providing social harmony and economic development (e.g., China). Either way, a political leader's primary obligation is to provide order and security, and if the protection of human rights interferes with that duty, then human rights must be sacrificed for the greater good. This is not by virtue of a leader's preferences, but of necessity. As the political philosopher Machiavelli (1469–1527) famously argued in *The Prince,* effective states require leaders who are able to retain power, and those leaders must sometimes resort to deception, manipulation, and even brutality if the state's security is threatened. The ends (increased security) justify the means (human rights violations).

Human rights are therefore best viewed as secondary or illusory interests of the state. In other words, states may be willing to protect human rights, but only when human rights happen to coincide with their fundamental interests. However, when a state's security or a leader's power is threatened, then that leader can (and indeed must) cast off the restraints of human rights and maintain order by any means necessary. This is illustrated by the similar responses to violent rebellion in 2011 taken by the authoritarian leader Muammar Qaddafi in Libya, and by the so-called reformist Bashar al-Assad in Syria. In both cases, these leaders found that some level of brutality was required in order to maintain the state's power. Likewise, when the security of the United States has been threatened, even this advanced democracy has not hesitated to violate its own citizens' rights, as demonstrated by the internment of Japanese Americans during World War II, the blacklisting of suspected communists during the Cold War, and the invasion of privacy during the post–September 11 war on terrorism. Human rights may sometimes be incorporated into a state's domestic policies when convenient, but they are epiphenomenal in the sense that the state's more fundamental interests are the actual motivation for its policies.

For realists, what is true at the domestic level is exaggerated in the international sphere. Because there is no world government to provide international order and security, states must rely on themselves to protect their sovereignty and their survival. Under these circumstances, given these limitations in the international system, the only way for a state to survive and prosper is to prioritize its national interests above all else.[3] While a political leader may hold private ethical positions about human rights, as a public official he or she must act as an agent of the state, and the state's objective interests are to increase its power. Pursuing national interests over human rights is therefore not merely a policy preference, but a necessity, since those states that do not achieve their interests will weaken and ultimately lose their sovereignty. As the Greek historian Thucydides described more than two millennia ago during the Peloponnesian War, "The strong do what they will, and the weak do what they must."

As in the domestic sphere, then, a state will use its foreign policy to protect human rights only when this is convenient, inexpensive, or advantageous for the state itself. For example, the United States is willing to support human rights around the globe, particularly when this reinforces its alliances, bolsters its international reputation and influence, and secures access to resources. For example, its denunciations of human rights violations in communist countries helped the United States win the Cold War by destabilizing and ultimately breaking apart the Soviet Union. When President George H. W. Bush initiated Operation Restore Hope in 1992, committing 25,000 troops to provide order and protect humanitarian aid in war-torn Somalia, this allowed the United States to claim the mantle of the "world's policeman" and establish a military foothold in the Horn of Africa. Currently, US defense of human rights in Burma (Myanmar), North Korea, and Tibet is designed to contain China's growing influence in East Asia.

> **Think Again**
>
> In your opinion, how far would the United States be willing to go to defend its interests? Are there any rights that the United States would not violate under any circumstances whatsoever? Is the United States different from other countries in this regard? Would your answer depend on the political leaders currently in power?

These foreign policies that appear to be motivated by a concern for human rights are actually led by national interests, as they must be from the realist perspective. Indeed, the realist explanation becomes clear when we consider how US foreign policy manifested itself when the country's core national interests were threatened. During the Cold War, the United

States was fond of denouncing communist states, but it had no qualms about supporting—financially, diplomatically, and militarily—some of the worst human rights violators on the planet, so long as they were right-wing, anticommunist dictators. US support for the Somozas in Nicaragua, Mobutu in Zaire, the Shah in Iran, and Marcos in the Philippines during the Cold War led to persisting civil war, instability, and underdevelopment. After the United States embarked on a humanitarian intervention in Somalia in 1992, during which eighteen soldiers were killed in battle, President Bill Clinton immediately withdrew US forces, realizing that supporting human rights in Somalia was no longer in the national interest of the United States. The impact of the failed mission in Somalia was felt two years later, as the United States and Belgium led a charge to withdraw 80 percent of the UN peacekeepers in Rwanda even as 800,000 civilians were being slaughtered in one of the worst genocides of the twentieth century. As a Clinton administration official told a Rwandan activist at the time, "The United States doesn't have friends, it has interests; and the United States has no interests in Rwanda."[4] In the case of China, the United States is content with containing the country's influence in the region and publicly criticizing its human rights record, but the United States would not threaten its economic trade with China or its Treasury bond ratings (since China holds roughly $1 trillion in US public debt) over human rights concerns. Secretary of State Hillary Clinton made this clear during a 2009 visit to China when she stated, "Our pressing on [China's human rights] can't interfere with the global economic crisis, the global climate change crisis and the security crisis."[5]

These are but a few examples of states prioritizing their national interests above human rights. I focus on the United States not to single out one country as any worse than the others, but because the United States prides itself on being the "city on the hill," the liberal democracy that serves as the world's human rights policeman.[6] I also am not saying that US policymakers don't care about human rights personally; but as agents of the state, they must prioritize state sovereignty and national interests above all else. Even the United States, the world's most powerful state, which was founded on the principle of the constitutional protection of rights and has been instrumental in building the global human rights system, cannot afford to disregard its national interests in favor of human rights.

In sum, according to the realist argument states may protect human rights when this is convenient, inexpensive, or consistent with their national interests. However, in an international system of sovereign states, national interests come first, and human rights typically are (and must be) disregarded when those interests are at stake. Therefore, the best way to guarantee that human rights are protected is to link them together with the material interests of powerful states.

Argument 2
States can and will sacrifice their narrow self-interests to protect human rights.

In contrast to the realists, liberalists argue that human rights can and actually do become a determining factor in states' policymaking. Human rights are not merely used as manipulative rhetoric, or ignored in favor of other concerns; they often are used by states to circumscribe their domestic and foreign policy choices. This is not because states follow human rights norms or international law instead of their national interests, but because states come to define national interests in ways that are consistent with human rights standards.

At the domestic level, liberalists argue that the rule of law and the respect for individual rights are the most solid foundation for social order and security, not vice versa. Liberalists side with Locke in his view of the social contract—that rights provide the basis for order—rather than with Hobbes in his vision of rights being exchanged for order. As a result, democracies—meaning those governments that respect liberal rights—act much differently than dictatorships. Political leaders in democracies stay in power by being responsive to their constituents' interests, and brutality and political deception are therefore often punished rather than rewarded. In this context, state sovereignty belongs properly to the citizenry itself, rather than to the ruler. Through participating in the democratic process, the citizenry is empowered to define the nation's interests and determine how to pursue them. Through the checks and balances within government, the availability of constitutional protections, and the mechanisms that hold political leaders accountable for their actions, established democracies are able to ensure that political order is achieved in a way that protects human rights.

Just as liberalists envisage a pathway for states to protect human rights at home, they also argue that states can best achieve their national interests by incorporating human rights into their foreign policies. This is because, even in the midst of an international arena characterized by anarchy and state sovereignty, states can define their interests in terms of absolute gains, rather than through the relative gains that realists imagine. In other words, states are often able to achieve their interests through mutual cooperation that benefits all states, rather than worrying about how much one state benefits compared to others. Human rights provide just this kind of basis for mutual cooperation. So long as the state's policies are reciprocated by others, it makes sense for that state to protect human rights, because all states are better off in the long term if their prisoners of war are not mistreated, if genocides are prevented, and if free speech is protected.

Liberalists therefore point to the importance of international institutions like the United Nations, which facilitate cooperation and raise the political cost of violating human rights. Once a state signs and ratifies a human rights treaty, and participates in the treaty's implementation through regular evaluation by its peers, it is able to receive some of the collective benefits that accompany treaty membership. Thus, although a state may see some short-term benefit to violating human rights, international institutions can impose diplomatic, economic, and military costs for noncompliance, making it far more likely (though not universally guaranteed) that the state will comply. This is known as the **collective enforcement** of human rights. Even in the absence of an overarching world government, the more that states are integrated into a dense web of international human rights institutions, the more that they will calculate that the protection of human rights is in their national interests. Therefore, states care about human rights because they have much to gain collectively from their protection.

Liberalists also note that if people have successfully created coercive institutions at the domestic level that protect their rights (i.e., governments), it is theoretically possible for humans to achieve this at the global level as well. Although this has not yet happened, it is imaginable that states would give up some of their sovereignty in exchange for the protection of their citizens' human rights at home and abroad. The creation of the International Criminal Court in 2002, which is authorized to prosecute war crimes and gross violations of human rights wherever they occur, is one small step in this direction. Even though a state might suffer some short-term costs by having its leaders or soldiers prosecuted for war crimes, the 120 member states of the ICC have determined that they have a greater long-term interest in the collective enforcement of human rights.

According to one of the founders of liberalism, Immanuel Kant (1724–1804), democratic states are uniquely crafted to care about human rights both at home and abroad.[7] Because democratic republics respect their own citizens' rights, they are more likely to cooperate with other democracies. Kant predicted that this would establish a "zone of peace" within which democracies do not go to war with each other, which is exactly what has occurred among the roughly 100 democracies in the world. Kant also predicted that democracies would be more likely to go to war with dictatorships, in order to convert them into states that protect human rights. Liberalists therefore argue that human rights become important to democracies in determining both peace and war.

Constructivism offers a slightly different reason why states should care, and often do care, about protecting human rights in their domestic and foreign policies. Based on the philosophy of social constructivism discussed in Chapter 1, constructivists claim that people, and therefore states, are motivated by their *ideas* more than any objective interests.[8] These ideas about the world are created through a process of social dialogue and interaction. Ideas that are widely viewed as legitimate gain strength through socialization, modeling, education, and habitual behavior. These ideas literally define our interests and determine the range of action that is considered appropriate to achieve those interests. In other words, our values drive us, and states' actions are limited by what their leaders, their populations, and other states deem to be proper behavior.[9]

Human rights are one set of ideas that has gained increasing global legitimacy over the past century. States therefore follow human rights because they believe that this is the right thing to do, not because they will gain anything from compliance. However, human rights compete with other ideas that could potentially guide state policy, such as ethnic nationalism, religious doctrine, laissez-faire economics, and realpolitik. It is this competition over ideas that ultimately determines whether states care about protecting human rights and what policies they will implement toward this end. The competition takes place in the media, in school classrooms, in political debates, and in daily conversations—anywhere ideas are exchanged.

For constructivists, it is clear that human rights have (at least partially and temporarily) won this competition, because some state actions that were once routinely practiced are now so widely condemned that they are unthinkable in a modern context. Recall, for example, how realists point to the Peloponnesian War of ancient Greece as an example of states' invariable pursuit of their own power and self-interests at the expense of potential rivals. Constructivists would point out how much has changed since the fourth century B.C.E. In the Peloponnesian War, after the democratic Athenians conquered Melos, they enjoyed the spoils of victory by killing all adult males and enslaving the Melian women and children. Indeed, as Thucydides described, this was relatively common practice among warring societies at the time. Constructivists would ask: Today, in the twenty-first century, why don't we continue to slaughter and enslave populations that we conquer? Is it because the victors calculate that slaughter is not in their self-interests, or that they do not have the power to "do what they will"? No, it is because genocide and enslavement have become unthinkable in most modern civilizations. Protecting the human rights even of one's enemies has become a social norm. While such norms are still sometimes violated, constructivists argue that human rights play an important role in how states conduct wars, engage in foreign policy, and treat their own populations at home. Human rights help to shape the way that state leaders think about the range of appropriate actions they can take in order to provide order and security.

Does concern for human rights depend on enlightened leaders who care about common moral sentiments? For constructivists, not necessarily. Following realist logic, states may initially promise to uphold human rights out of a self-interested or manipulative intent. However, a state's public commitments often inspire its own population to hold it accountable to those promises, which results in public pressure upon the state from within and abroad. The state may then be forced to enact human rights reforms; and if these reforms take hold, eventually they can become institutionalized by the state as a matter of habitual practice. This has been called the **spiral model** of human rights enforcement, as states with leaders who may not inherently care about human rights can still be led down a path of increasing the state's concern for those very rights.[10]

In sum, liberalists and constructivists argue that states do care about human rights, because they increasingly define their interests in accordance with human rights standards. States still care about power and security, but they are unwilling to incur any cost to achieve these interests, because their populations are now empowered to hold them accountable to human rights norms. For liberalists, democracy has empowered people within the state, and involvement in international institutions has empowered outsiders to pressure or encourage the state into human rights compliance. For constructivists, states care about human rights because their populations have internalized these values and imposed them upon the state. While violations of human rights continue, modern states must increasingly justify their actions in human rights terms in order to be considered legitimate and responsible. Their security depends on human rights protection, not vice versa.

* * *

Conclusion

Do states really care about protecting human rights? In the complex world of international politics, it is certainly possible to find compelling evidence on both sides of the argument (see Figure 2.1). In this context, we should remind ourselves of our own cognitive biases. We tend to interpret new

Figure 2.1 Interpreting the US War in Iraq

In March 2003, President George W. Bush led a "coalition of the willing" to invade Iraq, depose Saddam Hussein, and occupy the country. Although the US-led military invasion was successful, the war remained highly controversial, as Iraq subsequently devolved into civil war and the human and financial costs of the war proved far higher than Bush administration officials had promised.

President Bush's primary justification for starting this war was to prevent Iraq from supporting terrorism and to remove suspected weapons of mass destruction from Iraqi possession. Another key justification for the war, however, was grounded in human rights. The Bush administration argued repeatedly that the invasion and occupation of Iraq would transform the country into a democratic society and free the Iraqi people from decades of oppression under Hussein. Toward this end, the US military invasion was dubbed Operation Iraqi Freedom.

This case raises the question of whether US policymakers really cared about human rights in Iraq. Realists might contend that Bush's rights-based justification was nothing more than a Machiavellian attempt to engender international and domestic support for a war that served US national interests. From this perspective, the United States was overwhelmingly concerned about terrorist attacks against its citizens, the proliferation of weapons of mass destruction, and the regional balance of power in the Middle East, but it was (at best) only secondarily concerned about the protection of human rights in the region. Indeed, criticisms at the time from the major US-based human rights organizations seemed to lend credence to the realist perspective. NGOs like Amnesty International and **Human Rights Watch** declared that the rights-based justifications for the war in Iraq were vacuous and without merit, and even called for the arrest of senior Bush administration officials for war crimes.[11] Realists would also note that the United States was able to execute this war despite widespread international protest and the refusal of the United Nations Security Council to endorse the invasion. As Thucydides said, the strong do what they will.

Liberalists might counter that the war in Iraq really was motivated, in large part, by a concern for human rights, even if applied in an inconsistent and ineffective manner. While the fundamental motivation was clearly national security, the United States spent a tremendous amount of human, political, and financial capital on transforming Iraq into a democracy, as Kant would predict. The United States could have withdrawn from Iraq soon after failing to uncover weapons of mass destruction, but it remained for a decade in the attempt to maintain peace, hold elections, and enshrine new rights into the Iraqi constitution. Liberalists would also point out that, although the Bush administration circumvented the United Nations in executing the war, it still

(continues)

Figure 2.1 continued

---

felt compelled to justify the invasion before the Security Council and required some international support for the operation.

Finally, constructivists would argue that the battle of ideas largely determined how much the United States cared about human rights in Iraq. In the immediate aftermath of the events of September 11, 2001, concern about terrorism and weapons of mass destruction probably trumped concerns about human rights in the collective mind of the American public. Most Americans were probably willing to support the war, irrespective of the impact it had on Iraqi human rights. Constructivists might further note how the **Abu Ghraib** scandal in 2004 demonstrated the ongoing impact of human rights on US foreign policy. When the American public learned about abuses committed by its own soldiers against Iraqi prisoners, it widely condemned these violations as morally repugnant, and eventually elected a president committed to reversing some of the most egregious violations.

---

events in ways that are consistent with our preexisting beliefs, rather than question the accuracy of those beliefs. If one is accustomed to thinking like a realist, then one would tend to interpret states' human rights policies as self-interested or manipulative. If one is a liberalist or constructivist, one would likewise see states' human rights policies as a result of the growth of democracy, international engagement, or the internalization of values.

In the twenty-first century, the international system of human rights protection is characterized by two notable features. On the one hand, we have witnessed a dramatic expansion of international treaties and organizations designed explicitly for the protection of human rights. On the other hand, these international bodies are still overwhelmingly governed and controlled by sovereign states. The question of whether these states meaningfully incorporate human rights into their domestic and foreign policies makes a huge difference in the practical implementation of human rights. If states are fundamentally and inherently oriented toward the pursuit of self-interest and power, then the best that human rights activists could hope for is a temporary coincidence between the protection of rights and the interests of powerful states. Until and unless sovereign states are replaced by some other form of governance, human rights would remain a secondary concern or epiphenomenon in international affairs. Perhaps some redefinition of state sovereignty is already occurring in small ways, as the ICC and the **Responsibility to Protect (R2P)** doctrine have attempted to make sovereignty conditional upon the protection of rights. If states can be counted on to protect human rights, then we can be more hopeful about the efforts around the world to pressure states into fulfilling the numerous public commitments they have already endorsed.

Notes

1. Upendra Baxi, "Human Rights Education: The Promise of the Third Millennium?" December 19, 1995, http://www.pdhre.org/dialogue/third_millenium .html.

2. Max Weber, *Politics as a Vocation* (Minneapolis: Fortress, 2000).

3. See, for example, the six principles of political realism specified in Hans Morgenthau, *Politics Among Nations: The Struggle for Power and Peace* (New York: Knopf, 1948).

4. See the documentary film *Ghosts of Rwanda*, May 10, 2005, http://www .pbs.org/wgbh/pages/frontline/shows/ghosts.

5. Richard Spencer, "Hillary Clinton: Chinese Human Rights Secondary to Economic Survival," *The Telegraph*, February 20, 2009, http://www.telegraph.co.uk /news/worldnews/asia/china/4735087/Hillary-Clinton-Chinese-human-rights -secondary-to-economic-survival.html.

6. Ronald Reagan, "Farewell Address to the Nation," January 11, 1989, http:// www.reaganfoundation.org/pdf/Farewell_Address_011189.pdf.

7. Michael Doyle, "Liberalism and World Politics," *American Political Science Review* 80, no. 4 (1986): 1151–1169.

8. Alexander Wendt, *Social Theory of International Politics* (Cambridge: Cambridge University Press, 1999).

9. For a primer on constructivism, see Alice Ba and Matthew J. Hoffman, "Making and Remaking the World for IR 101: A Resource for Teaching Social Constructivism in Introductory Classes," *International Studies Perspectives* 4, no. 1 (March 2003): 15–33.

10. Thomas Risse and Kathryn Sikkink, "The Socialization of International Human Rights Norms into Domestic Practice: Introduction," in *The Power of Human Rights: International Norms and Domestic Change*, edited by Thomas Risse, Stephen C. Ropp, and Kathryn Sikkink (Cambridge: Cambridge University Press, 1999), p. 3.

11. Kenneth Roth, "Was the War in Iraq a Humanitarian Intervention?" *Journal of Military Ethics* 5, no. 2 (2006): 84–92.

3

How Can Western States Promote Human Rights in China?

On April 22, 2012, a blind lawyer named Chen Guangcheng boldly escaped from his village in China, where he had been under house arrest for four years, and made his way to the US embassy in Beijing. Chen's amazing escape included climbing over walls, swimming through rivers, slipping past dozens of guards, and walking for several hours in the middle of the night. Chen, a human rights activist who had exposed abuses resulting from China's one-child policy, such as forced sterilizations, had been imprisoned without any formal charges. He entered the US embassy seeking protection for himself, his family, and fellow dissidents who had helped him escape.

This episode sparked a diplomatic crisis, as US secretary of state Hillary Clinton was simultaneously in Beijing for delicate talks with China over economic policy, nuclear proliferation, territorial disputes, and other thorny issues. Chen hoped that the US government, by providing him refuge, could actively demonstrate its long-professed commitment to defending human rights in China. Secretary Clinton, however, indicated that she would be careful not to anger China over Chen's case, so as not to threaten the "constructive relationship" between the two countries.[1] Ultimately, Clinton negotiated a compromise with China, as Chen voluntarily left the embassy but was subsequently allowed by the Chinese authorities to study abroad with his family in the United States.

Chen's case highlighted a decades-long dilemma for Western states in their relationships with China. Successive US presidents and European leaders have consistently criticized the Chinese Communist Party for its human rights abuses at home and abroad. In negotiations over issues ranging from

39

security to climate change, Western diplomats frequently admonish their Chinese counterparts over human rights abuses. The criticisms appear to have some merit, as China is well known for jailing its political dissidents, restricting access to information, limiting religious freedom, and propping up repressive regimes in places like Sudan and Iran. Chinese leaders typically do not respond kindly to these accusations, replying with their own condemnation of the human rights records of Western states, especially the United States, and claiming that Americans have no right to lecture them on human rights. The Western states and China often find themselves at an impasse over human rights, and so they seem content to rebuke each other rhetorically even as they continue to deepen their economic and diplomatic ties.

Some political analysts (such as the realists, as discussed in Chapter 2) would look at this behavior and conclude that the Western states are not truly interested in the protection of human rights in China, and that both sides are merely trading rhetorical barbs in order to appease their nationalistic populations at home. No country seems willing to risk its vital national interests in order to pursue human rights abroad. Other analysts, however, would allow that policymakers may be genuinely interested in protecting human rights, but perhaps are unsure about the most effective strategies, or lack sufficient power to achieve their goals. Assuming for the moment that the Western states are committed to improving human rights in China, what approaches are most likely to prove effective? What set of foreign policies can a government take in order to improve the protection of rights in another state?

In this debate, the stakes could not be higher. The United States, European Union, and China are the world's three largest economies, collectively accounting for over half of the world's total gross domestic product (GDP).[2] Any economic dispute that were to harm these economies would certainly result in a major global recession. Likewise, these actors are also nuclear powers and possess some of the world's strongest militaries (with the United States unrivaled in this regard), with contrasting positions on security issues ranging from Taiwan, to the South China Sea, to Iran and Syria. Any major military dispute between these states would certainly result in a third world war. On a wide range of measures, for better or worse, the United States and China will likely form the most important bilateral relationship in the world in the twenty-first century.

This chapter presents two sides in the debate over human rights and foreign policy. One side argues in favor of **confrontation**—in other words, that Western states should use their considerable leverage to pressure or compel China into reforming its human rights record. Confrontation is a time-tested strategy that human rights activists have used to change the behavior of their opponents. The other side argues that **engagement** with China is a more effective way to ensure that any improvements in human rights are locally owned, durable, and based on cooperation with the West rather than conflict. By further linking China into the globalized world, the Chinese people will eventually become empowered enough to achieve their own rights protection in their own ways.

Argument 1
Western states should pressure China to improve its human rights record.

According to the confrontation perspective, human rights should be at the top of the international foreign policy agenda, and the situation in China demands an urgent response. This is because China is indeed one of the world's worst human rights violators, as many suspect. Civil rights and political freedoms are notably lacking in China. The country is controlled by a one-party regime that does not submit itself to public accountability through the electoral process and does not tolerate dissent. Activists such as Chen Guangcheng or the artist Ai Weiwei, who speak out against the abuses committed by the Chinese Communist Party, are routinely jailed without receiving a fair trial. It is estimated that China executes thousands of its prisoners each year, vastly exceeding every other country in the use of the death penalty.[3] Most Chinese citizens do not have free access to information, as the Internet is censored and private media outlets are blocked.

The Chinese government also systematically violates the economic, social, and cultural rights of its people. Minority groups such as Chinese Christians, Tibetan Buddhists, and Uyghur Muslims are persecuted for their religious practices and denied cultural protections. Chinese workers, who produce so many of the manufactured goods for the developed world, often suffer in sweatshop-like factories that lack basic health protections or labor rights. When Chinese families have more than one child, they are penalized economically and sometimes forced to endure sterilization or abortion.

China regularly violates human rights in its foreign policy as well. When Sudanese president Omar al-Bashir committed genocide against the people of Darfur, China blocked stronger economic sanctions in the UN Security Council so that it could continue to import much of Sudan's oil. In North Korea, China remains the only bastion of support for the totalitarian, nuclear-armed regime of the Kim family, which has led its people into multiple famines and international isolation. China is suspected of selling nuclear technology to the dictatorial government of Iran, and has blocked stronger UN sanctions against Iran for its nuclear weapons program. In sub-Saharan Africa, China is leading the push to invest in the extraction of oil, natural gas, and other minerals, which leads to local environmental destruction and contributes to global climate change.

According to the confrontation perspective, these human rights violations require urgent and immediate action, not only because they affect China's 1.3 billion citizens, but also because China is now a major global power. Abuses by the Chinese state affect a large swath of the world's population. The Western powers cannot sit by and wait for China to reform itself. China is clearly on the rise economically and militarily, and must be pressured to improve its commitment to human rights.

Thus, when Chinese officials respond to external criticism by condemning the human rights record of the West, we should recognize this for what it is: a cynical attempt to deflect attention from their own deplorable behavior. Western states certainly do not have a perfect record on human rights, but they include the most advanced liberal democracies, which are generally the world's strongest defenders of human rights. In contrast with China, Western states are world leaders in protecting religious and ethnic minorities, holding free elections, respecting due process, and protecting free speech. The West's strong reputation for defending human rights gives it the moral authority to judge China's record, and the United States and its allies are the only group in the world with both the power and the international legitimacy to pressure China on human rights.

It is vital that Western states use this power in the service of human rights. Chinese officials (and foreign policy isolationists) argue that the Western states should mind their own business, because under the principle of sovereignty, states should not interfere in the domestic affairs of other states. As long as China is not threatening international peace and security, it should be left alone. According to the confrontation perspective, however, the West is part of an international community that is merely trying to hold China accountable to its own promises. China has agreed to over twenty international human rights treaties, including conventions protecting economic and social rights, civil and political rights, women's and children's rights, and freedom from torture and discrimination.[4] In 2006, China also affirmed the Responsibility to Protect doctrine, which makes state sovereignty conditional upon the respect for human rights. By signing and ratifying these documents, the Chinese government has ex-

plicitly committed itself to protecting these rights, and thereby opened itself up to the mechanisms of enforcement available to the international
community.

Thus, given that international pressure to improve human rights in
China is both urgent and legitimate, confrontation is a better strategy to
pursue than engagement, because confrontation involves methods that
have been tested over the decades by human rights activists, and have
proven to be successful in a wide variety of cases. One of the most basic
confrontational tactics is known as **naming and shaming,** or publicly
condemning human rights abuses by specifically identifying the violation
and the violator. Naming and shaming is effective because individual
leaders (and therefore states) care about their reputations in the international community. Even when leaders do not care about their reputations,
naming and shaming can also work by generating outrage among like-
minded populations and states, thereby expanding support for more coercive forms of enforcement. This is why Amnesty International, today the
world's largest human rights NGO, has used naming and shaming tactics
since its inception in 1961. Its letter-writing campaigns have resulted in
the release of thousands of political prisoners.[5] When IGOs such as the
United Nations Human Rights Council (UNHRC) monitor and report
on human rights abuses by its member states, they too are relying on naming and shaming tactics.

As an emerging global power, China certainly does care about its international reputation. Thus, states like China make an effort to avoid or
blunt the criticism that they receive from the international community.
Even though it seems hypocritical for countries like the United States to
condemn China publicly as they continue to cooperate with China privately, these words still matter in pressuring China to comply with human
rights standards. One way that states can blunt international criticism is by
enacting small reforms, such as China's allowing of Chen Guangcheng to
study abroad in the United States. These small changes may eventually
build momentum toward more substantial reforms, as the spiral model
would predict.

As a mechanism for the international enforcement of human rights,
naming and shaming is a relatively weak tool. But there is a wide range of
confrontational tactics that states can use to pressure human rights violators. Western states could apply diplomatic sanctions against China, such
as denying Chinese officials travel visas or closing their overseas embassies in Beijing. They could apply targeted military sanctions against
China, such as restricting the sale of weapons or nuclear technology. They
could levy financial sanctions, which might include freezing the foreign

bank accounts of Chinese officials and denying them access to their assets abroad.[6] Or they could even enforce broader economic sanctions against China, boycotting all exports or banning all foreign investment.

These confrontational tactics are designed not only to send a strong message in support of human rights, but also to coerce Chinese decision-makers by punishing them for noncompliance. If sanctions are not effective in changing China's behavior, then more forceful measures could be employed, even including military action. Of course, no leader would start a full-scale war with China, as the result would be devastating to everyone involved. However, policymakers may be willing to take actions short of direct military confrontation, such as selling advanced weapons technology to Taiwan, or mobilizing foreign navies in the South China Sea as a show of force.

Public condemnation, economic sanctions, and military action are more effective when undertaken universally rather than unilaterally. The United States cannot expect to change China's behavior by itself. However, according to the confrontation perspective, the United States, as the most powerful Western actor, must lead the international effort to pressure China toward human rights reforms, because no other state has both the power and the moral authority to lead. China retains a veto in the UN Security Council, which essentially prevents the United Nations from taking any forceful action against it. Therefore, the United States should lead a coalition of like-minded allies in compelling China to implement reforms, as it successfully did to end apartheid in South Africa and to promote democratic reforms in Burma. The United States did not appoint itself the world's human rights policeman, but because no other state or international institution is able to fulfill that role, the United States must maximize its use of power if human rights are to be protected. As a collection of powerful democratic states, the West can collectively pressure China to improve its respect for human rights.

Confrontational tactics such as sanctions and military action are clearly costly in the short run. They risk the erosion of political stability in China, economic prosperity, and international cooperation. These tactics would be even more costly in the case of China, which is far more powerful than South Africa or Burma, and therefore more able to resist external pressure. However, given the economic and military strength of the West, it still maintains tremendous leverage over China. As China continues its rapid pace of growth, this window of superiority will gradually close. While a conflict over trade or financial sanctions would likely be destructive in the short term, it would still prove more beneficial to long-term collective interests than the existence of a future authoritarian China as a superpower. Because of the seriousness of China's human rights violations and its support for the world's worst regimes, the international community will suffer tremendous damage should China continue to increase its power without taking more responsibility for protecting human rights.

So far, though, the West has not stood up to China's human rights abuses. The United States and European Union have largely chosen a failed policy of "unconditional engagement" with China; in other words, they have not made economic and political cooperation conditional upon the protection of human rights.[7] The European Union maintains an arms embargo on China in response to its human rights violations, but this does not affect the overwhelming majority of trade between the two economies. And while individual states such as Germany and Denmark frequently use bilateral or multilateral diplomacy to excoriate China over its abuses, this has not resulted in a coherent Western policy of confrontation and pressure.

Proponents of engagement with China believe that political reforms will occur almost naturally, as China becomes ever more integrated into the global economy and socialized into the global community of states. However, as the list of China's human rights violations indicates, there is no historical evidence to support this belief. At least since the Deng Xiaoping era of the 1980s, China has opened itself to foreign trade and investment. China actively participates in the political bodies of the United Nations, as well as other IGOs such as the **World Trade Organization (WTO)**. China's extensive international engagement has not resulted in sufficient progress on human rights because China knows that it will not be held accountable for its violations. The Tiananmen Square massacre of 1989 clearly demonstrated to the world the Chinese government's repression of dissent and free assembly. The final straw proved to be the 2008 Olympics in Beijing, which were offered to China by the International Olympic Committee with the specific goal of promoting political reforms through international cooperation. Instead, China further disregarded human rights in the lead-up to the Olympics, displacing poor communities to make way for sporting events, jailing political dissidents, and restricting access to the media.

In sum, according to the proponents of confrontation, engagement has not proven effective in constraining China's egregious human rights violations. As citizens in the West continue to buy the products made in Chinese sweatshops by people who do not have the ability to protest their own conditions, they become complicit in those violations. As Western governments continue to prioritize their economic and security interests over the protection of human rights in China, they also become complicit in those violations. Engagement policies are therefore tantamount to complicity. While confrontational tactics would likely entail short-term economic and political risks, these risks are preferable to the continuation of the status quo, which likely will result in an authoritarian China as a superpower. Western states are powerful enough to lead the international community to constrain China's rise and pressure it to improve its human rights record.

Argument 2
Western states should engage rather than confront China.

From this perspective, engagement is a more effective strategy than confrontation if the West wants to reform China's human rights practices. Indeed, the expansion of confrontational tactics might result in both lack of progress on human rights and far more destructive outcomes.[8]

Engagement is an approach that the West has pursued since President Richard Nixon first visited China in 1972, involving the opening of China to trade and foreign investment, the increasing of diplomatic linkages, and encouragement of China's participation in a wide range of international institutions. The Clinton administration expanded US engagement with China in the 1990s by offering it most-favored-nation status (thus making China eligible for full trade privileges) without taking into account its human rights record. Since China joined the WTO, it has established similar trade relations with other Western countries. The West chose this path in China because of its belief that "the only route to progress on human rights lay in economic growth and a larger middle class."[9] Despite the occasional public criticism of China's human rights abuses, Western officials have largely continued this policy to the present.

Engagement works by fostering economic and social trends that lead to internal pressure for political reforms, rather than trying to force these reforms from the outside. **Modernization theory** predicts that as a state becomes wealthier, it develops a middle-class population that is more educated, urbanized, and empowered to speak up for human rights. Together, the United States and European Union trade roughly $1 trillion in goods and services with China each year, accounting for half of China's total exports.[10] Between 2000 and 2007, China increased its trade with the world nearly sixfold, to $3 trillion annually.[11] China's rapid economic growth since the reforms of Deng Xiaoping increased the average annual income of its citizens from $250 in 1980 to over $7,500 in 2010.[12] This is important for civil and political rights, as researchers have found that countries that are near China's current level of income are more likely to transition from dictatorship to democracy, and democracies above this level of income nearly always survive.[13]

Although China has not yet embraced democracy, the policy of engagement has led to significant strides toward the protection of human rights.[14] Politically, China has instituted relatively free and competitive elections at the local level, even though the Chinese Communist Party still dictates policy at the national level. Although media censorship and corruption remain common, the Chinese government has slowly become more transparent and has opened itself to some criticism in private media outlets. Economically, China has made extraordinary progress, pulling more than 600 million of its citizens out of extreme poverty since the 1970s (more than double the entire population of the United States).[15] This pace of improvement is literally unprecedented in human history. The majority of China's people still do not live in prosperity by Western standards, but they can now meet their basic needs, and attain their economic and social rights. The Chinese state provides free primary and secondary education to its citizens, and is committed to ensuring universal access to basic health care.[16] This record compares quite favorably to that of capitalist democracies in the West, and it gives the Chinese government a significant amount of legitimacy among its people, even though it is not democratic. Pressure from the United States to improve human rights in China probably reveals more about the US bias against economic and social rights than it does about China's actual record.

By fostering China's involvement in regional and global institutions, a policy of engagement also encourages China to follow the rules of the global community. By participating in institutions such as the WTO and various United Nations bodies, China regularly interacts with democratic states and can increasingly model its behavior after states that follow the institutions' rules. According to the engagement perspective, this process is best facilitated not by coercion and enforcement from the outside, but by socialization and learning. Cultural and diplomatic exchanges with the West can strengthen the constituency within China who advocate for political reforms of their own accord. As China increases its role as a global power, the internal pressure for it to become a responsible world leader will also increase.

Granted, this process of improving human rights through internal economic and cultural changes is incremental and often slow. Those who promote confrontation often promise rapid and dramatic changes in behavior. The problem is that confrontational tactics are likely to backfire in China, producing more harm than good. China's growing power, its nationalistic sentiment, and its history of foreign intervention make it particularly resistant to coercive tactics.[17] When China's policies are publicly criticized, as occurred in the run-up to the Beijing Olympics, its people often respond with nationalistic demonstrations, supporting their own government and accusing the West of ethnocentric bias.[18] This nationalist backlash is partly grounded in China's history of being invaded by Western powers during the 1900 Boxer War, and by Japan during World War II. In its international relations, China has held fairly consistently to the principle of sovereignty, warning against external interference in the domestic affairs of states. It views pressure from the West over human rights as a violation of its sovereignty, and remains staunchly opposed to such pressure.[19]

As a result, according to the engagement perspective, Western states, even the United States, have neither the leverage nor the legitimacy to pressure China to improve its human rights record. China possesses several hundred nuclear weapons, and holds roughly $1 trillion in US debt. Any attempt to impose broad economic sanctions or military pressure on China would likely inflict significant damage to global security and prosperity, without even achieving the goal of improving the protection of rights in China. Major confrontation between the West and China would certainly threaten global stability.

Likewise in support of the engagement perspective, the United States, despite its superpower status, does not necessarily occupy the moral high ground when it admonishes China for its human rights violations at home or its support for dictators abroad. The United States loses credibility when it preaches to China about human rights while practicing torture against detainees, invading countries under false pretenses, and supporting its own authoritarian allies in places like Saudi Arabia and Yemen. China rightly responds to US criticism by pointing out the failures in US security, immigration, health, and economic policies. The hypocrisy evident in US criticism of China makes it clear that US policy is based on self-interest rather than a consistent concern for human rights. The Chinese people have good reason to believe that US pressure is a thinly guised attempt to weaken or contain China's rising power. Therefore, if the United States genuinely cares about human rights in China, it would be better served by setting a moral example and improving its own human rights record. By consistently defending human rights at home, the United States can gain more credibility when it advances those same rights abroad.

> **Think Again**
>
> Do you think that the United States has the moral authority to criticize China's human rights record? Given the fact that no state has a perfect record, should any state try to incorporate human rights conditions into its foreign policy?

In sum, engagement is a sometimes slow and frustrating approach to promoting human rights, but its benefits far outweigh the risks. Because the West lacks the appropriate leverage to force China's hand, confrontational tactics could potentially backfire, causing a global economic recession, the violent breakup of China, or a major war. As Secretary of State Clinton has stated, the world is already undergoing too many crises for the United States and China to threaten their delicate relationship over human rights. Instead, the West should continue to engage China economically and diplomatically in order to encourage the positive trends already occurring as China embraces globalization. When the Chinese people are empowered enough to achieve the realization of their own rights through their own methods, the reforms they adopt will prove more sustainable than if they were pressured by the West.

* * *

Conclusion

Do Western policymakers really care about human rights in China? Realists would suggest that support for human rights in China is fundamentally self-interested, and that the West is merely trying to weaken or destabilize China by pushing human rights. Realists are correct when they predict that rhetoric urging greater freedom in China will not be matched by any costly enforcement action. They are not surprised when states do not practice what they preach, as they believe all states must compromise their values in the pursuit of their interests. Realists are also skeptical about the liberalizing influence of economic trade, cultural exchanges, and participation in international institutions. Although they see confrontation as an inevitable part of international relations, most realists would urge caution in pursuing policies that might threaten instability. If the authoritarian Chinese state is able to achieve economic growth and political stability by restricting certain rights, then we should not upset the status quo and violate China's sovereignty simply to protect human rights.

On the other hand, liberalists would argue that human rights should receive primary consideration in foreign policy decisions. Because the protection of human rights is the best pathway to ensure long-term interests, states do not need to sacrifice human rights in the name of short-term interests. Most liberalists would place their trust in the power of economic interdependence and multilateral diplomacy to improve human rights, rather than unilateral coercive measures. Better that the West continue to trade, negotiate, and promote educational exchanges with China, than apply economic sanctions. To the extent that coercive measures might be necessary, they should be enforced under the universal authority of the United Nations, rather than applied by the United States and a group of like-minded supporters alone. Constructivists too might see engagement as an effective approach to encourage a change of values in China. The more Chinese citizens exposed to Western people and ideas in a positive rather than punitive context, the more they will learn to mobilize for their own rights.

The case of China is unique in some regards, because of its growing power, its possession of nuclear weapons, and its veto in the UN Security Council. However, a similar debate between confrontation and engagement arises in addressing human rights violations in many other countries around the world. For example, the West has imposed harsh economic and diplomatic sanctions on Burma since 1988 in response to the military regime's brutal suppression of political protest and its discriminatory treatment of ethnic minorities. However, as Burma began to institute some democratic reforms in 2010, including the release of political prisoners and the election to parliament of Nobel Prize–winning activist Aung San Suu Kyi, the West has rewarded the Burmese government by removing some sanctions and widening its diplomatic engagement. Recent developments in Burma may point to the success of confrontational tactics in pressuring the military regime to reform itself, as the West's leverage over a relatively poor Burmese government was far greater than it has been over a rising China. Yet many Burmese democracy activists are still wary of the West opening up too quickly to a government that is still largely authoritarian. Western states have no vital national interests to protect in Burma, and thus liberalists and constructivists would view their promotion of human rights as relatively genuine. Realists, however, would suggest that the West is beginning to engage Burma in order to counter China's growing influence there.

Likewise, in Cuba, the United States has continuously pursued a policy of confrontation since 1960 in response to the Castro government's suppression of civil and political rights. Although it would seem that the United States would have tremendous leverage over a poor island nation ninety miles from its border, a strict economic embargo against Cuba has proven ineffective in removing the Castro family from power, or in promoting democratic reforms. In part, this is because US sanctions have largely been unilateral, unsupported by the rest of the world. Thus, in 2009, the Obama administration began easing travel and financial sanctions against Cuba, hoping that economic trade and an exchange of ideas would prove more effective in encouraging democracy there. This change in US policy was very controversial domestically, particularly among the Cuban exile community concentrated in the state of Florida. For most of the past half-century, it seems that the US approach toward human rights in Cuba has been driven as much by domestic political interests as by international politics or a concern for human rights.

And so, whether a state chooses confrontation or engagement to promote human rights is determined by a combination of different concerns: political interests at home, economic and security interests abroad, the severity of human rights violations, and the amount of leverage the state has over the violator. Although globalization has made many different actors important in international relations, states are still the primary actors entrusted with the military and economic power to enforce human rights at home and abroad. So long as sovereignty precludes the establishment of a world government, states still have the most coercive leverage to change the behavior of other states. However, as this chapter demonstrates, the power of the United States to influence human rights in China is limited by the counterbalancing power of China, the national interests of the United States, and the inconsistency of its own human rights record. Even the world's most powerful state cannot enforce human rights wherever and whenever it pleases.

If not states, then who? As this book illustrates, there are myriad actors that have some influence, for better or worse, over human rights enforcement. For example, NGOs and international institutions (such as United Nations treaty bodies) can investigate and condemn human rights violations wherever they occur. NGOs and IGOs certainly do not possess the coercive power of states, but they typically maintain greater moral authority than states, and can sometimes influence states' behavior by damaging their reputation among other states. Thus a group like Amnesty International has the credibility to criticize China's human rights violations in ways that the US government cannot. Indeed, multiple actors may be able to promote human rights in China more effectively through a combination of confrontation and engagement, as NGOs can play the "bad cop," using more confrontational tactics such as naming and shaming, while governments play the "good cop" and utilize strategies of engagement.[20] Depending on the actors involved, confrontation and engagement are not necessarily mutually exclusive.

Notes

1. Michele Kelemen, "Activist's Escape Complicates Clinton's China Visit," *National Public Radio*, April 30, 2012, http://www.npr.org/2012/04/30/151707162 /activists-escape-complicates-clintons-china-visit.

2. Central Intelligence Agency, "GDP (Official Exchange Rate)," in *The World Factbook*, 2012, https://www.cia.gov/library/publications/the-world-fact book/fields/2195.html.

3. Amnesty International, "Death Sentences and Executions in 2011," March 2012, http://www.amnesty.org/en/library/info/ACT50/001/2012/en.

4. Sanzhuan Guo, "Implementation of Human Rights Treaties by Chinese Courts: Problems and Prospects," *Chinese Journal of International Law* 8, no. 1 (2009): 161–179.

5. See Stephen Hopgood, *Keepers of the Flame: Understanding Amnesty International* (Ithaca: Cornell University Press, 2006).

6. For a defense of targeted sanctions, see David Cortright and George A. Lopez, eds., *Smart Sanctions: Targeting Economic Statecraft* (Boulder: Rowman and Littlefield, 2002).

7. John Fox and François Godement, *A Power Audit of EU-China Relations* (London: European Council on Foreign Relations, 2009), p. 1.

8. Yitan Li and A. Cooper Drury, "Threatening Sanctions When Engagement Would Be More Effective: Attaining Better Human Rights in China," *International Studies Perspectives* 5, no. 4 (2004): 378–394.

9. David Forsythe, *Human Rights in International Relations* (Cambridge: Cambridge University Press, 2012), p. 214.

10. US-China Business Council, "U.S.-China Trade Statistics and China's World Trade Statistics," https://www.uschina.org/statistics/tradetable.html, accessed June 13, 2012.

11. Ibid.

12. Measured in GDP per capita, adjusted for purchasing power parity (PPP) by current international dollars. Statistics from Google Public Data, http://www.google.com/publicdata, accessed June 13, 2012.

13. Adam Przeworski and Fernando Limongi, "Modernization: Theories and Facts," *World Politics* 49, no. 2 (1997): 155–183. Przeworski and Limongi's findings were based on a per capita income threshold of $6,000, adjusted for PPP in 1985 dollars.

14. See the comments from Jacques Delisle in Carnegie Endowment for International Peace, "Reframing China Policy: U.S. Engagement and Human Rights in China," public debate, Washington, DC, March 5, 2007, http://www.carnegieendowment.org/files/cds4_transcript.pdf.

15. Shaohua Chen and Martin Ravallion, "The Developing World Is Poorer Than We Thought, but No Less Successful in the Fight Against Poverty" (Washington, DC: World Bank, August 2008).

16. Winnie Chi-Man Yip et al., "Early Appraisal of China's Huge and Complex Health Care Reforms," *The Lancet* 379, no. 9818 (March 2012): 833–842.

17. Li and Drury, "Threatening Sanctions," p. 385.

18. See, for example, Preeti Bhattacharji and Carin Zissis, "Olympic Pressure on China," Council on Foreign Relations, June 17, 2008, http://www.cfr.org/china/olympic-pressure-china/p13270#p7.

19. Delisle in Carnegie Endowment for International Peace, "Reframing China Policy."

20. Ibid.

4

Is the United Nations Human Rights Council Effective?

Many different types of actors contribute to the protection or violation of human rights: NGOs such as Amnesty International, transnational corporations such as Walmart, regional organizations such as the European Union, and most important, individual states like China. When all of these actors fail to ensure that human rights are upheld, people tend to fall back on a familiar refrain: "Call in the United Nations!" As if it were a cavalry waiting to intervene anywhere to rescue the vulnerable, the United Nations is often perceived to be the global enforcer of human rights.

This perception is not entirely accurate. The UN is not a world government that stands above, or operates independently from, sovereign states. It does not have any legislative authority, or the power to impose taxes, or any coercive power independent of its member states. Other than the International Criminal Court, it does not have any judicial authority. Like most IGOs, the UN is a political organization composed of sovereign states as its members, and most of its actions are initiated and carried out by those states. The UN can best be described as a forum through which states act, rather than an actor of its own accord.

Despite these limitations, the United Nations is still important as the most universally inclusive IGO. Every population that has achieved statehood has obtained membership in the UN. States have chosen to create dozens of committees and agencies within the UN that help protect human rights around the world, and some of these bodies are able to act independently. States have worked together under UN auspices to negotiate and sign dozens of human rights treaties. Once those treaties have undergone a process of **ratification** in enough states, they become legally binding. Many

53

of those treaties also establish UN committees that monitor states' compliance with those treaties (see Figure 4.1). These UN committees comprise independent human rights experts who can receive complaints, investigate states' behavior, and file public reports.[1] States have also created dozens of specialized programs and agencies within the UN that facilitate economic and social development around the world. These include agencies such as the UN Development Programme, the UN Children's Fund, the UN High Commissioner for Refugees, the World Food Programme, the World Health Organization, and the UN Population Fund. UN personnel staff these autonomous agencies, and most of them have incorporated human rights principles directly into their mission. The UN also maintains an Office of the High Commissioner for Human Rights, whose job is to serve as the UN's main spokesperson on human rights, and to coordinate all of the human rights–related activities occurring through the UN.

Operating somewhat differently from these committees and agencies is the United Nations Human Rights Council.[2] Created in 2006, the UNHRC comprises political representatives of the forty-seven states that are elected to the council by a vote of the General Assembly. States are elected to the UNHRC for three-year terms, and seats on the council are distributed broadly among all of the world's geographical regions. In order for the UNHRC to adopt any resolution, it must receive a majority vote by the forty-seven state members. Although the UNHRC is a political body, and not a legal institution, it does employ some independent experts in an advisory role or as **Special Rapporteurs** on specific human rights issues. The UNHRC replaced the **United Nations Commission on Human Rights**, which had functioned since 1946 under a similar structure. The Commission on Human Rights received intense criticism and ultimately lost credibility,

---

Figure 4.1   Selected Human Rights Treaties and the UN Committees They Created

ICESCR (1966)	Committee on Economic, Social, and Cultural Rights
ICCPR (1966)	Human Rights Committee
ICERD (1966)	Committee on the Elimination of Racial Discrimination
CEDAW (1979)	Committee on the Elimination of Discrimination Against Women
CAT (1984)	Committee Against Torture
CRC (1989)	Committee on the Rights of the Child
CRPD (2006)	Committee on the Rights of Persons with Disabilities

primarily due to the fact that many of the states serving on the commission were systematically abusing human rights themselves.

The purpose of the UNHRC, like the commission it replaced, is to monitor and report on human rights violations around the globe, and make recommendations for their improvement. The UNHRC has three main avenues to receiving reports about human rights violations. First, its advisory committees and Special Rapporteurs can bring an issue to its attention. Special Rapporteurs and other independent advisers exist to investigate specific human rights themes (such as torture, food, and indigenous rights) or certain countries that find themselves under the UNHRC's scrutiny (such as North Korea, Iran, and Burma). Second, the UNHRC has a complaint procedure that allows individuals and NGOs to bring gross violations of human rights to the council's attention. Third, the UNHRC has established the **Universal Periodic Review** mechanism, which requires every UN member state to report to the UNHRC every four years and identify the gaps in its own human rights practices and explain the steps it is taking to improve the protection of rights.

We should remember that the UNHRC, when it discovers cases of severe human rights violations, has no power to impose sanctions on the perpetrator or use coercive intervention. The only mechanism in the United Nations with this kind of coercive power is the UN Security Council, which can act to prevent gross human rights violations if they threaten international peace and security. The idea behind the UNHRC is that, by exposing violations that would harm a state's reputation, and by providing technical assistance to improve human rights policies, the UNHRC will provide a form of peer pressure that will encourage states to implement reforms voluntarily.

The United States initially voted against the creation of the UNHRC in 2006, and it did not run for a seat on the new council, as it was skeptical of the UNHRC's ability to solve the problems inherent in the former Commission on Human Rights.[3] In 2008, the United States refused funding to the UNHRC and withdrew its observer status, complaining that the UNHRC was overly concerned with condemning Israel for its actions in the Palestinian territories, to the exclusion of more obvious and systematic abuses elsewhere. In 2009, the Obama administration changed course and the United States was voted in as a member of the UNHRC, although the United States continues to voice strong opposition to some of the decisions taken by the UNHRC.[4]

This debate addresses the question of whether the UNHRC is an effective institution to promote and protect human rights. As a political body, does the UNHRC have the legitimacy to condemn human rights violations in a fair and consistent manner? As an institution with no coercive enforcement power, can the UNHRC effectively encourage human rights reforms? Do states take its reprimands and advice seriously, or does the UNHRC represent a diplomatic smokescreen with no real effect? Supporters of the UNHRC argue that, despite its imperfections, it is the most legitimate political body exclusively designed to monitor human rights globally. By forcing states to report and listen to the UNHRC's recommendations, it provides an important form of peer pressure on violating states. In contrast, critics of the UNHRC argue that it is still affected by political manipulation, ideological bias, and hypocrisy. Even when the UNHRC does target the worst human rights abusers, it has neither the legitimacy nor the power to change their behavior.

Argument 1
The UNHRC is an effective promoter of human rights.

This is not an argument that the UNHRC is free from political manipulation or bias, but that it is an important and effective institution to promote human rights at the global level, despite its faults. In a world of sovereign states, no global institution exists that both is free from political bias and has the coercive power to enforce human rights across national borders. By definition, sovereignty prevents that. In this context, the most fair and effective way to promote human rights is to have a representative body of rights-respecting states shame and pressure rights-abusing states into reforming themselves. The UNHRC uses the power of socialization, modeling, and learning rather than coercive enforcement. It is the only global political body that reviews all human rights in all places.

Clearly there are limitations inherent in a political organization like the United Nations that is based on state membership. Some of these limitations were manifested clearly in the former Commission on Human Rights, as many of its members had terrible human rights records of their own. At some point in the commission's history, the authoritarian states of Algeria, China, Nepal, Saudi Arabia, Vietnam, and Zimbabwe were all members.[5] Perhaps the last straw was the election of Muammar Qaddafi's Libya to chair the commission, and the reelection of the genocidal regime of Sudan to the commission in 2004. It comes as no surprise that these states chose to focus the UNHRC's scrutiny on Israel, rather than on the human rights abuses that they or their allies were perpetrating.

The UNHRC, however, is a vast improvement over the now-defunct Commission on Human Rights. The rules of membership were changed so that states elected to the UNHRC must explicitly pledge to uphold the highest human rights standards, and they can be suspended by a two-thirds vote of the General Assembly if they fail to uphold their commitment.[6] These rules were enforced for the first time in 2011, against Libya, after Colonel Qaddafi ordered attacks against civilian protesters. Thus, while the states that compose the UNHRC do not have perfect human rights records (and we should recall that some observers might include the United States on this list), the majority are predominantly rights-respecting states. There is now a mechanism in place to exclude the world's worst human rights violators, such as Libya and Sudan. The failed bid from Belarus to join the UNHRC in 2007, thanks to protests from human rights activists in that state, demonstrates that UNHRC membership is now more restricted.[7]

It is true that the UNHRC, like its predecessor, focuses a tremendous amount of attention on Israel's treatment of the Palestinians. Roughly half of the council's country-specific resolutions to date have condemned Israel for violating the laws of war in Lebanon and the Gaza Strip, and expanding Israeli settlements in the West Bank.[8] This disproportionate focus on Israel's violations compared to violations perpetrated by other states could be perceived as anti-Semitic. However, it can be argued that the work of the UNHRC still legitimately advances human rights because it is the only global political body that can realistically hold Israel to account for its actions. When Israel does violate the rights of Palestinians, it should be held accountable, just as Palestinians should be held accountable for targeting Israeli civilians. However, when resolutions on Israel are brought before the UN Security Council, the United States consistently exercises its veto in order to protect its ally. Resolutions against Israeli policies are supported by Latin American, Asian, and European democracies. Because Israel is shielded from criticism in other important international venues, this disproportionate focus can serve to redress an existing imbalance, and put pressure on Israel to conform to universal standards.

While the former Commission on Human Rights was completely fixated on condemning Israel, the UNHRC has expanded its scope to expose human rights abuses around the world. The UNHRC has passed resolutions condemning abuses in Afghanistan, Burma, the Democratic Republic of Congo, North Korea, Somalia, Sri Lanka, Sudan, Syria, and elsewhere. In addition, the establishment of the Universal Periodic Review mechanism ensures that every state must open its human rights record to the light of public scrutiny. Initial research has shown that many states, especially emerging democracies in the global South, do interpret the Universal Periodic Review mechanism as a serious evaluation of their human rights record.[9] Unlike the UN Security Council, which is dominated by five permanent members who wield a veto, the UNHRC has roughly an equal number of members from all geographic regions of the world, and each state has an equal vote. This makes the UNHRC the most representative, legitimate political body to monitor human rights.

Even though it is a legitimate body, is the UNHRC actually effective in causing states to implement human rights reforms? Yes, according to this argument, because effectiveness in the promotion and protection of human rights does not depend on coercive enforcement. Liberalists remind us that states gain benefits from participating in international institutions like the UNHRC, and so these states gradually come to see that their interests are better served by following the rules. Constructivists add that, because states and their leaders care about their reputation, peer pressure is an effective way to encourage repressive states to model their behavior after that of democratic states. The naming and shaming mechanisms of the UNHRC are ways of putting this kind of peer pressure on states.

What if states do not take their reporting requirements seriously? There is plenty of evidence to show that in their reports to the UNHRC, states tend to gloss over their worst violations and overstate their reform efforts.[10] However, as the spiral model predicts, even these cynical commitments by abusive states can be used later, by human rights advocates within the state, to increase the pressure for reform. Of course, this kind of pressure does not work in every case, but it is currently the most cost-effective, sustainable, and legitimate tool available to the international community for advancing human rights.

There is also ample evidence to show that most states do care about their reputations and take their reporting requirements seriously. This is demonstrated by the fact that, when states become the target of UNHRC investigations, they go to great lengths to avoid international criticism. For example, Sri Lanka made an extensive effort to prevent the UNHRC from passing a resolution condemning its indiscriminate killing of civilians in a civil war in 2009.[11] When the resolution did pass, the Sri Lankan government reaffirmed its commitment to universal human rights, even as it disputed the specific findings of the UNHRC. Likewise, the Israeli government has shown its sensitivity to international criticism by vigorously disputing the UNHRC's resolutions and accusing it of anti-Semitic bias. Although Israel ultimately withdrew from the UNHRC, international criticism has led Israel to conduct internal investigations of its military actions in Lebanon and Gaza.

In sum, while the member states of the UNHRC do not have perfect human rights records, and while the methods the council uses do not guarantee improvement, the work of the UNHRC can be improved by ensuring that no state can escape fair scrutiny. In a world constrained by the political interests of sovereign states, the UNHRC can be seen as a laudable institution whose work should be supported. It does not *enforce* human rights; rather, it *promotes* human rights by encouraging voluntary participation and compliance among its members. The primary alternative to this approach is enforcement through the UN Security Council, an institution that is often perceived as unrepresentative and even more prone to political manipulation by powerful states.

Argument 2
The UNHRC is illegitimate and ineffective.

Taking the opposite position, this argument acknowledges that although the UNHRC is an improvement upon the former Commission for Human Rights, the changes are largely cosmetic and represent an attempt to mask the fundamental structural problems inherent in the UN human rights system. According to this argument, the UNHRC is a biased institution that reflects the political interests of its member states, not a global promoter of universal rights. As a result, its pronouncements lack credibility and are easily dismissed by human rights abusers.

Although Libya was suspended from the UNHRC and Sudan is no longer a member, the council still accepts members such as Azerbaijan, Bahrain, China, Cuba, Russia, and Saudi Arabia,[12] authoritarian regimes that are often perceived as having no business judging the human rights practices of democracies through the Universal Periodic Review process. As supporters of this perspective argue, the regulations designed to prevent human rights abusers from participating in the UNHRC are still weak and ineffective. There is no rigorous process in place that a state must endure to make it eligible to serve on the UNHRC; a simple majority vote in the UN General Assembly will suffice. While UNHRC member states do pledge to respect human rights, these promises are empty so long as the council remains a politically divisive institution run by hypocritical states.

While it is true that the UNHRC has expanded the targets of its criticism beyond Israel, it is still overwhelmingly focused on it, resulting in one-sided condemnations and inaccuracies. The United States, the European Union, Canada, and even UN diplomats have denounced the UNHRC for its "pathological obsession with Israel."[13] The UNHRC often criticizes Israel for the way it conducts its war against Palestinian militants, without ever mentioning the rocket attacks directed by Hamas against Israeli civilians. As in every military action, it is possible that Israel has crossed ethical and legal lines, but according to this argument it is up to the Israeli legal system to deal with any abuses that have occurred. Israeli policies, enacted in the context of their own war on terrorism, are certainly no worse than those of most of the UNHRC member states. When countries like China and Saudi Arabia criticize Israel for killing or oppressing civilians, it does not put any real pressure on Israel to reform itself. Instead, it turns the UNHRC into a laughing stock, exposes the hypocrisy of its member states, reeks of anti-Semitism, and erodes any credibility in the institution. It causes a state like Israel to entrench its current policies, not to reexamine them.

These institutional biases are not something that can be reformed with minor changes to the UNHRC's rules and procedures. They are an inherent characteristic of an institution run by states with their own political interests. The UNHRC's anti-Israel bias is not the only sign of its dysfunction. Each year until 2011, the UNHRC passed a controversial **Defamation of Religion** resolution that was sponsored by the council's Islamic member states.[14] This resolution, in the aftermath of some cartoons in the European media depicting the prophet Muhammad, decried the "deliberate stereotyping of religions, their adherents, and sacred persons in the media," and condemned the "intolerance and discrimination toward Islam or any other religion."[15] Whether the intent of this resolution was sincere or not, human rights activists and Western governments feared that it would be used by Islamic and other governments to justify so-called antiblasphemy laws that restrict the freedom of speech and religion. Governments that impose a single state religion on their citizens often use antiblasphemy laws to imprison political dissidents who speak out against the regime's policies, or to silence independent thinkers who question religious orthodoxy. As a result, each year the Western states would vote against this resolution in the UNHRC, while the Muslim states would vote in favor, and the resolution would pass. Ultimately the Defamation of Religion resolution was abandoned by the UNHRC, but the recent history of the council shows a pattern of bloc voting on ideological or political grounds, rather than an impartial assessment of universal rights gained through consensus.

The UNHRC's lack of legitimacy is the reason why the United States initially opposed its creation, despite the US desire for a more effective UN mechanism to monitor human rights. The United States criticized the failings of the Commission on Human Rights, seeking an institution that could fairly assess human rights violations across the globe, rather than being dominated in its membership by human rights abusers themselves.[16]

But according to this criticism, the reforms that produced the UNHRC did not go far enough, reflecting a problem endemic to the United Nations system as a whole: that it is an unrepresentative body trying to impose a sense of moral authority on the world, without sufficient legitimacy or power to do so effectively. While the UN is the most globally inclusive organization, it is inclusive only of states, not of their individual citizens. Many of the authoritarian states that are members of the UN do not represent their people at all, and do not have the legitimacy to evaluate the human rights records of democratic states. A more credible organization to monitor human rights, it is argued, would be composed of more democratic and rights-respecting states, states that have the legitimacy to judge the human rights records of others. The UN's inclusivity in welcoming authoritarian states, which is one of its strengths in resolving international conflicts, becomes one of its major weaknesses when it comes to monitoring human rights.

Even if the UNHRC could speak with a sense of moral authority, it still does not possess any enforcement mechanism, so states are not required to listen to its advice. The worst sanction that the UNHRC can impose is a public slap on the wrist. Only the UN Security Council can impose economic sanctions or authorize a military action to stop human rights abuses. Only the International Criminal Court can prosecute suspected human rights abusers, and only if they are arrested and extradited to The Hague. As a result, states do not take UNHRC reporting requirements seriously, often sugar-coating their own human rights records because there is no penalty for obstructing the council's mission. To paraphrase President Theodore Roosevelt's famous phrase, the UNHRC speaks loudly, but does not carry any stick.

In sum, according to this argument the UNHRC possesses neither the legitimacy nor the power to effectively promote human rights. It is an institution that manifests some of the UN's major flaws, particularly the inability to achieve a political consensus about universal values in the midst of competing ideologies and interests. As realists would suggest, in the absence of any real moral authority or coercive power, the UNHRC is a mouthpiece through which states preach about compliance with human rights standards while often disregarding those standards themselves.

* * *

Conclusion
Everyone acknowledges that the United Nations is an imperfect institution that is composed of states that often act according to their own interests rather than in the collective interest. The UN is often asked to solve some

of the world's biggest problems, such as monitoring and enforcing human rights everywhere, without being given the proper authority or power to accomplish its task. The question remains: Does the UNHRC represent a step forward, toward the effective monitoring and implementation of human rights on a global scale? Or do the weaknesses inherent in the UNHRC diminish the legitimacy of international human rights, permitting states to ignore the council's strictures? Given the UNHRC's limitations, are there any better alternatives for making the collective enforcement of human rights more consistent and effective?

Recall that sovereign states overwhelmingly have the most legitimacy to enforce human rights domestically, and the most power to influence human rights through their foreign policies. NGOs, IGOs, regional organizations, and corporations may have some influence as well, but states (at least those that are politically stable) are the only actors with the authority to collect taxes, imprison people, and go to war on behalf of an entire population. The UN Security Council and the International Criminal Court have some coercive mechanisms, but these mechanisms too must be triggered by the decisions of sovereign states. Yet as discussed in Chapter 2, states may not care about implementing human rights at all, if this does not accord with their national interests or particular values. As such, it should be clear that there is no perfect mechanism in place to promote, protect, and enforce human rights consistently, even if we accept that human rights are universal in theory. Human rights activists must do their best with the tools that are available, which is why they often work at multiple levels (with NGOs, IGOs, states, and corporations) to use any source of leverage at their disposal.

Some US leaders have suggested that the United States should bypass the United Nations and use alternative mechanisms to collectively enforce human rights. Presidential candidate John McCain recommended in 2008 that the United States establish a so-called **League of Democracies** that could enforce the US vision of human rights around the world. According to McCain,

> The new League of Democracies would form the core of an international order of peace based on freedom. It could act where the UN fails to act, to relieve human suffering in places like Darfur. It could join to fight the AIDS epidemic in sub-Saharan Africa and fashion better policies to confront the crisis of our environment. . . . It could bring concerted pressure to bear on tyrants in Burma or Zimbabwe, with or without Moscow's and Beijing's approval. It could unite to impose sanctions on Iran and thwart its nuclear ambitions.[17]

This proposal for a permanent group of like-minded democracies received a mixed reaction within the United States. Because no such institution exists on a global scale, the process of establishing it would certainly be controversial, as there is no consensus definition of a democracy or a rights-respecting state. The group would largely be self-selected, similar to the "coalition of the willing" that the United States put together in 2003 to invade Iraq. It would serve the purpose of excluding the worst human rights abusers (some of which would presumably be US allies) from collective decisionmaking processes, but it would clearly not resolve the political and ideological divides that infuse the enforcement of human rights internationally. And it would certainly be an embarrassment if the United States, based on its own human rights record, did not qualify for a league it helped create. Considering the drawbacks of more restrictive groups of human rights enforcers, keeping states like China, Russia, Pakistan, and Saudi Arabia involved in decisions regarding human rights may be a better approach than excluding them from the discussion altogether.

If nothing else, the debate over the UNHRC demonstrates that human rights are neither a sterile package of legal instruments, enforceable only in courts, nor a set of absolutist claims that people can

> **Think Again**
>
> Do you think a League of Democracies would be more credible than the UNHRC in condemning human rights violations? How might China and Russia react if the league were to authorize the bombing of Iran or Syria without Chinese or Russian consent?

use as a "trump card" in political debates. Human rights are more accurately thought of as the moral and legal ground upon which political debates are fought. To the extent that the values of human rights are universally accepted, the UNHRC does encourage states to implement some progressive reforms. Yet because the values and interests of different states can diverge so dramatically, political debates about human rights (such as the clashes over the Israeli-Palestinian conflict and the defamation of religion in the UNHRC) will continue to characterize international relations.

Notes

1. United Nations Office of the High Commissioner for Human Rights, "Human Rights Bodies," http://www.ohchr.org/EN/HRBodies/Pages/HumanRightsBodies .aspx, accessed June 22, 2012.

2. For more information, see the United Nations Office of the High Commissioner for Human Rights, "Background Information on the Human Rights Council," http://www.ohchr.org/EN/HRBodies/HRC/Pages/AboutCouncil.aspx, accessed June 22, 2012.

3. United Nations News Centre, "In Historic Vote, General Assembly Creates New Human Rights Council," March 15, 2006, http://www.un.org/apps/news/story .asp?NewsID=17811&Cr=rights&Cr1=council.

4. John R. Crook, "State Department Hails U.S. Accomplishments in UN Human Rights Council; United States to Seek Election to Another Term," *American Journal of International Law* 105, no. 3 (2011): 592–594.

5. Editorial, "The Shame of the United Nations," *New York Times,* February 26, 2006.

6. Lauren Vriens, "Troubles Plague UN Human Rights Council," Council on Foreign Relations, May 13, 2009, http://www.cfr.org/un/troubles-plague-un-human -rights-council/p9991.

7. Eli Rosenfeld, "The Human Rights Council One Year On: Are We Any Better Off?" Report from a discussion hosted by the Century Foundation, Open Society Institute, and Friedrich Ebert Foundation, June 19, 2007, http://tcf.org/events/2007 /ev188.

8. Eye on the UN, "Human Rights Actions by the Human Rights Council," http://www.eyeontheun.org/browse-un.asp?ya=1&sa=1&u=344&un_s=0&ul=1 &tp=1&tpn=Resolution, accessed June 22, 2012.

9. Edward McMahon and Marta Ascherio, "A Step Ahead in Promoting Human Rights? The Universal Periodic Review of the UN Human Rights Council," *Global Governance* 18, no. 2 (2012): 231–248.

10. See, for example, Human Rights Watch, "Sri Lanka: Report Fails to Advance Accountability," December 16, 2011, http://www.hrw.org/news/2011/12/16 /sri-lanka-report-fails-advance-accountability.

11. Nick Cumming-Bruce, "In Resolution, UN Council Presses Sri Lanka on Civilian Deaths," *New York Times,* March 22, 2012.

12. Vriens, "Troubles Plague UN Human Rights Council."

13. "UN's Ban Faults Rights Council over Israel," *Israel News,* June 21, 2007, http://www.ynetnews.com/articles/0,7340,L-3415619,00.html.

14. Laura MacInnis, "UN Body Adopts Resolution on Religious Defamation," *Reuters,* March 26, 2009, http://www.reuters.com/article/2009/03/26/us-religion -defamation-idUSTRE52P60220090326.

15. See, for example, United Nations Human Rights Council, Resolution 7/19 (on combating religious defamation), March 27, 2008.

16. Philip Alston, "Reconceiving the UN Human Rights Regime: Challenges Confronting the New UN Human Rights Council," *Melbourne Journal of International Law* 7, no. 1 (2006): 185–224.

17. Michael Goldfarb, "John McCain's League of Democracies," *Weekly Standard,* May 3, 2007, http://www.weeklystandard.com/weblogs/TWSFP/2007/05 /mccains_league_of_democracies_1.asp.

5

Does the International Community Have a "Responsibility to Protect"?

Rwanda, 1994. In this central African country, the Hutu government was fighting a civil war against a Tutsi rebel group to maintain control over the state. Decades of Tutsi domination in Rwanda, enabled by Belgian colonial rulers, had left Hutus poor and oppressed, and they sought revenge against their ethnic rivals. As part of a strategy to win the war, Hutu leaders ordered the army and civilian militias to commit genocide against the Tutsi population. Armed with guns and machetes, the Hutus carried out the nationwide massacre with brutal efficiency. In roughly 100 days, they had killed over 800,000 of their neighbors, in one of the worst genocides in modern history.

The international community reacted with understandable horror at this tragedy, and yet they stood aside as it unfolded. At the time the genocide started, roughly 2,000 UN peacekeepers were positioned in Rwanda to monitor a fragile peace agreement between the Hutus and Tutsis. The commander of the UN peacekeepers, General Roméo Dallaire, learned of a Hutu plan to exterminate the Tutsis. He contacted UN headquarters in New York, and asked for troop reinforcements and the authority to stop the killers. Instead, the UN Security Council, led by pressure from the United States and Belgium, voted to withdraw almost 90 percent of the peacekeepers, leaving only a token force in place. The genocide ultimately ended not by any action of the international community, but by the Tutsi rebels sweeping through the country and defeating the Hutu army.

Four years later, US president Bill Clinton visited Rwanda and apologized for his failure to respond, acknowledging that "we in the United States and the world community did not do as much as we could have and should have done to try to limit what occurred" in Rwanda.[1] He vowed that the international community would "never again" stand aside while mass atrocities were being committed, repeating a familiar phrase that was used after the Nazi Holocaust, the Khmer Rouge genocide, and the ethnic cleansing in Bosnia. Certainly, if the international community could agree on anything, they could agree that mass slaughter should be stopped.

But it did not take long for these words to ring hollow again. In 2003, a civil war was raging in Darfur, a region in Western Sudan. Sudanese president Omar al-Bashir adopted a tactic similar to that of the Rwandan government, arming militia groups to massacre civilians and wipe out entire villages in Darfur. Over the next several years, up to 300,000 people died in Darfur, and over 2 million were displaced from their homes.[2] The international community's response was perhaps an improvement on its actions in Rwanda, but it was nevertheless slow and incomplete. After gaining President Bashir's consent, the African Union sent a peacekeeping force of 7,000 lightly armed troops to Darfur in 2005, which was supplemented by approximately 20,000 UN peacekeepers in 2007. Combined with economic sanctions and diplomatic pressure against Sudan, this finally led to a reduction in violence, the division of the country into Sudan and South Sudan, and a fragile peace that now holds in Darfur.

These events raise a vital question in the international politics of human rights. To what extent is the international community responsible for protecting civilians from mass atrocities committed by their own government? Can the UN Security Council effectively enforce international human rights? While the world's leaders continue to repeat the phrase "never again," do they have any interest in intervening to prevent these abuses? The UN Security Council has always maintained the authority, under Chapter VII of the UN Charter, to intervene when a conflict crosses national borders and becomes a threat to "international peace and security." But what if the atrocities occur within a state's territorial boundaries? The Security Council can also authorize a force of UN peacekeepers to intervene, but it must first gain the consent of the host country's government, and peacekeepers typically have a limited mandate to use military force.[3] What if the host government does not accept a strong international peacekeeping force, and the UN Security Council does not authorize more coercive measures? Who in the international community has the authority to stop civilians from being massacred within their own state, and when should they act? Can military intervention be used effectively to stop human rights violations, or does war inevitably destroy more than it saves?

In order to try to resolve these questions, and to prevent the kinds of slaughter that the world witnessed in the twentieth century, an international

What Would You Do?

Imagine that it is April 1994, and you are President Bill Clinton. Your advisers have just informed you that widespread slaughter has begun in Rwanda, and almost 10,000 Tutsi civilians are being killed every day. How would you respond?

Human rights NGOs are lobbying for you to stop the genocide; however, there is not much public support for US involvement. Members of Congress have declared that "Africans just do this to each other from time to time," and your advisers have said that the United States has no strategic interests in Rwanda. Just two years earlier, the US military did intervene in Somalia to protect the flow of humanitarian aid, but you chose to withdraw from Somalia after eighteen US soldiers were killed in battle. The American public is clearly not eager to risk a large number of American lives to support a humanitarian mission in Africa.

At the same time, human rights groups are also calling for the United States to intervene in Bosnia, where ethnic cleansing has been occurring for two years, and UN peacekeepers appear incapable of stopping it. As the president of the United States, you do not want to repeat the mistakes of Somalia, and the United States cannot afford to intervene in both Rwanda and Bosnia. And yet, your administration has promised to uphold the international rule of law and to "never again" allow these kinds of atrocities to occur.

Would you contribute US troops, money, or military equipment to an expanded UN peacekeeping mission in Rwanda or Bosnia? If not, what policies could you employ, short of US military intervention, that might prove effective? Does the United States have any strategic interest in preventing genocide in Rwanda or ethnic cleansing in Bosnia?

group of human rights experts came together in 2001 to develop the Responsibility to Protect doctrine. The R2P doctrine elaborates a set of principles that can be used to determine when it is appropriate for states to forcibly intervene to stop mass atrocities from occurring in other states. These principles are not legal requirements, but rather ethical guidelines. The R2P doctrine was approved by the UN General Assembly in 2005, and by the UN Security Council in 2006, which means that all states have expressed their intention of following the R2P guidelines.[4]

The basic principles of the R2P doctrine are as follows. Above all, states have the primary responsibility to protect their own citizens from gross human rights violations. Whenever a state is unable or unwilling to do so, it loses its sovereignty. The international community has not only the right, but also the obligation, to intervene to stop these atrocities, using any methods that would prove effective. This principle is a substantial change to the centuries-old notion of Westphalian sovereignty, in which a state had almost complete protection from foreign intervention in its internal affairs. The R2P doctrine gives the international community the responsibility to prevent imminent abuses from occurring, to intervene forcibly when atrocities are in progress, and to rebuild the country after the intervention ends. The R2P doctrine then outlines a set of criteria, based on the religious traditions of theologians such as St. Thomas Aquinas and the secular traditions of humanist jurists such as Hugo Grotius, known as the **Just War doctrine**, which is used to determine when **humanitarian intervention** would be appropriate.[5] These criteria are necessary to prevent states from using the R2P doctrine cynically to justify military intervention according to their own interests. Because virtually all states claim that their wars are for humanitarian purposes, these criteria exist to determine whether states are genuinely intervening to protect human rights.

There are six basic criteria for a humanitarian intervention to be considered legitimate, according to the R2P doctrine. First, the intervention must be for a just cause, meaning that the human rights abuses planned or carried out by the target state must result in death or ethnic cleansing on a large scale. Because military intervention inevitably causes a significant loss of human life, the war must be designed to protect more lives than are lost in the conflict. Second, the intervention must have the right intention, meaning that saving innocent lives must be the primary goal. States and their leaders always have some ulterior motives for going to war, but preventing atrocities should be the primary motive. Third, military intervention should be employed only as a last resort, after all other measures have been deemed ineffective. This does not necessarily mean that other measures such as economic sanctions or diplomatic negotiations must be tried first, but that they are almost certain to prove ineffective in this particular case. The fourth criterion is **proportionality**, meaning that the scale and intensity of the military intervention should match the goals it seeks to accomplish. This does not mean that the weapons and tactics used should match the opponent, but that interveners should use the minimum amount of force that would prove effective in stopping atrocities. The amount of force therefore depends on the goal of the intervention, whether it be a change in the target state's regime, or more limited ends such as delivering humanitarian aid or preventing the state's army from entering a particular territory. Military forces should also seek to distinguish combatants from civilians, and make every effort to reduce civilian casualties. Fifth, the intervention should have a reasonable chance of success, meaning that the international community should have a long-term plan of action that would lead to victory and a reduction in suffering. Sixth, and perhaps most controversial, the intervention should be approved by the right authority. The R2P doctrine envisions that the UN Security Council is the most legitimate body to authorize humanitarian interventions, but it recognizes that the Security Council is also a political institution with competing interests that may fail to fulfill its responsibility, as it did in Rwanda. As a result, the R2P doctrine allows for other actors to authorize an intervention, such as the UN General Assembly, or a regional organization such as the **North Atlantic Treaty Organization (NATO)** within its own geographic region. In the most extreme cases of genocide and mass slaughter, the R2P doctrine even allows a single state to go to war against another, if all other routes have failed.

So, for the first time in history, the international community has developed a set of norms that legitimizes intervention in a state's internal affairs in order to protect human rights. Yet the dilemmas of humanitarian intervention remain. Does starting a war to protect human rights, or even applying economic sanctions, end up causing more long-term damage than it prevents? Can we truly separate humanitarian intentions from political interests? Since only a few states have the power to go to war across the world, and thus cannot be counted on to intervene in every case of mass atrocity, does this render the R2P doctrine invalid?

These questions were brought to the forefront in 2011 when the UN Security Council authorized NATO to enforce a no-fly zone over Libya. It represented the first time that the R2P doctrine was explicitly cited to justify a humanitarian intervention. The Arab Spring protests were surging through the Middle East and northern Africa, and they made their way to Libya as demonstrators were challenging Muammar Qaddafi's regime. Having seen the success of the Arab Spring protests in bringing down dictators in Egypt and Tunisia, Qaddafi was determined to hold on to power and violently repress the protesters. This resulted in a civil war, but the lightly armed and poorly organized opposition was no match for Qaddafi's armed forces, and the Libyan government began to push through rebel-held cities, killing many civilians along the way. The UN Security Council responded by imposing financial and diplomatic sanctions on the Qaddafi regime, and requesting the International Criminal Court to investigate the regime for possible crimes against humanity. Then, in March 2011, as Qaddafi's forces were approaching the rebel strongholds of Benghazi and Misrata, the UN Security Council passed Resolution 1973. This resolution called for an immediate cease-fire, and authorized the international community to establish a no-fly zone over Libya and use all necessary measures (excluding troops on the ground) to protect civilians.[6] The United States led its NATO allies and a handful of Islamic states in implementing Resolution 1973, by shooting down Libyan military aircraft, enforcing a naval blockade, and bombing Libyan armed forces throughout the country. With the aid of the international community, the Libyan rebels were able to achieve victory within seven months, and they ultimately captured and killed Muammar Qaddafi.

Did this foreign military intervention really protect human rights? Was this an appropriate and legitimate invocation of the R2P doctrine, or did this represent another war for political interests, masked by humanitarian justifications? It is to this debate that we now turn.

Argument 1
The international community fulfilled its responsibility to protect civilians and advance human rights with the NATO bombing of Libya.

From this perspective, the bombing of Libya was legitimate and appropriate, and successfully protected the human rights of the Libyan people.[7] Although war is always a painful endeavor, the NATO bombing of Libya closely followed the R2P criteria and will result in better long-term outcomes than if the international community had failed to act.[8]

First, the war was for a just cause, to prevent the large-scale loss of innocent life. Qaddafi had ordered his military to fire on unarmed civilian protesters, causing some of his own security forces and his interior minister to defect to the opposition.[9] Qaddafi enlisted civilian militias and hired foreign mercenaries to fire machine guns into civilian demonstrations, killing dozens of protesters.[10] In a nationally televised speech, Qaddafi tagged the protesters as "drug addicts fomented by Islamic fundamentalists" and ordered his supporters to "get out of your homes and fill the streets. Leave your homes and attack them in their lairs."[11] This is tantamount to ordering a widespread massacre, and this is part of the evidence that the ICC used to indict Qaddafi for crimes against humanity. Although the number of people killed in Libya had not yet reached genocidal proportions, it was clear by March 2011 that many innocent people would have been massacred or wrongfully imprisoned had Qaddafi continued to march through rebel-held areas.

From this perspective, the bombing of Libya was conducted with the right intentions, and as a last resort. Diplomacy, peace negotiations, and financial sanctions were tried, but failed to persuade Qaddafi to step down. An attack by the Libyan forces on the people of Misrata and Benghazi was imminent. If the international community wanted to act to protect human rights, they had no other choice than to impose more coercive measures. While political interests are inescapable when fighting a war, this war was fought largely for humanitarian purposes. The protection of civilians was the explicit mandate that governed military action. Qaddafi was certainly no friend of the United States or NATO countries in 2011, but there were no significant underlying economic or security interests that motivated their intervention. Although some would claim that the United States was interested in Libya's oil,[12] Western oil companies already held major contracts with Qaddafi, and the intervention was just as likely to hurt Western economies as it was to help them.

The conduct of the war in Libya was also proportional to the international community's goals. Allied forces used a minimal amount of violence in order to protect civilians. Critics of the war (including some, like Russia, which had abstained from the Security Council vote) argued that NATO forces went beyond their original mandate by bombing the Libyan army in coordination with rebel advances. Yet these actions, and the ultimate removal of Qaddafi from power, were necessary in order to protect the Libyan people over the long term. More limited military action, such as simply enforcing the no-fly zone, would have resulted in a stalemate and a damaging, drawn-out civil war. While some civilians are always victims of war, NATO forces also made their best effort to target military assets and command structures of the Libyan government while avoiding civilian neighborhoods. Although the Libyan government claimed that thousands of civilians were killed by the UN intervention, human rights groups estimated between fifty-five and seventy-two civilian deaths caused by NATO.[13] In any war, each side has a strong incentive to overstate the number of casualties caused by its opponent.

It is impossible to predict the outcome of any war with certainty; nevertheless, this military intervention had a reasonable chance of success. NATO forces held huge tactical advantages over the Libyan military, and could easily dominate the air and sea, even without any ground forces. The Libyan opposition was broadly supported, and thus had a reasonable chance of victory, as well as the probability of success in democratic elections. The R2P criteria

> **Think Again**
>
> Wars are typically judged by the public according to their outcomes, not the reasonableness of the decision itself. If a war ends in victory, it is usually deemed legitimate. This is different than the criteria that the R2P doctrine proposes. How do you think that war should be justified?

are clear in saying that coercive measures are not appropriate in every case of gross human rights violations. Instead, intervention can only be used when the supportive states on the UN Security Council have sufficient power to accomplish their mission. This criterion rules out intervention in places like Russia (in its conduct of the war in Chechnya), China (in its treatment of Tibet), and perhaps Syria, which are all powerful enough to resist foreign intervention. Libya, however, was not like these countries; it possessed neither a formidable military nor powerful allies to come to its aid. In this case, humanitarian values, political interests, and military power were properly aligned to achieve a victory for human rights.

In hindsight, the clearest evidence that there was a reasonable chance for success in Libya is that the Libyan opposition was victorious after only seven months of conflict. Qaddafi has been killed (to be fair, in a way that violated his own rights), and Libya is now run by a transitional government that has committed itself to human rights and held a national election in 2012.[14] Critics of the war argue that the UN intervention in Libya is still far from successful, as political instability is widespread, violence is intermittent throughout the country, and the transitional government continues to violate human rights. However, temporary instability is a common feature of states transitioning into democracy. With continued aid and political support from the international community, Libya can gradually strengthen the rule of law, build democratic institutions, and protect its people's rights far better than the regime it replaced.

Perhaps most important, the bombing of Libya received the proper authorization from the UN Security Council. The vote in favor of Resolution 1973 was unanimous, with Brazil, India, Germany, China, and Russia abstaining. Moreover, the UN military intervention received regional approval, as the Arab League also supported the no-fly zone. The intervention was welcomed by the majority of the Libyan population, as demonstrators themselves called for foreign military support. The participation of states like Jordan, Qatar, and the United Arab Emirates in the UN intervention showed that this was not a Western imperialist war, as Qaddafi had claimed. It was a military action to enforce a universal norm, initiated under the legal authority of the UN Security Council under Chapter VII of the UN Charter.[15]

As a point of contrast, we can compare the war in Libya to the US war in Iraq in 2003.[16] Despite the rationale claimed by the George W. Bush administration, the war in Iraq was not fought for a just cause, as Saddam Hussein's most severe human rights violations were neither recent nor imminent. Protecting Iraqi civilians from suffering was clearly not the primary motivation for the war, as security concerns dominated US decisionmaking. The war was not fought as a last resort, as the United States refused to negotiate with Hussein in the months leading up to war.

While the United States quickly won the war and occupied Iraq, it did not adequately distinguish civilians from combatants in the fighting that ensued, and the ongoing instability resulted in roughly 100,000 Iraqi deaths. While the United States had a successful plan to win the war, it did not prepare any strategy for winning the peace and establishing security in the country it occupied. And of course, the United States led a coalition of states to invade Iraq without the authorization of the UN Security Council or any other legitimate international institution. Libya is qualitatively different from Iraq in nearly all respects.

The purpose of the R2P doctrine is to allow the international community to make exactly these distinctions between politically motivated interventions and truly humanitarian ones. Every intervention will result in some violence and turmoil, so the R2P doctrine helps us determine when an intervention will, on balance, produce more good than harm. The 2011 bombing of Libya did meet the standards of the R2P doctrine, and it has produced net benefits, not only for the Libyan people, but also for international human rights in general. It makes a statement to leaders around the world that the protection of human rights takes precedence over state sovereignty. The reinforcement of this global norm helps to deter future leaders from repressing their citizens' rights and following the path of Qaddafi.

Argument 2
The international community did not fulfill its responsibility to protect civilians and advance human rights with the NATO bombing of Libya.

According to this perspective, the bombing of Libya was a setback for human rights, and an unwise policy decision, because although some of the normative principles of the R2P doctrine are valid, others are too vaguely defined, allowing for politically motivated wars conducted under the guise of humanitarianism. The R2P doctrine would be beneficial if all states valued human rights over an absolute notion of state sovereignty. However, because military intervention is so destructive and destabilizing, it should only be used in the most extreme circumstances, with truly universal consensus among the international community. War is generally not an effective approach to protecting human rights, because war produces so many unintended and unforeseen consequences. As such, according to this perspective, Libya is not a good test case for the R2P doctrine. In fact, the war in Libya seems more analogous to Iraq in 2003 than to Rwanda in 1994.[17]

Why did the bombing of Libya not fit the R2P criteria for engaging in war? First, there was no just cause. There is no doubt that Muammar Qaddafi was a dictator who, like Saddam Hussein in Iraq, systematically denied basic rights to his people. There is no doubt that he responded to the Arab Spring protests with violence and repression. However, the intensity of his abuses in Libya did not amount to the large-scale loss of life or ethnic cleansing that the R2P doctrine sets out as the threshold for justifying war. While there were some initial attacks against civilians, the violence in Libya did not increase until after the rebellion itself turned violent. In cases of civil war, the government has a legitimate right to defend itself by targeting combatants. Qaddafi rigidly defended his position of power, and ordered his supporters to fight for him, but his public statements did not amount to a call to genocide or mass slaughter. Indeed, Qaddafi may have been correct in labeling some of the opposition fighters as mercenaries and terrorists. Even a rebel commander admitted that some of his troops had come to Libya after fighting for al-Qaeda in Iraq.[18] In the midst of the civil war, abuses against civilians were committed by both sides.

The R2P doctrine sets a high threshold for intervention precisely because its drafters knew that war typically results in human suffering and political conflict that may take generations to heal, and so they intended to authorize war only in the most extreme circumstances. Libya's political repression was brutal, but not qualitatively worse than that witnessed recently in Syria, Bahrain, Iran, Equatorial Guinea, Burma, North Korea, and elsewhere. If military intervention was justified in Libya, why was it not warranted in those countries? Supporters of the war in Libya argue that this was because there was a reasonable chance of success in Libya, but not in those other countries. However, critics suspect that Libya was targeted due to political interests rather than humanitarian ones. Qaddafi was a thorn in the side of the United States for several decades, as he contributed to driving up oil prices in the 1970s, supported the bombing of the Lockerbie jet in the 1980s, and began to develop chemical and nuclear weapons programs in the 1990s. Qaddafi regularly allied himself with enemies of the West, and he was attempting to unite African countries under the umbrella of opposition to the West.

Although it is impossible to discern the underlying motivation for the UN intervention in Libya, it appears that removing Qaddafi from power was the real purpose of the intervention, rather than protecting civilians as Resolution 1973 had stated. Its purpose was political rather than humanitarian. This is further demonstrated by the fact that, when the government of Bahrain repressed its own Arab Spring protests, the West supported the Bahraini monarchy as its ally and oil supplier. Thus, when the UN Security Council authorizes a military intervention in Libya, but remains silent in the face of many other atrocities, it de-legitimizes human rights in the long run. The R2P doctrine loses credibility when it is applied inconsistently, according to political rather than humanitarian interests.

Like the war in Iraq, the military intervention in Libya also fails to meet the R2P criteria stating that war must be a last resort and have a reasonable chance of success. The international community had other options available to pressure Libya into respecting its citizens' rights, but these options were not given adequate time to take effect. Although the United States had applied economic sanctions on Libya since 1996 in response to Libya's support for terrorism, UN sanctions were applied in February 2011, only a few weeks before the UN intervened with force. The UN Security Council could have ratcheted up sanctions, while promoting diplomacy and a peaceful resolution to the emerging civil war. Instead, it chose to side with the Libyan rebels, whose democratic credentials themselves were questionable.

Ultimately the UN intervention proved successful in aiding the rebels to victory and toppling the Qaddafi regime. However, from the vantage point of March 2011, when Resolution 1973 was passed, a successful outcome was by no means clear. Many political analysts were predicting a drawn-out civil war and a political stalemate that would have led to widespread destruction and many thousands of deaths. Most experts suggested that a bombing campaign, in the absence of significant ground troops, would not be enough to overthrow the Qaddafi government. The fact that the outcome fortunately exceeded NATO's expectations does not make the decision any less risky and reckless.

More important, the R2P doctrine defines "success" as not only winning a war and preventing immediate atrocities, but also rebuilding a society so that human rights are protected over the long run. This requires the interveners to make a commitment to promote political stability and build democratic institutions in Libya. The military intervention in Libya neither planned for nor achieved success according to this criterion. As in Iraq and Afghanistan, the United States supported undemocratic militants in order to topple an undemocratic government. It should be no surprise that, under these circumstances, human rights may deteriorate in the ensuing transition, as different groups continue to fight over their share of national resources.

In addition, while national elections were established, they were established far too early and haphazardly, and as a result the new government appears to be protecting human rights no better than the Qaddafi regime. Reports of torture and arbitrary detention remain widespread in

Libya, and the transitional government passed a law in 2012 banning any speech that "insults the people of Libya" or praises Muammar Qaddafi.[19] Likewise, an initial draft of Libya's new constitution declares that legislation will be grounded in Islamic sharia law, which has historically been in tension with women's rights and Western values.[20] As in Iraq and Afghanistan, holding elections can provide a shell of democracy, but it ensures neither the political stability nor the protection of basic rights that is ultimately necessary for a society to thrive. For true democracy to thrive in a postconflict society, a country must first rebuild its civic organizations and reconstruct political parties across traditional divides, not simply rush off to the polls.[21]

In terms of the last R2P criterion—right authority—the bombing campaign in Libya did receive some international support and official authorization from the UN Security Council. This support, however, was narrowly focused on a no-fly zone, not on a widespread bombing campaign that would initiate regime change. When NATO forces expanded their operations to bomb Libyan government and military assets, much of the international support ran dry, and some human rights experts deemed this expanded bombing to violate international law.[22] Critics of the war began to label the intervention as just another example of Western imperialism. For example, the *China Daily* stated that "no matter what the well-decorated excuses are, the latest military action in Libya is part of Western political and strategic intentions."[23] Indeed, even the war in Iraq received some international support from the so-called coalition of the willing, which included countries from the region such as Kuwait, Ethiopia, Eritrea, and Turkey. In contrast, there was no real international consensus in favor of a war in Libya. When NATO expanded the bombing campaign with the intention of removing Qaddafi from power, this undermined the credibility of the R2P doctrine, and made future interventions to protect human rights even more politically complicated.

In sum, according to this perspective, the bombing of Libya did not advance human rights, because it did not meet the R2P criteria for going to war. Libya's violations were not severe enough to justify a war. The R2P doctrine recognizes that war frequently results in widespread destruction and the loss of human life, and so it should be reserved for only the most extreme circumstances. War often requires the interveners to ally themselves with undemocratic partners, and results in long-term consequences that are unintended and unforeseen. Because the R2P doctrine was applied inappropriately in Libya, it was perceived as a tool of Western imperialism, to be applied in the service of Western interests, rather than as a global norm to protect human rights. When human rights are enforced inconsistently and hypocritically in this manner, it does not encourage deterrence and the rule of law. It simply encourages dictators to become allies with the United States, or else build up sufficient leverage (as Iran and North Korea have done with their nuclear programs) to resist such an intervention.

*   *   *

Conclusion

Recall that constructivists believe that respect for human rights is best strengthened by gaining universal consensus to a set of agreed-upon values. They might hope that the principles outlined in the R2P doctrine can gradually gain international legitimacy, so that states would no longer consider it acceptable to violate their people's rights in the name of national security, and so that major powers would accept their obligation to respond to atrocities committed outside their borders. For constructivists, this is why it is so important that military interventions like the war in Libya strictly follow the norms laid out in the R2P doctrine. Likewise, liberalists hope that the UN-sponsored intervention in Libya might be a small step toward building a system of collective security—that is, a multilateral institution that has sufficient legitimacy and power to intervene consistently to enforce international law. To the extent that the states on the UN Security Council can put aside their own political interests and enforce the rule of law, truly representing the interests of the international community, they could deter future leaders from committing abuses.

The international community's failure to protect civilians in Syria, at the same time that NATO was bombing Libya, might represent a disappointment for liberalists and constructivists. For any system of collective security or norm enforcement to work, the international response to such a widespread violation of human rights must be consistent. As the Arab Spring protests arrived in Syria in 2011, President Bashar al-Assad reacted with brutal force toward the opposition, thereby sparking a civil war that has killed over 100,000 people. Assad's violation of human rights has arguably been more grotesque than Qaddafi's actions in Libya, particularly with the alleged use of chemical weapons in 2013, all of which would amount to a just cause to trigger the R2P doctrine.[24] However, the R2P doctrine was never invoked by the major powers as a justification for possible intervention in Syria. Perhaps this is because the R2P doctrine contains a mixture of principled and pragmatic criteria, and the international community deemed that while intervention might be justified in Syria, it would not prove to be effective in actually protecting civilians.[25]

Realists would respond with the critique that there really is no "international community" with any set of common interests and values, which is why there is no agreement on when to invoke the R2P doctrine. Humanitarian intervention was authorized in Libya not because the atrocities in Libya triggered action, but because Libya had no powerful allies in the UN Security Council to defend its interests. Syria, on the other hand, maintains strong alliances with Russia and Iran, which have prevented any aggressive action to protect civilians caught in the Syrian civil war.[26]

For realists, the international community is divided, and there is no system of collective security, because powerful states cynically use the justifications provided by the R2P doctrine to pursue their own interests. Since Western states currently hold a monopoly on the power to project their militaries across the globe, their inconsistent enforcement of human rights is understandably perceived by the rest of the world as Western imperialism. This is why realists are skeptical about the ability of states to cooperate in a system of global human rights enforcement. If atrocities like the Rwandan genocide are to be prevented in the future, the best we can hope for is that powerful actors like the United States find that intervention aligns with their strategic interests in particular cases.

The UN-sanctioned bombing of Libya in 2011 highlights an important dilemma inherent in the international enforcement of human rights. When sovereign states fail to protect their own citizens' rights, who has the right and the obligation to intervene, if anyone? Because the legal authority to intervene rests with the UN Security Council, it is impossible to separate humanitarian concerns from political interests. Because war causes human suffering and instability, even as it tries to relieve suffering, using war to protect human rights is a difficult balancing act. Because war often produces unintended consequences, it is impossible to apply R2P criteria in a formulaic way in every case. Military intervention may be appropriate to prevent the atrocities committed by relatively weak or small states, but not for larger, more powerful, and politically connected states. This inevitably produces some inconsistency in how the international community responds to grave human rights violations. Even actors with the best intentions must balance their moral considerations with a sense of pragmatism, if they seek to be effective in protecting human rights. This is why NGOs, states, and IGOs must continue to strengthen and widen the range of tools that they can use in responding to abuses committed within sovereign states. It makes sense that the protection of human rights sometimes involves public condemnation, and other times diplomatic negotiation; sometimes sanctions and boycotts, and other times economic engagement.

Notes

1. Samantha Power, "Bystanders to Genocide," *The Atlantic*, September 2001.

2. John Hagan, "Voices of the Darfur Genocide," *Contexts* 10, no. 3 (Summer 2011): 22–28.

3. The power to deploy UN peacekeepers is often called "Chapter VI½" authority, because it falls between the Security Council's power to forcibly intervene under Chapter VII of the UN Charter, and its power to pursue peaceful resolution of conflict under Chapter VI.

4. For the full report outlining the R2P, see the International Commission on Intervention and State Sovereignty, *The Responsibility to Protect,* December 2001, http://responsibilitytoprotect.org/ICISS%20Report.pdf.

5. Lynn H. Miller, "The Contemporary Significance of the Doctrine of Just War," *World Politics* 16, no. 2 (January 1964): 254–286.

6. United Nations Security Council Resolution 1973, adopted March 17, 2011.

7. For a selection of international responses to the no-fly zone in Libya, see Eleanor T. West, "World Voices: The Libya Debate," *World Policy* Blog, March 23, 2011, http://www.worldpolicy.org/blog/2011/03/23/worldvoices-libya-debate. For a selection of arguments for and against the intervention, see Chris R. Albon, "The Libyan No-Fly Zone Debate: A Cheat Sheet," *UN Dispatch*, March 7, 2011, http://www.undispatch.com/the-libyan-no-fly-zone-debate-a-cheat-sheet.

8. Thomas G. Weiss, "RtoP Alive and Well After Libya," *Ethics and International Affairs* 25, no. 3 (2011): 287–292.

9. "Interior Minister Resigns Rather Than Carry Out Gadhafi Orders," *CNN*, February 22, 2011, http://www.cnn.com/2011/WORLD/africa/02/22/libya.protests/.

10. Kareem Fahim and David Kirkpatrick, "Qaddafi's Grip on the Capital Tightens as Revolt Grows," *New York Times*, February 22, 2011.

11. "Defiant Gaddafi Blames World Leaders for Violence in Rambling TV Address," *Daily Mail*, February 23, 2011.

12. Robert Dreyfuss, "Obama's NATO War for Oil in Libya," *The Nation*, August 23, 2011, http://www.thenation.com/blog/162908/obamas-nato-war-oil-libya#.

13. Sebastian Moffett, "NATO Underplayed Civilian Deaths in Libya: HRW," *Reuters,* May 14, 2012, http://news.yahoo.com/nato-underplayed-civilian-deaths -libya-hrw-040710456.html.

14. See Amnesty International, "Libya Human Rights," http://www.amnestyusa .org/our-work/countries/middle-east-and-north-africa/libya, accessed June 26, 2012.

15. Alex J. Bellamy and Paul D. Williams, "The New Politics of Protection? Côte d'Ivoire, Libya, and the Responsibility to Protect," *International Affairs* 87, no. 4 (2011): 825–850.

16. See Kenneth Roth, "Was the War in Iraq a Humanitarian Intervention?" *Journal of Military Ethics* 5, no. 2 (2006): 84.

17. For a range of critical approaches to the intervention in Libya, see Aidan Hehir and Robert Murray, eds., *Libya, the Responsibility to Protect, and the Future of Humanitarian Intervention* (New York: Palgrave Macmillan, 2013).

18. Praveen Swami, "Libyan Rebel Commander Admits His Fighters Have al-Qaeda Links," *The Telegraph,* March 25, 2011.

19. Human Rights Watch, "Libya: Revoke Draconian New Law," May 5, 2012, http://www.hrw.org/news/2012/05/05/libya-revoke-draconian-new-law.

20. Adam Serwer, "The Great Libya-Shariah Freakout of 2011," *Mother Jones,* October 26, 2011, http://www.motherjones.com/mojo/2011/10/great-libya-shariah-freakout-2011.

21. Dawn Brancati and Jack Snyder, "The Libyan Rebels and Electoral Democracy," *Foreign Affairs,* September 2, 2011, http://www.foreignaffairs.com/articles/68241/dawn-brancati-and-jack-l-snyder/the-libyan-rebels-and-electoral-democracy.

22. Geir Ulfstein and Hege Fosund Christiansen, "The Legality of the NATO Bombing in Libya," *International and Comparative Law Quarterly* 62, no. 1 (2013): 159–171.

23. Li Qinggong, "Politics Behind Attacks on Libya," *China Daily,* March 22, 2011, http://usa.chinadaily.com.cn/opinion/2011–03/22/content_12207695.htm.

24. International Federation for Human Rights, "Bashar al-Assad: Criminal Against Humanity," Report no. 570a (Paris, July 2011).

25. Ian Williams, "Applying 'Responsibility to Protect' to Syria No Cakewalk," *Washington Report on Middle East Affairs* 31, no. 4 (2012): 35–36.

26. Spencer Zifcak, "The Responsibility to Protect After Libya and Syria," *Melbourne Journal of International Law* 13, no. 1 (2012): 9–93.

6

Should the United States Join the International Criminal Court?

On March 14, 2012, Thomas Lubanga Dyilo was found guilty of committing war crimes in the Democratic Republic of Congo, in central Africa. As the founder of a rebel militia, Lubanga had been accused of ordering the massacre of rival ethnic groups, widespread rape and mutilation, and forcing children to fight in his army over a period of several years.[1] The severity and scope of his atrocities were not unprecedented, but Lubanga's case was unique in that he was the first person convicted by a new global institution, the International Criminal Court.

As already discussed, the international system for human rights protection is still dominated by sovereign states. For the past few centuries, states have held a monopoly on the coercive power to hold human rights violators accountable, but they have often used this power inconsistently or selfishly. To the extent that the perpetrators of human rights violations have been punished, it has occurred through prosecution by the courts of their own state or an occupying state. Many human rights violators have therefore been left to continue their abuses with impunity.

Recent years have witnessed a significant change in the international human rights system. Many states have voluntarily given up some of their sovereignty in order to submit themselves to some of the enforcement mechanisms of international law. They have agreed to follow a set of binding international rules and procedures when severe abuses of human rights occur.

The International Criminal Court embodies this change. Created in 2002 by the **Rome Statute**, the ICC is the first permanent court in history that operates across national borders to prosecute individuals for gross human rights violations. As of 2013, 121 states have ratified the Rome

Statute to become members of the ICC, thereby submitting themselves to the Court's jurisdiction. The ICC is authorized to prosecute acts of **genocide**, **war crimes**, and **crimes against humanity** that have occurred since the Court's inception. The ICC is physically located in The Hague, Netherlands, and it maintains its own prison, independent prosecutor, public defenders, and panels of judges who are elected by the member states. The ICC has jurisdiction over anyone who is a citizen of one of the ICC's member states, or anyone who has committed genocide, war crimes, or crimes against humanity on the territory of a member state. Typically, a criminal investigation is initiated by the Office of the Prosecutor. In special cases, the ICC can also prosecute other individuals referred to it by the UN Security Council. In addition, the ICC operates on the principle of **complementarity**, which means that it gets involved only after it has determined that national courts are unwilling or unable to provide a fair trial for their alleged perpetrators. The ICC is also limited in its enforcement power because it relies on states to voluntarily extradite criminal suspects to the Court for trial.[2]

It is important to keep in mind that the International Criminal Court is designed to prosecute individuals, not states. The **International Court of Justice (ICJ)** is a court that arbitrates disputes between states, but its decisions are binding only if the disputing states accept its jurisdiction, and it does not conduct individual criminal trials. The idea that individual persons can be held accountable to international law is itself a fairly recent development in the human rights system. The ICC is not the first court to prosecute individual human rights violators, but it is the first permanent court that has been established by international treaty. Previous international criminal courts have been created on an ad hoc basis, beginning with the tribunals in Nuremberg and Tokyo after World War II, in which the Allied powers prosecuted some of the German and Japanese leaders who ordered the Holocaust and committed other acts of brutality. The Nuremberg and Tokyo tribunals were important in establishing the principles of individual accountability and **command liability**; in other words, that both the leaders who give orders to commit human rights abuses and the soldiers who carry out those orders are criminally responsible. However, the Nuremberg and Tokyo tribunals were also criticized for carrying out a form of **victor's justice**. For example, the United States refused to prosecute some Nazi scientists in order to allow them to work on US weapons programs during the Cold War.[3] And certainly the Allies were not interested in investigating their own leaders for possible crimes committed during World War II, including the firebombing of major Axis cities and the dropping of the atomic bomb on Hiroshima and Nagasaki.

Several other ad hoc criminal trials were created after the end of the Cold War to deal with atrocities that were committed in the midst of particular civil wars. International tribunals were instituted to investigate ethnic cleansing in the former Yugoslavia and genocide in Rwanda, and **hybrid courts** (with a mixture of international and national elements) were created to deal with abuses committed in Kosovo, East Timor, Sierra Leone, and Cambodia.[4] There is considerable debate about the effectiveness of these courts. Even when they have been effective in prosecuting high-profile human rights violators, these courts have been limited in time and scope to the specific countries they are authorized to investigate. The ICC, on the other hand, is designed to prosecute any acts of genocide, war crimes, or crimes against humanity that are committed by or within any of its member states.

Why would a state give up some of its sovereignty and permanently submit itself to the rules of the ICC? Following liberalist and constructivist principles, the 121 member states of the ICC have determined that their long-term interests are best achieved if everyone is held accountable to the same set of international rules, which are based on widely accepted values. For example, everyone agrees that genocide is a heinous crime that should be punished. These states believe that an international court with independent authority is the best way to ensure that severe violations of human rights are prosecuted fairly and consistently, isolated from the political interests of sovereign states.

The United States, however, has not taken this position. Although the United States was involved in the drafting of the Rome Statute, and President Bill Clinton reluctantly signed the treaty in the final days of his tenure, he never had any intention of submitting the treaty for ratification in the US Senate. After George W. Bush took office, he officially "unsigned" the Rome Statute, publicly declaring the opposition of the United States to the ICC. In 2002, once the ICC began its operations, the US Congress passed the American Service-Members' Protection Act, which authorizes the president to use "all means necessary and appropriate" to protect US soldiers and government officials from any "criminal prosecution by an international criminal court to which the United States is not party."[5] This act gave the president the power to withhold military aid from countries that have joined the ICC, the power to refuse to extradite US defendants to the ICC, and even the power to intervene militarily to free any US citizens held at The Hague. The United States subsequently used diplomatic pressure to make other ICC member states promise not to extradite US citizens to The Hague if indicted.

In recent years, US opposition to the International Criminal Court has softened, at least insofar as the targets of ICC investigations are not US citizens. The George W. Bush administration voted to abstain in the UN Security Council resolution that authorized an ICC investigation into genocide in Darfur. Likewise, in 2011, the Obama administration voted to refer to the ICC the case of Muammar Qaddafi massacring civilian protesters in Libya. The Obama administration has assisted the Court with several of its investigations, but the official US policy on the ICC is still under review as of 2013, as Obama continues to consult with his military advisers before deciding whether to re-sign the Rome Statute and press for ratification in the Senate.

Should the United States join the International Criminal Court? We now turn to the arguments for and against US participation in this international court.

Argument 1
The United States should ratify the Rome Statute and join the ICC.

From this perspective, the ICC is an important positive step toward the global enforcement of human rights. So long as human rights enforcement is conditional upon the political whims of sovereign states, the realization of these rights will always be inconsistent and incomplete. As liberalists would suggest, when states give up a small amount of their sovereignty to submit to the rules of an international court, they receive even greater benefits by having an impartial and independent body hold the world's worst violators accountable for their crimes. If the United States does in fact practice democratic values to the extent that it preaches them, then the existence of the ICC should be no cause for concern.

In order to truly possess human rights, victims of human rights abuses must be able to seek and receive a remedy. Legally prosecuting those who commit atrocities is the most common way that victims can receive a remedy and societies can deter future crimes. The problem is that some of the worst crimes—genocide, war crimes, and crimes against humanity—are committed in states where such a remedy is politically or legally impossible. Political leaders like Omar al-Bashir in Sudan and Muammar Qaddafi in Libya are often responsible for gross violations of human rights in their own state, and certainly they will not arrest themselves or their cronies. They may also have powerful allies in the UN Security Council who would support them and prevent outside intervention. The purpose of the ICC is to separate criminal prosecution from national political considerations, and place it in the hands of international legal experts who are committed to universal rights rather than the interests of their own nations.

The current policy of the United States is to apply the rules and procedures of the ICC to other nations, but not to its own soldiers and government officials. This is a blatant double standard that the rest of the world recognizes as hypocritical. While the United States claims to have substantive problems with the ICC, its underlying reason for avoiding the ICC's jurisdiction is clear: it does not want its own officials arrested for war crimes. This may appear to be in the national interest of the United States, as no nation would welcome the negative publicity attached to having its citizens, much less its leaders, prosecuted for human rights violations. However, by doing this, the United States is sacrificing its long-term interests for short-term gains, and is missing the opportunity to help build an effective institution to enforce human rights.

By making a claim of **American exceptionalism**, the United States is acting as though it deserves an exemption when it comes to human rights simply because it is already a liberal democracy that contributes so much to global security. But this is not how the system of human rights works; a state does not receive credit for good behavior so that its citizens can violate human rights elsewhere. Human rights represent a universal standard, a threshold that everyone must reach, no matter who or where they are. No individual who commits a mass atrocity should be able to do so with impunity; exceptions should not be allowed, even for the most powerful state. Because human rights are universal, it is important to develop a mechanism for the consistent application of international law. The predominant mechanism in place today, in which states enforce human rights according to their own particular interests and values, decreases the credibility of international law. As an impartial tribunal designed to hear the worst cases of human rights abuses, the International Criminal Court is a small but important step in making human rights enforcement more predictable and legitimate.

The International Criminal Court is not a perfect institution, but it is a dramatic improvement on the global human rights system. Critics of the ICC argue that it does not provide sufficient procedural safeguards to protect a defendant's right to a fair trial. But supporters counter that the ICC provides extensive due process rights, including the presumption of innocence, the right to a speedy trial, the right to legal counsel, and evidentiary standards similar to those of the US Constitution.[6] Even the American diplomats who negotiated the Rome Statute acknowledged this. As a former legal adviser to the State Department stated, "The list of due process rights guaranteed by the Rome Statute is, if anything, more detailed and comprehensive than those in the American Bill of Rights. . . . I can think of no right guaranteed to military personnel by the U.S. Constitution that is not also guaranteed in the Treaty of Rome."[7] While critics note that the ICC does not provide a traditional trial by a jury of one's peers, this does not represent a fundamental conflict with the US Constitution: "The United States has long accepted that its citizens (including U.S. service members) will not get jury trials when accused of crimes in countries like France or Japan, where juries are not used. The United States has signed extradition treaties with many countries that explicitly permit Americans to be tried without a jury."[8] Because the ICC supplements rather than replaces the US legal system, the US Constitution would not need to be amended in order to ratify the Rome Statute.

Critics also argue that, without any checks and balances against the power of the ICC's Office of the Prosecutor to initiate a legal proceeding, the Court will engage in politically motivated prosecutions that undermine US sovereignty. But supporters counter that any ICC investigation must be approved by a panel of judges who, under the principle of complementarity, must allow the US legal system the opportunity to pursue its own investigation. The ICC's judges are elected by its member states, and the overwhelming majority of these states are democratic nations that are US allies. Many of the world's authoritarian regimes, such as China, North Korea, Burma, and Libya, have joined the United States in rejecting the Rome Statute. They are likely fearful of opening themselves to ICC prosecutions for their own crimes. It is extremely unlikely that a group of independent judges elected by democratic states, with a mandate to try only the worst human rights abusers, would engage in a politically motivated prosecution against the United States. Even in this improbable event, the UN Security Council could vote to suspend such an investigation indefinitely, or the United States could protect its sovereignty by refusing to extradite specific individuals to The Hague.

Opponents of the ICC also claim that the crimes covered by the Court are vaguely defined, opening up the possibility of frivolous prosecutions. But supporters counter that legal definitions are always subject to interpretation; this is the reason why judges exist. The relevant question is, Who should have the authority to interpret international law? Those who think that the United States should join the ICC believe that international human rights experts, who are not bound to any state's political interests, are in the best position to make these legal judgments.

Additionally, it is not just with regard to the ICC that the United States claims exception in applying international rules to others that it does not enforce upon itself.[9] It has refused to sign and ratify several important human rights treaties that have gained universal consensus, such as the 1989 **Convention on the Rights of the Child** and the 1997 **Ottawa Treaty**, which bans landmines, because of perceived national interests or domestic political concerns. Similarly, US courts have claimed jurisdiction over foreign citizens, even in another state's territory, when this serves US interests.[10] But those same courts have refused to accept jurisdiction or apply the same law when the US government is the abuser.[11] When US citizens are accused of committing a crime on foreign territory, the US government vigorously enforces their rights under the 1963 **Vienna Convention on Consular Relations** to receive counsel from a US embassy. However, the United States does not consistently enforce these same Vienna Convention rights for foreigners who are arrested on US soil. The United States maintains the world's largest stockpile of nuclear weapons, and supports its allies (e.g., Pakistan and Israel) when they develop a nuclear program, but cries foul when Iran and North Korea contravene international law in this regard. Another example is that when Saddam Hussein invaded Kuwait in 1990 without Security Council approval, the United States led a military invasion to remedy this violation of international law, but when the United States invaded Iraq in 2003 without Security Council approval, it declared itself a guarantor of freedom.

This kind of human rights enforcement practiced by the United States, dubbed the "unidirectional model"[12] or "exceptional exceptionalism"[13] by human rights scholars, is nothing more than rank hypocrisy. While it may achieve some short-term national interests, it results in even greater costs to US credibility and moral leadership around the world. The United States does not practice exceptionalism because it has uniquely substantive objections to international law, but because it is the world's lone superpower. Citizens of the United States need to be held accountable to the same human rights standards as everyone else, precisely because the US military is more engaged around the globe than are the militaries of other states. With great power comes great responsibility. If US citizens wantonly disregard those standards, as witnessed with the torture of prisoners at Abu Ghraib in 2004, then they should be held accountable for their crimes.

Indeed, the US response to the abuses at Abu Ghraib is instructive for the debate about the ICC. Eleven US soldiers who participated in the abuses were court-martialed and received relatively minor prison sentences, but no senior military or civilian personnel received any punishment whatsoever. The torture of detainees that has occurred elsewhere in the US war on terrorism, from Afghanistan to Guantanamo Bay to secret Central Intelligence Agency (CIA) prisons, has been committed with impunity. The failure to prosecute those responsible is not the result of any significant gaps in US or international law, but rather a result of the lack of political will in the United States to hold US leaders accountable. The fact that alleged war criminals in the United States have been given de facto amnesty for their actions points to an even greater need for the United States to join the ICC.

In sum, according to this perspective the United States cannot be relied on to enforce human rights in its own time, by its own means, and according to its own interests. While some rights are indeed protected in this way, their inconsistent application erodes the legitimacy of international law and reduces the credibility of the United States. If the international community truly cares about protecting human rights, then it needs to move away from the one-sided enforcement of rights by powerful nations, and toward the collective enforcement of rights by institutions that are impartial, consistent, and legitimate.

Argument 2
The United States should not join the ICC.

From this perspective, the United States should continue its current policy of cooperating with the ICC's investigations, so long as US citizens are exempted from the Court's jurisdiction. The supporters of the ICC promise the fair and independent enforcement of universal norms, which sounds attractive in theory. In practice, however, the ICC is a foreign court that provides fewer protections to its defendants than does the US Constitution, and enforces norms that have not yet achieved universal consensus. This results in the likelihood of politically motivated prosecutions against US citizens, and the loss of US sovereignty.

Although it may seem like the United States follows a double standard by assisting with ICC investigations in other countries but refusing to subject its own citizens to the ICC's authority, upon closer inspection US policy is not inconsistent if the notion of American exceptionalism is accepted as valid. The United States is in fact different from other countries, and therefore cannot be held to the same rules and procedures of international law. The United States is exceptional in two ways. First, as the only global superpower, it has unique responsibilities to provide security and promote development throughout the world. As US ambassador

David Scheffer explained in the international negotiations that led to the drafting of the Rome Statute,

> The reality is that the United States is a global military power and presence. Other countries are not. We are. Our military forces are often called upon to engage overseas in conflict situations, for purposes of humanitarian intervention, to rescue hostages, to bring out American citizens from threatening environments, to deal with terrorists. We have to be extremely careful that the [ICC] does not limit the capacity of our armed forces to legitimately operate internationally. We have to be careful that it does not open up opportunities for endless frivolous complaints to be lodged against the United States as a global military power.[14]

Because the United States has taken on most of the responsibility for protecting global stability, and is involved in more violent conflicts, it is more vulnerable to politically motivated prosecutions. An enemy may want to prosecute a US official simply to constrain US power. Therefore, to the extent that the world asks the United States to provide security, it must allow the United States to act with some degree of independence. This is actually a routine request for national armed forces acting in the service of international security. For example, virtually all nations that contribute soldiers to United Nations peacekeeping missions sign status-of-forces agreements with the host country, keeping their soldiers immune from prosecution by the host country.[15] Without similar assurances for US soldiers, the United States would be less likely to join missions that support human rights throughout the world. This would harm the very people the ICC is aimed at helping.

Second, the United States is exceptional in the extent to which its own legal system already protects the right to a fair trial. The Fifth and Sixth Amendments to the US Constitution provide citizens with the right of due process, which includes safeguards such as a speedy trial, reasonable bail, the ability to confront witnesses, and the restriction of evidence based on hearsay. Until the ICC develops a substantial body of case law, there is some doubt that it will provide the same procedural safeguards as does the US Constitution. Even more important, there are areas where the Rome Statute directly contradicts the US Constitution. The Sixth Amendment states that all criminal trials should be heard "by an impartial jury of the State and district wherein the crime shall have been committed"— meaning the right to a trial by a jury of one's peers. According to the Heritage Foundation, the "Supreme Court has long held that only the courts of the United States, as established under the Constitution, can try [criminal] offenses."[16] Since ICC cases are tried in The Hague before a panel of international judges, this provision clearly violates the US Constitution.

This inconsistency has led many legal analysts to conclude that the United States would have to amend its Constitution in order to ratify the Rome Statute. In the meantime, it is unreasonable to require US citizens to submit to a court that provides fewer procedural safeguards than does their own legal system. The US legal system is strong enough to prosecute its own war criminals, as it did in response to William Calley's massacre at My Lai in the Vietnam War, and for the eleven soldiers who committed abuses at Abu Ghraib in Iraq.

Joining the ICC would therefore result in a loss of sovereignty and a reduction in legal rights for US citizens. As US representative Ron Paul stated, the ICC is "inherently incompatible with national sovereignty. America must either remain a constitutional republic or submit to international law, because it cannot do both."[17] Supporters of the ICC argue that the principle of complementarity protects national sovereignty because the ICC acts only when national court systems have failed to prosecute. In fact, even if the state has put a suspect on trial, the ICC still grants itself the authority to prosecute the same person if it determines that the "proceedings were not conducted independently or impartially."[18] This is particularly troubling given the fact that the ICC's Office of the Prosecutor has the power to initiate a proceeding entirely on its own. The United States has argued that trials at the ICC should be initiated only through a vote of the UN Security Council, which would protect US sovereignty by virtue of its Security Council veto. The United States could simply veto any prosecution of its own citizens. As it stands, the ICC prosecutor is authorized to indict a US citizen for war crimes even though the United States is not a member to the Rome Statute, so long as the act occurred on the territory of an existing member state. The ICC is therefore in the awkward position of allowing nondemocracies (which participate in the selection of ICC staff) to prosecute the behaviors that take place in democracies.

The threat of unreasonable or reckless prosecution against the United States is compounded because the crimes over which the ICC has jurisdiction are not clearly articulated. For example, in addition to genocide, war crimes, and crimes against humanity, the Rome Statute lists the crime of "aggression" as falling under the jurisdiction of the ICC. At a conference in Uganda in 2010, the ICC member states agreed to define aggression as "the planning, preparation, initiation or execution . . . of an act of aggression which, by its character, gravity and scale, constitutes a manifest violation of the Charter of the United Nations."[19] This is a vague definition, and one that is particularly subject to political manipulation in its interpretation. Because of these difficulties, the ICC will not have the authority to prosecute crimes of aggression until at least 2017; but after that point, the threat of frivolous prosecutions will increase. Similarly, what constitutes a war crime is open for interpretation under international law. Under international law, combatants in war are permitted to cause civilian deaths, so long as civilians are not directly targeted, the action was a military necessity, and basic precautions were taken to distinguish civilians from combatants. But where does one draw the line in these situations? Would President Harry Truman have been subject to prosecution for using a nuclear weapon in World War II? Would President George W. Bush have been subject to prosecution for invading Iraq in 2003 without Security Council authorization? Could President Barack Obama be prosecuted for causing civilian deaths with drone strikes in Afghanistan and Pakistan? However one might personally answer these questions, it is easy to imagine an ambitious ICC prosecutor, spurred on by pressure from enemies of the United States, initiating a legal proceeding in any of these cases. The political instability that would be caused by such proceedings, both domestically and internationally, would be destructive to human rights.

> **Think Again**
>
> Do you think that the dropping of atomic bombs on Japan in World War II, which killed over 200,000 people, was a war crime? How would you determine whether this was a "military necessity"? What do you think the political consequences would be if those responsible were brought to trial?

Constructivists would argue that international cooperation should be based on a consensus about the norms of international law. To the extent that definitions are ambiguous and values are contentious, we cannot expect compliance with the law. The international reputation of the United States will not suffer from a refusal to participate in a fundamentally flawed institution. Instead, the United States is judged based on how well it respects human rights in its own courts and its foreign policy. Realists would argue that no powerful state should voluntarily relinquish its sovereignty under these conditions. While the United States can continue to cooperate with ICC investigations on a case-by-case basis, it should protect its sovereignty by refusing to ratify the Rome Statute. US citizens are better protected by their own Constitution, and international human rights are better protected when the United States has the operational freedom to play an active role in global security.

* * *

Conclusion

Does the International Criminal Court represent the first step toward the impartial and nonpolitical enforcement of human rights at the global level? Or is the ICC an inherently political institution that violates US sovereignty and threatens US interests and values? This debate reflects more broadly on the question of how human rights are best enforced across national borders. Within a state's own borders, most people would agree that civil rights are best protected by a national constitution and the rule of law.

Liberalist supporters of the ICC argue that the neutral application of law is the most reliable way to enforce human rights in the international arena as well. Because human rights are based on the law, liberalists would expect that the rule of law should be applied consistently among all states, extending it to the global level. Realists, however, are skeptical about the value of international law in a world still dominated by sovereign states. Because human rights are best protected at the national level by sovereign states, realists rely on states pursuing their national interests to enforce rights across borders. Politics and the balance of power determine whether rights are upheld, rather than international law, and realists would not expect the mixture of conflicting political interests to produce consistent enforcement of international law.

Now that the International Criminal Court has been operational for more than a decade, what is its record to date? Has it functioned as an impartial court, or as a tool to be used for political manipulation? A bit of both, analysts might say. To date, the ICC has convicted only one war criminal, Thomas Lubanga Dyilo. His trial did demonstrate the need for the Court, as Lubanga could not be tried fairly in the Democratic Republic of Congo, and it showed the Court's commitment to the right of due process. The ICC judges suspended Lubanga's trial briefly in 2008 when the prosecutor failed to give the defense evidence it had obtained, and the Court was generally praised for its fairness to the defendant throughout the proceedings.[20]

On the other hand, of the thirty-six alleged war criminals indicted by the ICC over the years, fifteen still remain at large. National authorities have either failed to arrest these suspects, or refused to extradite them to The Hague. Perhaps the most notable case is Sudan's President Omar al-Bashir, who was indicted by the ICC in 2009 for his role in committing genocide in Darfur. President Bashir has openly defied the ICC indictment, and responded by expelling many of the international aid agencies that were operating in the Sudan. Perhaps most troubling to the ICC, Bashir later traveled to an African Union summit in Libya, where Africa's leaders joined together in a declaration saying that they would neither arrest nor extradite Bashir to the ICC.[21] This openly contradicted many of their own legal obligations as members of the Rome Statute. Sudan's foreign minister praised the decision, saying, "It's the confirmation of what we always said: The indictment is a political thing, not a legal thing."[22] This shows that, despite the ICC's attempt to be impartial, many African governments perceive the Court as a legacy of European colonialism that represents political interests and is only concerned about human rights abuses in Africa.[23] Indeed, all of the ICC's indictments to date have targeted African individuals. Ironically, at the same time that the United States was refusing to join the ICC, it was also self-righteously urging African states to extradite Bashir to the Court. Having failed to pressure other states to adopt its preferred stance on the ICC, the United States has begun to support the Court's aims.[24]

Despite the attempts by the International Criminal Court to remove human rights from the realm of power politics, it seems that political considerations will still play an inevitable role in how human rights are enforced. Perhaps this is not such a bad thing, as courts have so far achieved mixed results in holding war criminals accountable and promoting reconciliation after a society endures mass atrocities.

Notes

1. Human Rights Watch, "DR Congo: ICC Arrest First Step to Justice," March 18, 2006, http://www.hrw.org/fr/news/2006/03/17/dr-congo-icc-arrest-first-step-justice.

2. For more information, see the International Criminal Court website, at http://www.icc-cpi.int/Menus/ICC, accessed June 18, 2012.

3. David Forsythe, *Human Rights in International Relations* (Cambridge: Cambridge University Press, 2012), p. 121.

4. Ibid., p. 126.

5. See US Department of State, *American Service-Members' Protection Act,* June 30, 2003, http://www.state.gov/t/pm/rls/othr/misc/23425.htm.

6. Human Rights Watch, "Myths and Facts About the International Criminal Court," http://www.hrw.org/legacy/campaigns/icc/facts.htm, accessed June 20, 2012.

7. Ibid.

8. Ibid.

9. For numerous examples, including those mentioned in the successive discussion, see Mark Gibney, *Five Uneasy Pieces: American Ethics in a Globalized World* (Boulder: Rowman and Littlefield, 2004).

10. See the precedent-setting *Filártiga v. Peña-Irala* case of 1980, in which it was ruled that the Alien Tort Claims Act applied to acts of torture that occurred in Paraguay among Paraguayan citizens.

11. See, for example, the US Supreme Court's refusal to apply the Alien Tort Claims Act to an alleged victim of torture by the CIA, in *El-Masri v. Tenet* of 2006, http://www.aclu.org/national-security/el-masri-v-tenet.

12. Jamie Mayerfeld, "Who Shall Be Judge? The United States, the International Criminal Court, and the Global Enforcement of Human Rights," *Human Rights Quarterly* 25, no. 1 (February 2003): 93–129.

13. Julie Mertus, "The New U.S. Human Rights Policy: A Radical Departure," *International Studies Quarterly* 4, no. 4 (November 2003): 371–384.

14. Barbara Crossette, "World Criminal Court Having Painful Birth," *New York Times,* August 13, 1997, p. A8.

15. Roisin Burke, "Status of Forces Deployed on UN Peacekeeping Missions: Jurisdictional Immunity," *Journal of Conflict and Security Law* 16, no. 1 (2011): 63–104.

16. Lee Casey and David Rivkin, "The International Criminal Court vs. the American People," Backgrounder no. 1249 (Washington, DC: Heritage Foundation, February 5, 1999).

17. Ron Paul, "A Court of No Authority," April 8, 2002, http://www.rumormill news.com/cgi-bin/archive.cgi?read=18922.

18. Kristafer Ailslieger, "Why the United States Should Be Wary of the International Criminal Court: Concerns over Sovereignty and Constitutional Guarantees," *Washburn Law Journal* 39, no. 1 (1999): 88.

19. Marina Mancini, "A Brand New Definition for the Crime of Aggression: The Kampala Outcome," *Nordic Journal of International Law* 81, no. 2 (2012): 231.

20. Alison Cole, "A Landmark Decision for International Justice," March 14, 2012, http://www.lubangatrial.org/2012/03/14/a-landmark-decision-for-international -justice/.

21. Kurt Mills, "'Bashir Is Dividing Us': Africa and the International Criminal Court," *Human Rights Quarterly* 34, no. 2 (2012): 404–407.

22. Alfred de Montesquiou, "African Union Leaders Refuse to Extradite Sudan's President, Denounce International Court," *Minneapolis Star Tribune,* July 3, 2009.

23. Marc Glendening, "Why Is Botswana Behaving As a European Puppet?" (London: ICCwatch, March 19, 2010), http://www.iccwatch.org/pressrelease_19 mar10.htm.

24. Alexander Dukalskis and Robert C. Johansen, "Measuring Acceptance of International Enforcement of Human Rights: The United States, Asia, and the International Criminal Court," *Human Rights Quarterly* 35, no. 3 (2013): 569–597.

7

How Should Human Rights Violators Be Held Accountable?

Mobutu Sese Seko ruled the central African country of Zaire (now known as the Democratic Republic of Congo) for thirty-two years. During his dictatorial and corrupt reign, he personally expropriated $5 billion from the resource-rich state, and was accused of crimes against humanity that included widespread torture and murder. In 1997, when Congolese rebels were advancing on the capital to overthrow him, Mobutu fled into exile, first to Togo, then to France and Morocco. All of these countries, including the United States (which was Mobutu's Cold War ally), conspired to give Mobutu immunity for the crimes he committed. US president Bill Clinton claimed that Mobutu's luxurious exile was necessary for the Democratic Republic of Congo to move forward in a "transition to a genuine democracy."[1] After several months in exile, Mobutu ultimately died of cancer in his exclusive villa in Morocco.

   This was a common outcome for authoritarian leaders at the time, as the notion of **sovereign immunity** had long been the custom in international affairs.[2] In order to avoid conflict and maintain political alliances, nations have generally agreed not to prosecute other nations' leaders for crimes they committed while in office. Tyrants and warlords have also been able to resist arrest domestically because of their power over the military and judicial system. External actors wanting to stop these violations have had a limited set of foreign policy tools to use, most of which have been directed at the society as a whole (such as sanctions or military intervention) rather than at the individual leader. It was thought that the best way for societies to move beyond a period of mass human rights violations was to end the suffering as soon as possible, forgive and forget, and rebuild. The only way to preserve peace and stability was to give authoritarian leaders an inducement to leave by offering them amnesty and a comfortable exile. Many dictators have retired under similar conditions, including Charles Taylor of Liberia, Mengistu Haile Mariam of Ethiopia, Idi Amin of Uganda, Jean-Claude Duvalier of Haiti, and Augusto Pinochet of Chile.

However, just a few years after Mobutu's exile, some of these authoritarian leaders are instead appearing in court to be criminally prosecuted for the human rights violations they committed. The notion of sovereign immunity is eroding, and being replaced by the norm of **individual accountability**. Accountability implies that no one, not even leaders of states, should be able to perpetrate human rights abuses with impunity. States have shown an increased willingness to prosecute their own former leaders, or other nations' leaders, for crimes they have committed. New institutions such as the International Criminal Court have been created to prosecute violators almost anywhere in the world.

For example, Charles Taylor, the Liberian president who had supported a brutal civil war in neighboring Sierra Leone in the 1990s, initially enjoyed a comfortable exile in Nigeria, believing that he held immunity from prosecution.[3] However, when the newly elected president of Liberia requested Taylor's extradition in 2006, Taylor was ultimately captured and tried by the **Special Court for Sierra Leone** in The Hague, Netherlands. Taylor was convicted by the court in 2012 of eleven counts of war crimes and crimes against humanity, and sentenced to fifty years in prison. Yet despite the success in holding Taylor accountable for his crimes, analysts note that "the supporters of Charles Taylor are still a force to be reckoned with," causing ongoing instability in Sierra Leone.[4]

This is the dilemma for societies attempting to recover from a period of brutal human rights abuses. How can a nation work to end those abuses and hold the perpetrators accountable without threatening its own political stability? While the previous chapter examined whether these human rights prosecutions threaten national sovereignty, this chapter discusses the effectiveness of the institutions that are designed to hold violators accountable for their crimes. Because many of these crimes happen in the midst of violent conflict, political upheaval, and regime change, the trend toward providing accountability after a conflict is called **transitional justice**.

This debate arises because the mechanisms of transitional justice must serve several constituencies, each with different (and sometimes competing) goals and interests. International human rights activists have an interest in sending a strong message to the world that impunity will end and violations will no longer be tolerated. The society in transition has an interest in maintaining peace, preventing future atrocities, and rebuilding stable social, political, and economic institutions. The victims of human rights abuses need to have their stories heard, achieve some kind of emotional closure, and receive some compensation or remedy for their suffering. Perpetrators and their supporters obviously want legal immunity, but if they are indeed prosecuted for their crimes, they have an interest in receiving due process and the opportunity to reintegrate into society. Human rights are not well served by the kind of victor's justice that was seen when Libyan dictator Muammar Qaddafi was taken from his car by rebel forces in 2011 and summarily beaten and executed on the street.[5]

Clearly it is difficult to satisfy all of these competing interests simultaneously. Societies face real trade-offs between maintaining political stability and pursuing justice for human rights abusers. How effectively do the mechanisms of transitional justice balance these concerns? This is the debate we now confront. According to the first argument, criminal trials are the best way to ensure that a society (and indeed the international community) is able to hold perpetrators accountable, deter future crimes, and uphold the rule of law. According to the second argument, alternative mechanisms that can provide some individual accountability are available, and are often more effective than criminal prosecutions because they can bring a sense of justice without sacrificing peace and stability.

Argument 1
Human rights violators should be criminally prosecuted.

The premise of this argument is fairly straightforward, and is one that has been repeated throughout this book. Effective human rights enforcement requires the consistent application of the rule of law, and the rule of law by definition applies to everyone, including sitting presidents. If a political leader commits a crime, the rule of law requires that the leader be criminally prosecuted. Nations are bound by international treaties to investigate and prosecute anyone who has committed gross violations of human rights.[6] Impunity is the greatest threat to the rule of law, and thus the greatest threat to the protection of human rights. If leaders know that they are immune from prosecution, they would have little incentive to protect the rights of their people when it is politically inconvenient to do so.

Providing amnesty to human rights violators also profoundly disrespects the thousands of victims of those violations. People who have had their homes dispossessed and burned, or suffered imprisonment and torture, or had family members disappeared deserve an appropriate remedy to their suffering. Seeing their abusers retire to a luxury resort in the French Riviera is far from adequate compensation for the victims. Even worse, many human rights abusers play an influential role in government long after they have officially stepped down from power. In order to end political conflict, societies often sign power-sharing agreements, which legally ensure that a proportion of government offices remains in the hands of the same people who had committed atrocities. For example, in the hope of ending a civil war, Rwandan ethnic groups signed the Arusha Accords in 1993, which included a power-sharing agreement between Hutu leaders and Tutsi rebels.[7] This agreement failed on all counts, both in securing peace and in protecting human rights, as just a year later Hutu leaders began a campaign of genocide against the Tutsi population. Although Rwanda is an extreme case, similar kinds of power-sharing agreements have left human rights abusers in office in numerous other countries, including Cambodia, Côte d'Ivoire, Djibouti, Nigeria, Sudan, and Zimbabwe.[8] Rather than encouraging human rights abusers to participate in a smooth transition to democracy, impunity can have the opposite effect by emboldening them to thwart that transition, insofar as they know there will be no punishment for their corrupt actions.[9] As the famous Russian dissident Aleksandr Solzhenitsyn stated, "When we neither punish nor reproach evildoers, we are not simply protecting their trivial old age; we are thereby ripping the foundations of justice from beneath new generations."[10] Fortunately, societies have increasingly employed a number of old and new mechanisms to ensure that violators are held accountable. The exact mechanism may differ depending on the situation, but there is a range of institutions that can be used at the local, national, and international levels.[11] The key is that each of these mechanisms upholds the rule of law by criminally prosecuting those responsible for atrocities.

International law recognizes that the first line of defense against human rights violations should be the state itself. Human rights abusers should be prosecuted within their own national court system if possible. This is reflected in the principle of state sovereignty, and in the ICC's doctrine of complementarity. For example, in Egypt and Guatemala, former leaders Hosni Mubarak and Efraín Ríos Montt were tried in 2013 in national courts for human rights violations they had committed while in office. Saddam Hussein was convicted of crimes against humanity by a special Iraqi tribunal in 2006 and executed a month later. The advantage of prosecuting criminals in national courts is that it can add legitimacy to a democratic transition.[12] By demonstrating that an independent judiciary can enforce the rule of law in a well-publicized hearing, it gives strength to emerging democratic institutions. In trials that are conducted by the nation-

al authorities, victims and their advocates are often able to take part directly in the process. When prosecutions move forward successfully, it makes
a strong political statement that the society is ready to make a clean break
from the past.

Of course, national trials do not always proceed so successfully. Because they often take place within societies that are still riven with conflict, they are subject to political manipulation that can exacerbate the
conflict. For example, Saddam Hussein's trial in Iraq was criticized by
many independent analysts as a "show trial" carried out by Shiite prose-
cutors primarily as retribution against the Sunni minority group who had
ruled over them for decades.[13] The prosecution of Hussein and other
Baath party leaders ultimately did little to build democratic institutions
or forestall a sectarian civil war in Iraq. Political influence can also in-
hibit prosecutions when the human rights violator's political supporters
remain in important government posts. In Guatemala, the genocide trial
of Ríos Montt was suspended in 2013 amid claims by his allies in government that the trial would threaten the political stability of a fragile
democracy.[14]

In cases where fair trials are not possible within a country's own borders, there are other accountability mechanisms that can be employed at
the international level. The International Criminal Court can prosecute
gross violations of human rights that have occurred among its member
states after 2002. Beyond the jurisdiction of the ICC, ad hoc tribunals can
prosecute violations over a specific time period, such as the tribunals that
were created in the 1990s in Rwanda and the former Yugoslavia. The main
advantage of international trials is their impartiality; they are staffed by independent experts from outside the country who are far less vulnerable to
domestic political influences.[15] International courts are typically provided
with greater resources to hire attorneys and gather evidence, and thus the
chances for a fair trial are increased. When international courts prosecute
high-profile criminals, such as Serbia's former president Slobodan Milosevic, they send a clear message to the dictators of the world that the rule of
law will be upheld and impunity will not be tolerated. Although Milosevic
himself died in prison before his trial could be concluded, the **International Criminal Tribunal for the former Yugoslavia (ICTY)** has convicted
several dozen other high-profile war criminals. The ICTY also established
a new international legal precedent for prosecuting mass rape and sexual
violence as a war crime.[16] International courts therefore have the independence, expertise, and credibility to hold human rights violators legally accountable for their crimes.

While international courts can exact justice with greater impartiality,
they have also been criticized for being too distant from the society in

conflict to truly assist with its peaceful democratic transition. When the ICTY hearings were held in The Hague, or the **International Criminal Tribunal for Rwanda (ICTR)** hearings were held in Tanzania, few citizens in the former Yugoslavia or Rwanda followed or knew about the proceedings. These trials did nothing to help build a domestic judicial system to protect human rights in those countries.

Since both domestic and international trials have certain strengths and weaknesses, prosecutions can be pursued at both levels in a coordinated manner. For example, the highest-profile defendants could be sent to international courts, while lower-level accomplices could be tried at the national level. Alternatively, different courts could try different suspects depending on the nature or severity of the crime. The greatest amount of coordination can be found in hybrid courts, which combine elements of both domestic and international legal systems. Hybrid courts in Sierra Leone, East Timor, Kosovo, and Cambodia have included both national and international judges, and they apply a combination of national and international standards and procedures.[17] The parameters of these courts may be difficult to negotiate on a case-by-case basis, but when employed, hybrid courts can draw from the strengths of different kinds of accountability mechanisms.

A last option for providing accountability can be found at the transnational level; that is, human rights abusers can be prosecuted by national courts in other states. Under the principle of **universal jurisdiction**, several European states have claimed that their courts are entitled to prosecute anyone in the world for certain heinous crimes such as genocide and torture, even when neither the victim nor the perpetrator is a citizen of that state.[18] For example, in 1998 a Spanish judge indicted former Chilean dictator Augusto Pinochet for torture and murder that Pinochet was accused of committing in Chile decades before (see Figure 7.1). Similarly, in 2009 an Italian court convicted twenty-two agents of the US Central Intelligence Agency of illegally abducting Muslim cleric Abu Omar and transferring him to Egypt under the "extraordinary rendition" program. In this case, the court claimed the authority to try the US citizens in absentia because the crime occurred in Italian territory. Although Pinochet and the CIA agents were never extradited to Spain and Italy to stand trial and serve their sentences, these transnational prosecutions can send a message to the international community that the rule of law must be upheld.

In sum, according to this argument there are several effective mechanisms that can ensure that human rights violators are held criminally responsible for their actions. The legal institutions and procedures differ,

Figure 7.1 Holding Augusto Pinochet Accountable

Augusto Pinochet was a Chilean army general who came to power in 1973 through a US-sponsored military coup. Pinochet ruled Chile with an iron fist for seventeen years, implementing an array of economic reforms while allegedly committing widespread human rights violations that included murder, torture, and wrongful imprisonment.[19]

After a decade of nonviolent dissent and a national referendum to remove Pinochet, he peacefully stepped down in 1990. However, at the time, prosecuting Pinochet for his crimes was practically impossible.[20] The military regime had passed an amnesty law that gave government officials immunity from domestic prosecution, and Pinochet remained as commander-in-chief of the army until 1998 and held the position of "senator for life" in Chile. Given Pinochet's claims of sovereign immunity, the best form of accountability that the new Chilean government could carry out was to convene two national truth commissions, which detailed the various violations committed during his reign. These truth commissions recommended reforms in human rights, and provided compensation for victims and survivors.

Pinochet lived with impunity until 1998, when he was arrested while traveling in London. A Spanish judge named Baltasar Garzón had issued an arrest warrant based on the principle of universal jurisdiction, arguing that Pinochet's abuses were crimes against humanity rather than merely a concern for the sovereign state of Chile. The arrest made headlines around the world, as it represented the first time that sovereign immunity could not be applied as an excuse to commit gross human rights violations. Pinochet was imprisoned in the United Kingdom for over a year.

Although the British courts agreed to extradite Pinochet to Spain to face trial, the British government returned him to Chile on humanitarian grounds, due to his old age and deteriorating health. Upon his return in 2000, Chilean courts revoked his immunity, and put him on trial for various counts of corruption and human rights violations. Pinochet spent the next six years in and out of legal battles and house arrest. He died in 2006, before any of his criminal trials could come to a conclusion.

Pinochet's case highlights the fact that justice can be slow and imperfect, as it is limited by political realities at the national and international levels. However, it also demonstrates the power of human rights to change these realities and increasingly put pressure on dictators to be held accountable for their actions.

but each can provide due process for suspects and justice for victims. While each of these mechanisms is problematic in its own way, transitional justice can be achieved by combining different methods of prosecution in each case. Many of these legal institutions are relatively recent innovations; and as they continue to take on new criminal cases, the legal precedents will become clearer, enforcement will become more consistent, and future violators will be deterred from committing abuses. Indeed, although individual criminal accountability is still in its infancy, initial research shows that successful prosecutions do have a deterrence effect on future violations, both within societies and across national borders.[21] Dictators often calculate the costs and benefits of repressing their citizens, and the promise of future imprisonment can be a strong incentive for them to protect human rights. The consistent protection of human rights therefore requires the end of impunity.

Argument 2
Human rights violators should be held accountable without the use of criminal trials.

This second argument partially agrees with the first argument, in that transitional justice is seen as important for helping societies move beyond a period of conflict and mass atrocities. Human rights are not well served when abusers receive no consequences for their actions, and when societies are forced to ignore the past. However, according to this second argument, criminal trials are not the best method for holding human rights violators accountable and ensuring that human rights are respected in transitional societies. Other mechanisms are available that deter future violations, allow victims to be heard, and ensure that a society can peacefully move through a democratic transition. Instead of putting criminals in jail, human rights may be better protected by making the political compromises necessary to ensure peace and stability.

In societies torn by conflict and political repression, authoritarian leaders often have disproportionate power to manipulate courts and avoid legal accountability. In some situations, this power makes criminal prosecution politically and legally impossible at the national level. Many countries have passed amnesty laws as a precondition for ending a civil war, which make both dictators and rebel groups legally immune from prosecution. For example, in Argentina and Chile, military leaders gave themselves amnesty before leaving office; while in Sierra Leone and Haiti, amnesty laws were included in peace agreements that ended violent conflicts.[22] Even when authoritarian leaders may be indicted by an international court or tried in absentia by another state, they typically have the power to resist arrest or extradition, so these prosecutions are often only symbolic. The failure of the ICC to extradite Sudan's Omar al-Bashir, discussed in the previous chapter, is illustrative of this point.

Given the reality that leaders often retain the political and legal power to avoid prosecution, the attempt to hold them criminally accountable for their actions can actually be counterproductive. Rather than deterring future abuses, the threat of prosecution provides an incentive for leaders such as Bashir to stay in office and deny international peacekeepers access to their territory. The threat of punishment also induces warlords to continue fighting rather than sign peace agreements. For example, Uganda's Joseph Kony, infamous head of the rebel Lord's Resistance Army, continues to elude capture and operate in central Africa after he was indicted by the ICC in 2005 for war crimes and crimes against humanity. Efforts by the Ugandan military to arrest Kony have resulted in further conflict and suffering for the people of northern Uganda. Without any chance of being granted amnesty, there is little incentive for Kony to discontinue his crimes. This has made even the Ugandan victims of Kony's brutalities ambivalent about the ICC indictment and the international campaign to prosecute him.[23] For those suffering at the hands of a brutal warlord, peace and amnesty may be a better trade-off than an international prosecution.

Even when human rights prosecutions are possible, they do not always provide the best form of justice for societies and the individual victims. Though there are different kinds of criminal trials designed to hold violators accountable at the national, international, and transnational levels, all of these mechanisms have similar weaknesses that render them ineffective in

> **What Would You Do?**
>
> Imagine that you are US attorney general Eric Holder, responsible for prosecuting federal crimes and human rights violations committed by US citizens. You have been presented with detailed evidence that intelligence agents and senior George W. Bush administration officials have committed war crimes by authorizing and carrying out torture and other inhumane acts against terrorism suspects (see Chapter 8). International treaties and US law require you to prosecute human rights violators. Would you seek any arrest warrants for US officials? If so, whom would you target—senior administrators such as Bush, or lower-level agents? What would be the likely public response if you were to move forward with criminal investigations?

protecting human rights in transitional societies. First, criminal trials tend to be expensive, and produce results slowly. Because they employ legal experts who must compile evidence from hundreds of witnesses and follow a rigid legal procedure, it can take many years and millions of dollars to prosecute a single individual. For example, after ten years in operation and over $1 billion spent, the ICC has successfully convicted only one individual, Thomas Lubanga Dyilo, and even that case is still under appeal.[24] If this money were spent on disarming former combatants and rebuilding democratic institutions in war-torn societies, it could have a more lasting impact on human rights protection.[25] Second, proper criminal trials require proof of guilt beyond a reasonable doubt, and because evidence in war can be difficult to obtain, trials can result in acquittals on procedural grounds. This is what happened with the second case that the ICC concluded, in 2012, when it acquitted Mathieu Ngudjolo Chui, a Congolese army leader, of war crimes based on insufficient evidence that he ordered specific attacks.[26] For victims who must suffer the traumatization of being cross-examined in court, this outcome may be worse than amnesty. Third, because trials are slow and expensive, they simply cannot prosecute everyone who has committed atrocities within a particular conflict. Even when it might be possible to prosecute a handful of leaders who gave orders to commit abuses, no court can try the thousands of suspects who are accused of participating in human rights violations. A case in point is Rwanda after the 1994 genocide, where over 100,000 suspects awaited trial in a legal system that contained only a few dozen trained attorneys.[27] In all of these situations, attempting to put criminals in jail is economically inefficient, politically controversial, and legally problematic.

In sum, according to this argument the threat of criminal trials or their implementation can exacerbate conflict, forestall peace agreements, subvert justice, and prolong human rights violations. Ending conflict and political repression is a prerequisite for a democratic transition to occur. In order to resolve conflict, a society must enter into delicate negotiations and make political compromises with human rights violators. But this does not mean that human rights abusers can act with impunity, because there are alternative mechanisms available that can provide some accountability without disrupting social and political stability.

Truth commissions are the primary mechanism of transitional justice that can accomplish this delicate balancing act. Truth commissions have been increasingly used in postconflict settings to ensure that abusers are held publicly, though not criminally, accountable for their actions. Truth commissions come in a variety of forms, but the basic premise is that the society produces a historical record of the violations that occurred during a period of time so that they will not be repeated in the future.[28] Some truth commissions are officially sponsored by the state as part of a peace agreement (such as South Africa's post-apartheid **Truth and Reconciliation Commission [TRC]**), and some are privately organized (such as the Catholic Church–sponsored REMHI in Guatemala).[29] Some truth commissions operate in the context of a widespread amnesty and do not identify abusers by name. Others, such as South Africa's TRC, offer amnesty to violators on the condition that they admit their crimes in a public hearing. Some truth commissions allow victims the opportunity to tell their stories, have their suffering publicly acknowledged, and discover where their loved ones are buried, which can give them a sense of emotional closure. Although truth commissions can also be politically controversial, in divided societies they are far more feasible than criminal prosecutions, according to this argument. Truth commissions ask a society to forgive, but not to forget; this is the necessary political compromise that lets violators go free, but prevents them from committing future abuses.

Truth commissions employ a different model of human rights accountability—one that is based on restorative justice rather than retributive justice. Instead of putting criminals in jail, restorative justice seeks to repair social institutions, promote healing, and reintegrate former abusers back into society. Truth commissions often lay the foundation for reparations, which materially compensate victims for the suffering that they endured. According to this argument, it is far better to spend a state's limited resources on repairing victims' broken lives than on criminal trials for their abusers. The ultimate goal of truth commissions is to recommend governmental and societal reforms that can improve the protection of human rights moving forward. One such reform is a democratic constitution that includes a bill of rights and protections for minority groups. Although it may seem unwise to allow former abusers a power-sharing role in a democratic government, the experiences of Northern Ireland and South Africa have shown that human rights protection can improve dramatically if rights guarantees are built into the new constitutions.[30]

Truth commissions can also be paired with noncriminal sanctions such as lustration, which prohibits former human rights violators from serving in key government or societal positions. For example, in several postcommunist countries of Eastern Europe, former communist officials were barred from running for office for a set period of time.[31] This measure provided some form of punishment for abusers during a "cooling off" period without threatening the political stability of divided nations.

Because truth commissions and noncriminal sanctions require a lower standard of evidence than do criminal trials, they can be designed in a cost-effective way that applies to large numbers of perpetrators. While it may seem odious that some human rights violators receive legal immunity or mild sanctions for their actions, these are often the compromises that a transitional society must make in order to maintain stability and protect human rights moving forward. Indeed, research has shown that even public shaming has a deterrent effect on future violations, as potential abusers are motivated as much by their social reputation as they are by the threat of imprisonment.[32] Although some activists would claim that these accountability mechanisms violate the rule of law, according to this argument it is better to build the rule of law gradually within societies, than to attempt to enforce an absolutist notion of the law in places where it is politically ineffective.

* * *

Conclusion

Should criminals be prosecuted even at the risk of exacerbating conflict, or should human rights abusers walk free in order to ensure a more stable democratic transition? This debate has been framed as a choice between two mutually exclusive options, but in fact these different accountability mechanisms can often work hand in hand. A truth commission may be the only possible form of accountability immediately after a change in government, because political tensions are still high and former leaders have the power to negotiate an amnesty. However, years later political conditions may change, and the state itself may decide to withdraw the amnesty and move ahead with prosecutions, or extradite the same suspects to international tribunals. In these cases, the initial truth commission often gathers key evidence that can lay the foundation for future criminal prosecutions. This is what happened in places such as Guatemala, where two truth commissions in the 1990s (one official and one unofficial) spelled out the evidentiary basis for finally bringing former leader Ríos Montt to trial in 2013.[33] Similarly, Sierra Leone's truth commission provided evidence against Charles Taylor in 2004 that was used by the Special Court for Sierra Leone to convict him in 2012.[34] Human rights violators might be enticed by amnesty to give up power, only later to discover that the amnesty is irrelevant or overturned.

Another way in which the functions of truth commissions and criminal trials can be integrated is by applying different mechanisms to different types of crimes. Severe, widespread violations of human rights can be criminally prosecuted in high-profile court cases, while lower-level crimes can be dealt with through truth commissions or more flexible accountability mechanisms. This was the case in post-genocide Rwanda, where those who perpetrated the worst crimes and those who ordered the genocide were prosecuted in national courts or the ICTR, while lower-level participants were subject to village-level hearings (called *gacaca* trials) throughout the country. These *gacaca* hearings allowed the lowest-level perpetrators to atone for their crimes by compensating their victims with land or money, and provided other flexible solutions that promoted reintegration rather than retribution. If perpetrators admitted their violations in *gacaca* hearings, they were generally treated with leniency and avoided criminal prosecutions. This was the only feasible way that Rwanda could have held over 100,000 criminal suspects accountable for their actions while promoting some form of reconciliation between Hutus and Tutsis moving forward. In fact, some scholars have found that when criminal trials are paired with amnesties, either in a chronological sequence or for different levels of crime, it has a positive impact on democratization and the protection of human rights in the society moving forward.[35]

In sum, holding human rights violators accountable for their heinous actions is not always a simple and straightforward process. While we might wish to see every criminal stand trial in court and serve time in prison, it is often not politically, legally, or economically possible to carry this out in postconflict societies. There is often a trade-off between the long-term goal of deterring human rights abuses through a predictable justice system, and the short-term goal of ending human rights abuses through a stable democratic transition in a conflict-ridden society. These two goals are not always possible to accomplish simultaneously. Nevertheless, as a result of the accountability, authoritarian leaders and warlords can no longer assume that they can violate human rights with impunity. The doctrine of sovereign immunity is being replaced by an emerging norm of individual accountability. Although the mechanisms of accountability are still less than perfect, they are inching the world closer to the ideal of justice that human rights activists are striving to achieve.

Notes

1. Bruce Baker, "Twilight of Impunity for Africa's Presidential Criminals," *Third World Quarterly* 25, no. 8 (2004): 1487–1499.

2. Michael J. Kelly, *Nowhere to Hide: Defeat of the Sovereign Immunity Defense for the Crimes of Genocide and the Trials of Slobodan Milosevic and Saddam Hussein* (New York: Peter Lang, 2005), p. 77.

3. Baker, "Twilight of Impunity," p. 1489.

4. Daniel C. Turack, "Ending Impunity in Africa: The Charles Taylor Trial at the Special Court for Sierra Leone," *Journal of Third World Studies* 26, no. 2 (2009): 202.

5. Human Rights Watch, "Libya: New Era Needs Focus on Rights," October 20, 2011, http://www.hrw.org/news/2011/10/20/libya-new-era-needs-focus-rights.

6. These treaties include, but are not limited to, the 1948 Genocide Convention, the 1984 Convention Against Torture, and the 1998 Rome Statute. In certain cases, such as genocide, the obligation to prosecute criminals even extends across national borders. While virtually all states have ratified some of these treaties, the duty to prosecute can also be considered as part of customary international law and thus as binding on all states. See Diane F. Orentlicher, "Settling Accounts: The Duty to Prosecute Human Rights Violations of a Prior Regime," *Yale Law Journal* 100, no. 8 (1991): 2537–2615.

7. René Lemarchand, "Consociationalism and Power Sharing in Africa: Rwanda, Burundi, and the Democratic Republic of Congo," *African Affairs* 106, no. 422 (January 2007): 4.

8. Andreas Mehler, "Not Always in the People's Interest: Power-Sharing Agreements in African Peace Agreements," Working Paper no. 83 (Hamburg: German Institute of Global and Area Studies, July 2008).

9. Orentlicher, "Settling Accounts," p. 2543.

10. From *The Gulag Archipelago,* quoted in ibid, p. 2537.

11. Neil J. Kritz, "Coming to Terms with Atrocities: A Review of Accountability Mechanisms for Mass Violations of Human Rights," *Law and Contemporary Problems* 59, no. 4 (1997): 127–152.

12. Ibid.

13. Jeremy Peterson, "Unpacking Show Trials: Situating the Trial of Saddam Hussein," *Harvard International Law Journal* 48, no. 1 (2007): 257–292.

14. Emi MacLean, "Ríos Montt Genocide Trial Confronts Political Push-Back in Guatemala," Open Society Justice Initiative, April 18, 2013, http://www.open societyfoundations.org/voices/rios-montt-genocide-trial-confronts-political-push -back-guatemala.

15. Kritz, "Coming to Terms with Atrocities," p. 129.

16. Heidi Nichols Haddad, "Mobilizing the Will to Prosecute: Crimes of Rape at the Yugoslav and Rwandan Tribunals," *Human Rights Review* 12 (2011): 109–132.

17. Laura A. Dickinson, "The Promise of Hybrid Courts," *American Journal of International Law* 97, no. 2 (April 2003): 295–310.

18. Darren Hawkins, "Universal Jurisdiction for Human Rights: From Legal Principle to Limited Reality," *Global Governance* 9, no. 3 (2003): 347–365.

19. *Report of the Chilean National Commission on Truth and Reconciliation* (Notre Dame, IN: University of Notre Dame Press, 1993).

20. For an excellent analysis of the Pinochet case, see Rebecca Evans, "Pinochet in London, Pinochet in Chile: International and Domestic Politics in Human Rights Policy," *Human Rights Quarterly* 28, no. 1 (2006): 207–244.

21. Hunjoon Kim and Kathryn Sikkink, "Explaining the Deterrence Effect of Human Rights Prosecutions for Transitional Countries," *International Studies Quarterly* 54, no. 4 (2010): 939–963.

22. Elizabeth B. Ludwig King, "Amnesties in a Time of Transition," *George Washington International Law Review* 41, no. 3 (2010): 577–618.

23. Christian Noll, "The Betrayed: An Exploration of the Acholi Opinion of the International Criminal Court," *Journal of Third World Studies* 26, no. 1 (2009):

99–119. The international campaign to arrest Kony has been led by the US-based NGO Invisible Children, whose "Kony 2012" online video was viewed by over 100 million people worldwide.

24. Jon Silverman, "Ten Years, $900 Million, One Verdict: Does the ICC Cost Too Much?" *BBC News,* March 14, 2012, http://www.bbc.co.uk/news/magazine-17351946.

25. Kritz, "Coming to Terms with Atrocities," p. 150.

26. "ICC Acquits Congolese Armed Group Leader," *African Press Organization,* December, 18, 2012.

27. Kritz, "Coming to Terms with Atrocities," p. 150.

28. Priscilla B. Hayner, *Unspeakable Truths: Transitional Justice and the Challenge of Truth Commissions* (New York: Routledge, 2001).

29. Translated from Spanish, "REMHI" stands for the Interdiocese Project for the Recovery of Historical Memory. See Garrett FitzGerald, "The Truth Commissions of Guatemala: Pluralism and Particularity Within the Human Rights Paradigm," *Cult/ure* 5 (2010).

30. Christine Bell, *Peace Agreements and Human Rights* (Oxford: Oxford University Press, 2003). See also Christopher McCrudden and Brendan O'Leary, *Courts and Consociations: Human Rights Versus Power Sharing* (Oxford: Oxford University Press, 2013).

31. Kritz, "Coming to Terms with Atrocities," p. 139.

32. Kathryn Sikkink, *The Justice Cascade: How Human Rights Prosecutions Are Changing World Politics* (New York: Norton, 2011), p. 258.

33. See Human Rights Office, Archdiocese of Guatemala, *Guatemala, Never Again!* (Maryknoll, NY: Orbis, 1999). See also Commission for Historical Clarification, *Guatemala: Memory of Silence* (Guatemala City, 1999).

34. See Truth and Reconciliation Commission, *Witness to Truth: Report of the Sierra Leone Truth and Reconciliation Commission* (Cape Town, 2004).

35. Tricia D. Olsen, Leigh A. Payne, and Andrew G. Reiter, "The Justice Balance: When Transitional Justice Improves Human Rights and Democracy," *Human Rights Quarterly* 32, no. 4 (2010): 980–1007.

Part 2

Civil and Political Rights

8

Does the War on Terrorism Require Restriction of Rights?

September 11, 2001, stands as a date that will be etched into history books for years to come. On that day, nineteen members of al-Qaeda, a militant Islamist network at war with the United States, hijacked four commercial airplanes. They flew two of the planes into the World Trade Center towers in New York City, bringing both skyscrapers to the ground, and crashed one plane into the Pentagon in Washington, D.C. In total, almost 3,000 people died in the suicide attacks that day, including citizens of fifty-eight countries other than the United States.

Many commentators described September 11 as "the day that the world changed." And yet, acts of terrorism, even those involving suicide bombers and the hijacking of airplanes, were nothing new. Al-Qaeda, founded and led by the Saudi millionaire Osama bin Laden, had been attacking US targets around the world for over a decade. Terrorism itself, a tactic that deliberately targets civilians in order to strike fear into a population and gain a military advantage, had been used in wars for many centuries.

Perhaps what changed most on September 11 was the sudden sense of vulnerability felt by the people of the United States. The end of the Cold War in the 1990s had left the United States without a major global rival, and Americans entered the twenty-first century with a feeling of relative peace and stability. With the United States being the sole remaining military and economic superpower, many Americans perceived that there were no significant threats to its security. The terrorist attacks on September 11 reminded everyone that even a small group of nonstate actors, armed with weapons of mass destruction, could wreak havoc on US soil.

By declaring a "war on terror," the administration of George W. Bush responded to this "new" threat of terrorism with a range of policy initiatives. Some of these measures were relatively noncontroversial and accepted by a broad consensus domestically and internationally. For example, the United States created a new Department of Homeland Security, which was designed to facilitate information sharing and coordination among the intelligence-gathering agencies of the US government. With broad international support, the United States invaded Afghanistan to remove the Taliban from power and attack al-Qaeda camps. Although some peace activists protested the US war in Afghanistan, most human rights experts believed that the United States had the legitimate right to defend itself from further attacks by targeting al-Qaeda where it was hiding.[1]

Other policies implemented by the Bush administration after 2001 raised the hackles of human rights activists and were roundly criticized throughout the world. These policies allegedly violated some of the core civil and political rights that were so closely linked to the reputation of Western democracies such as the United States. These policies included the following:

• *Enhanced interrogation.* The Bush administration authorized representatives of the United States, including military police, CIA agents, and private contractors, to use harsh and coercive interrogation methods against people detained on suspicion of terrorism. These methods included **waterboarding**, physical beatings, sensory deprivation, sleep deprivation, exposure to hypothermia, mock executions, the use of stress positions, and similar interrogation methods that went beyond those authorized by the US Army Field Manual. Human rights activists claimed that these methods amounted to torture, violating the protections given to prisoners of war under the **Geneva Conventions**.

• *Indefinite detention of suspected terrorists.* The Bush administration created new prisons around the world to hold terror suspects whom it captured. In some cases, alleged terrorists have been held for many years without having the opportunity to challenge their detention in a court of law. In other cases, suspects were brought before US military tribunals, under more restrictive procedures than were available in civilian courts. Several hundred detainees have been held at the US naval base in **Guantanamo Bay**, Cuba, and many others have been held in prisons at military bases in Iraq and Afghanistan, or at secret **CIA black sites** in undisclosed locations. Human rights activists have protested that these policies also violate the Geneva Conventions, as well as the right of habeas corpus, which provides defendants with the right to confront the evidence against them in a court of law.

• *Extraordinary rendition.* The Bush administration transferred terror suspects across national borders without any judicial oversight. In addition to the prisons where suspects were detained indefinitely, some detainees were also transferred to third countries, such as Egypt, Jordan, Morocco, and Uzbekistan, in order to be interrogated by the authorities of those nations. Human rights activists claimed that the United States knowingly used these countries' interrogators in order to subject terror suspects to torture methods that went beyond even those approved under the "enhanced interrogation" program, such as the cutting of genitals and use of electrocution.

• *Expanded authority for surveillance and law enforcement within the United States.* The US Congress passed the **Patriot Act** in 2001, which gave the government greater power to gather intelligence on US citizens, regulate financial transactions, and secure the US border. The Patriot Act allowed for an increase in the wiretapping of phones, and the data-mining of e-mails, library, and financial records. It expanded the definition of terrorism to include material support for terrorist organizations, and increased the penalties for terror-related crimes committed in the United States. Using his assumed power under the Patriot Act, President Bush secretly ordered the National Security Agency (NSA) to create a terrorist surveillance program (otherwise known as warrantless wiretapping). Under this program, the NSA monitored phone calls, e-mails, and other communication going into and out of the United States without obtaining a warrant from a court of law. Human rights advocates argued that the Patriot Act and the surveillance program violated US citizens' right to privacy, and their rights to free speech and free association.

• *The invasion of Iraq.* The United States led a coalition of its allies to invade and occupy Iraq in 2003, arguing that Saddam Hussein was providing support to terrorists and was seeking to build weapons of mass destruction. The war succeeded in overthrowing Hussein and installing a quasi-democratic government in Iraq, but at the cost of roughly 100,000 Iraqi deaths, over 6,000 coalition deaths, and an estimated $3 trillion cost to the US economy.[2] Human rights activists from many countries protested against the war in Iraq, arguing that it was an illegal invasion that was not justified by self-defense against terrorism and not authorized by the UN Security Council.

The Bush administration's initial response to many of the criticisms from human rights organizations was one of denial. When human rights groups first interviewed terror suspects and reported cases of torture, enhanced interrogation, or extraordinary rendition, US officials denied that these programs ever existed. They claimed that al-Qaeda terrorists were trained to lie about their treatment in detention, and that terrorists often conduct psychological warfare against their enemies. Ultimately, however, the evidence of the existence of these programs became too overwhelming for the Bush administration to deny. Interviews with dozens of terror suspects were corroborated by physical evidence on their bodies, or in some cases their autopsy reports. US soldiers occasionally took pictures and videos of their interrogation tactics, and some of them went public about the methods they used. Infamous photos from prisoner abuses at the Abu Ghraib prison in Iraq were released to the public in 2004. Finally, in 2009 a series of internal memos were released showing that senior Bush administration officials explicitly approved the tactics used in the enhanced interrogation program.[3] Similarly, the Bush administration kept the NSA's warrantless wiretapping program secret until an article in the *New York Times* revealed its existence.[4]

Therefore, this debate is not about whether such programs and tactics really exist, but about whether they are necessary in order to defeat terrorists bent upon the destruction of the United States and its allies.[5] Supporters of these programs argue that, because suicidal terrorists operate differently from other kinds of combatants, they need to be confronted more aggressively than the traditional rules of warfare allow. Some human rights must be limited in this process, and the international law of human rights should be updated to account for the unique challenge of terrorism. On the other hand, opponents of these programs argue that terrorism is not so different from other forms of armed combat, and that human rights must not be sacrificed in order to win the war against al-Qaeda and other terrorist groups.

Argument 1
Some human rights must be restricted in the war on terrorism.

According to this argument, the war on terrorism is different than conventional war, and therefore it must rely on a different set of tactics. Human rights are certainly important, as a set of individual liberties that protect citizens from abuses by fellow citizens and by their own government. In the realm of **international humanitarian law**, human rights regulate what states can do to other states in the context of war. However, terrorists do not act like states in war, nor do they act like citizens. Thus, because of the unique nature of this threat in the twenty-first century, twentieth-century tools are insufficient to defeat terrorism. Some rights must be restricted in the war on terrorism, but only in order to protect the most fundamental human right, the right to security.

Terrorism has existed for many centuries, but what is unique about modern terrorism is the ability of a small group of unpredictable actors to project massively destructive power across the entire globe. Today's terrorists operate within secret, decentralized networks, rather than within a single, transparent, hierarchical command structure. With the possession of a chemical, biological, or nuclear weapon, a single person could potentially destroy an entire society. With the existence of global communication and transportation networks, terrorists can spread their ideologies and their weapons anywhere. For al-Qaeda, a radical fundamentalist ideology motivates people to commit suicide in order to kill not only Americans, but also anyone who disagrees with them. All of these factors make the threat of terrorism different than the threat of conventional warfare between territorial states.

Because of the secret, decentralized, and suicidal nature of terrorism, intelligence gathering may be the single most important weapon in the fight against terrorists. According to this argument, the only effective way to consistently stop secret attacks by small groups of people is to know about them in advance. Therefore, in order to collect this intelligence and protect innocent civilians' right to personal security, it may sometimes be necessary to derogate the rights of terrorists. The harsh interrogation tactics used by the Bush administration were not pleasant, but according to this argument they were effective in preventing terror attacks. According to former vice president Dick Cheney, "The activities of the CIA in carrying out the policies of the Bush Administration were directly responsible for defeating all efforts by Al Qaeda to launch further mass-casualty attacks against the United States."[6] The CIA's waterboarding of al-Qaeda mastermind Khalid Sheikh Mohammed led to vital information about the al-Qaeda network in Afghanistan, and helped prevent a planned attack on Los Angeles in 2001.[7] Enhanced interrogation led to actionable intelligence and the capture or death of many al-Qaeda operatives. The fact that there has not been a major terrorist attack on US soil since 2001 demonstrates that enhanced interrogation was effective. As former CIA director George Tenet stated, "I believe none of these successes would have happened if we had had to treat [Khalid Shaikh Mohammed] like a white-collar criminal—read him his *Miranda* rights and gotten him a lawyer."[8]

Furthermore, terrorists are explicitly trained to resist the interrogation methods outlined in the US Army Field Manual. They are religious fanatics who do not respond to appeals to reason or humanity. The harsh interrogation methods used after September 11 were often the only way to break them and get them to speak. Although human rights activists have labeled those methods "torture" and compare them to the methods of Nazi Germany's Third Reich or Cambodia's Khmer Rouge, supporters claim that US interrogation methods were not barbaric. They were carefully controlled, limited in time, and supervised by medical and psychological staff. When not directly under interrogation, terror suspects have lived in relative comfort at Guantanamo, which underwent a $38 million renovation in 2006 to improve the privacy and health of detainees.[9] Some individual soldiers went beyond the interrogation methods approved by the Bush administration, such as the military police at Abu Ghraib who committed sexual abuses against detainees. But when these abuses occurred, the soldiers responsible were prosecuted and the abuses stopped.

Abandoning these effective interrogation methods is therefore equivalent to sacrificing the security of civilians throughout the Western world in order to uphold the outdated mantle of the Geneva Conventions. The Geneva Conventions were drafted from 1864 to 1949, and envisaged warfare between uniformed soldiers of regular armies, taking place on a specific territory for a specific duration of time. These soldiers, when taken as prisoners of war, were protected from interrogation and torture, and were returned to their homes after the end of hostilities. With this kind of warfare, states could be expected to follow the norms of the Geneva Conventions because other states would realize that it was in their long-term self-interests to reciprocate. In other words, the United States could protect German soldiers whom it captured in World War II because it could reasonably rely on Germany to protect American prisoners of war. It was expected that after the war ended, Germany would become an ally of the West, as it did, and that there would be no reason to continue fighting. The Geneva Conventions, however, are not applicable in the fight against terrorism. Terrorists are unlawful combatants who are not provided the same protections by the Geneva Conventions as are prisoners of war. The war on terrorism is a global war without any territorial boundaries, and there is no foreseeable time in the future when the combatants might declare an end to hostilities. Could we even imagine what a peace agreement with al-Qaeda would look like? Therefore, we cannot apply the norms of conventional warfare to unconventional war. Al-Qaeda cannot be relied on to reciprocate US treatment of prisoners, as Germany did in World War II. In fact, al-Qaeda executes its prisoners without trial by beheading them and broadcasting these beheadings to the world. The United States would therefore receive no benefit to following the Geneva Conventions in the war on terrorism. Treating prisoners with complete respect, or returning them to their homes after a specified period of time, would certainly result in further attacks against the United States, according to this argument.

The United States has captured hundreds, perhaps thousands, of terror suspects, and it cannot return them to their places of origin. It also cannot reasonably be expected to prosecute them allowing all the legal safeguards provided for US citizens in civilian courts. In civilian courts, the standards of evidence and transparency are high, precisely because the conditions for collecting evidence in criminal cases are so tightly controlled. In warfare, however, the collection of evidence is entirely uncontrolled, and with the secrecy and global reach of terrorism, it is virtually impossible to collect evidence on terrorists that would stand up in a civilian court. Even if substantial evidence is collected, it would often be unwise to share secret evidence with terror suspects, who could potentially use that information to threaten US security. Therefore, the military tribunals set up by the Bush administration, and ultimately authorized by Congress in the **Military Commissions Act** of 2006, are the only reasonable way to hear evidence against terror suspects under lower standards of transparency than civilian courts offer. Military tribunals are the only way to provide terror suspects with a reasonably fair hearing while protecting the secrecy and national security of the United States. This is why the right to a fair trial in a civilian court is not listed by international treaties like the International Covenant on Civil and Political Rights as a **nonderogable** right; in other words, in times of emergency, states are allowed to restrict some due process rights.[10]

The same logic also applies to the program of extraordinary rendition. When a suspected terrorist is captured in another country, it is often impossible or unreasonable to conduct civilian legal proceedings to extradite that suspect to the United States. Therefore, the only way to ensure the safety of innocent civilians is to hold the terrorist in a secret site or transfer the terrorist to a third country for interrogation. While some of the interrogation methods used by other countries are harsher than those used by the United States, this would certainly not be the first time that the United States has had to ally itself with unscrupulous partners in order to win a difficult war. In World War II, the United States joined with Joseph Stalin of Russia, one of the worst human rights abusers of the twentieth century, in order to defeat Adolf Hitler. In war, as in politics, the lesser of two evils is sometimes the only reasonable choice.

In essence, according to this argument war inevitably produces a trade-off in human rights, and because terrorism is an extreme form of war, this trade-off is more profound. The human right to security is foundational—a precondition for the enjoyment of all other rights.

When security is threatened by emergency situations, then other rights must be curtailed, but only to the extent that is necessary to provide security. This is also the case with the Patriot Act, expanded wiretapping and data-mining programs, and expanded searches at airports. The right to privacy is limited by the need for security, and reasonable citizens are willing to give up some of their privacy and some personal conveniences in order to remain safe. It is therefore entirely legitimate for the United States to spy on potential terrorists in order to prevent another major attack, and law-abiding citizens should have nothing to fear from this kind of surveillance program.

Modern terrorism is a unique kind of war, in that it is secret rather than transparent, global rather than territorial, fought by small groups rather than states, and indefinite rather than bound in time. Another feature that characterizes modern terrorism is that it is often motivated by extremist religious ideology, not the rational pursuit of self-interests. This renders the conventional strategy of deterrence ineffective against terrorists, since the promise to retaliate does not deter someone who is already suicidal. The **Bush Doctrine** is based on this understanding of modern terrorism, and it calls on the United States to aggressively pursue terrorists, as well as state sponsors of terrorism, even if an attack is not imminent and the United States must act alone. Thus the invasion of Iraq was a legitimate war, even though it did not gain the support of the international community, because the United States could not stand by and allow a supporter of terrorism to gain access to weapons of mass destruction. Although some could reasonably criticize the way that the war was prosecuted, the United States had the right to attack Iraq because the United States had the right to defend itself against potential acts of terrorism. As Vice President Cheney argued in defending the war in Iraq, "With such an enemy, no peace treaty is possible; no policy of containment or deterrence will prove effective. The only way to deal with this threat is to destroy it, completely and utterly."[11]

On September 11, 2001, al-Qaeda declared a new kind of war against the United States. Article 51 of the UN Charter gives every nation the sovereign right to defend itself against foreign attacks. The US Constitution gives the president the authority as commander-in-chief to prosecute this war of self-defense as he deems necessary. As the former legal adviser to President Bush, John Yoo has argued that unless the president is expressly prohibited by Congress, he is allowed to restrict human rights during wartime in order to ensure the more fundamental right to security.[12] Because terrorism is a unique threat in the twenty-first century, the restriction of some rights in the war against it is not only allowable, but also necessary.

Argument 2
Human rights must remain inviolable
in the war on terrorism.

According to this argument, the idea that some human rights must be restricted in the war on terrorism is erroneous. Although modern terrorism has some unique features, it is not so fundamentally different that it requires ignoring the human rights standards that have functioned in some of the worst wars of the past century. By maintaining its commitment to human rights, the United States can ensure its security without sacrificing the most important elements of its national character. Violating human rights is not an effective way to defeat terrorism, and could even prove counterproductive in the long run.

According to this argument, although intelligence gathering is one of the most important weapons against a secretive and decentralized network of terrorists, torture is an ineffective interrogation tactic. Some of the top US interrogators have themselves argued that nonviolent methods work just as well, or perhaps better, than coercive methods. For example, Ali Soufan, who was involved in the initial interrogation of al-Qaeda operative Abu Zubaydah, has claimed that he was able to obtain far better intelligence from Zubaydah in the months before torture was used than after. According to Soufan, "When they are in pain, people will say anything to get the pain to stop. Most of the time, they will lie, make up anything to make you stop hurting them. That means the information you're getting is useless."[13] In other words, torture may be effective in coercing detainees to talk, but the information they provide is unreliable. When detainees give false information under torture, it wastes time and resources as the United States follows false leads.

The success of noncoercive interrogation methods was demonstrated by the killing of al-Qaeda's leader, Osama bin Laden, in 2011. The intelligence that located bin Laden's compound in Abbottabad, Pakistan, was gathered using traditional interrogation and surveillance methods over a period of several years. A plot to destroy a US-bound airliner with an underwear bomb was similarly foiled in 2012 by a double agent who had infiltrated al-Qaeda in Yemen, not by coercive interrogation.[14] Traditional law enforcement methods were also used effectively to prevent attacks on commercial buildings and Jewish synagogues in New York in 2009 and 2011.

Even in cases when torture is effective in gaining valuable information from terrorists, the costs of torture would still outweigh the benefits. The abusive conditions in the prisons at Guantanamo Bay and Abu

Ghraib have damaged the reputation of the United States around the world. This abuse has alienated US allies and made it more difficult for the United States to gain their cooperation on other human rights initiatives. The US torture program has enraged many Muslims at home and abroad, and enlarged the pool of potential enemies of the United States who would resort to terrorism. As President Obama has stated, Guantanamo Bay is "the best imaginable recruiting tool for Al Qaeda."[15] Thus, even as the United States is capturing and killing terrorists, its policies have simultaneously created more terrorists. Torture also makes it more difficult to prosecute a terror suspect in any reasonably fair court of law. Torture exacerbates the legal vacuum that detainees find themselves in, and makes it more difficult to protect their rights to habeas corpus and due process.

Beyond this, even if torture were an effective method of interrogation, it is patently illegal and contradicts the core values of the United States. The interrogation methods approved by the Bush administration were not merely uncomfortable; they were inhuman. They are indeed some of the same methods used by the Nazis, the Viet Cong, and the Khmer Rouge. They are the same methods that the US State Department regularly condemns in its annual human rights reports when other countries practice them. The fact that post–September 11 interrogations were often tightly controlled by medical professionals, to ensure that detainees did not die in custody, does not make the methods any less cruel. Several detainees who were subjected to stress positions, sleep deprivation, and hypothermia became so mentally unstable that they lost control of their regular bodily functions. Khalid Sheikh Mohammed was waterboarded 183 times by the CIA. Over 100 detainees have died in US custody in Iraq and Afghanistan, most of them violently.[16] The evidence over the past decade has made it clear that the kinds of abuses the world witnessed in Abu Ghraib in 2004 were not the result of a handful of "bad apples" in the US military police, but part of a system of abusive behavior that was authorized by senior US officials. These violations have been justified by the same "exceptionalism" rhetoric that the United States has used in many other contexts.[17]

These abuses not only were committed against hardened enemies of the United States, but inevitably reached innocent civilians as well. Much of the false intelligence provided to the United States in Iraq and Afghanistan led to the imprisonment of people who had no links to terrorism. For example, Khalid el-Masri, a German citizen who unfortunately shared the same name as a suspected terrorist, was kidnapped by the CIA in Macedonia in 2003 and transported to Afghanistan under the extraordinary rendition program. He was placed in solitary confinement for several months, denied sufficient nourishment, and beaten and sodomized during interrogation. When the CIA learned that they had captured the wrong man, they secretly flew him to a remote location in Albania and abandoned him with no explanation.[18] A similar fate awaited Maher Arar, a Canadian citizen who was arrested in New York in 2002 and rendered to Syria for interrogation under torture for ten months. Although Arar signed a false confession, he was ultimately cleared of all charges, and was issued a formal apology by the Canadian prime minister.[19]

Committing torture, ordering torture, or knowingly transferring a detainee to a third country for torture are all clearly illegal under both US and international law. Under US law, the Eighth Amendment to the Constitution prohibits "cruel and unusual punishment"; the 1996 War Crimes Act prohibits violations of the Geneva Conventions; and the Torture Statute in the US Code prohibits torture in the United States.[20] Under the Geneva Conventions, in Common Article 3, every prisoner captured in war must be protected from torture and other affronts to personal dignity, regardless of whether that prisoner is a lawful or unlawful combatant. US president Ronald Reagan signed the UN's **Convention Against Torture** in 1988, calling for anyone who authorized torture to be prosecuted.[21] Torture is explicitly listed in international treaties as a nonderogable right, which means that under no circumstances can it ever be used. Torture has been so consistently prohibited by international law that it is commonly seen as a **jus cogens** norm, meaning that no state is ever granted an exception from following it. This is why several US human rights organizations have called for the criminal prosecution of senior officials in the Bush administration.[22]

National and international laws also govern the criminal prosecution of terror suspects. Although the standards of evidence and transparency used in cases of terrorism cannot always be the same as those that operate in civilian courts, terror suspects nevertheless must receive a fair and impartial hearing that gives them the right to challenge the evidence against them in a court of law. The right of habeas corpus has been an important characteristic of Western civilization since King John of England signed the Magna Carta in 1215. The US Supreme Court reaffirmed that terror suspects should have the right to challenge their detention in a fair hearing, in the *Rasul v. Bush* decision of 2004. Military tribunals could potentially provide fair trials to terror suspects; human rights standards do not require all terror suspects to be tried in civilian courts. However, the military tribunals set up by the Bush administration did not provide a fair hearing to terror suspects, as found by the Supreme Court in the *Hamdan v. Rumsfeld* case in 2006. Defendants were often not provided with any of the evidence used against them, and were prosecuted based on evidence obtained under torture. The Supreme Court held that military tribunals must uphold these basic due process rights for terror suspects.

The US president does not have the authority to commit illegal acts, even in the process of fighting a war for national defense. He cannot order the torture of terror suspects, or transfer them to third countries for torture, or hold them indefinitely without a fair trial. The government cannot wiretap phone calls or collect e-mail records without a warrant from a court. The Bush administration's legal advisers, who argued that the president has virtually unlimited authority to prosecute a war, were wrong. The US Department of Justice declared in 2010 that President Bush's legal advisers had exercised poor judgment, inconsistent with legal precedents, in making this claim.[23] The United States must adhere to national and international laws in fighting the war on terrorism.

While suicidal terrorists present significant challenges to national security, the threat of al-Qaeda in the twenty-first century is not uniquely dangerous, or objectively worse than the threats of the twentieth century. The West defeated the nuclear-armed Soviet Union by expanding the protection of human rights at home and abroad, not by violating human rights in the name of national security. Similarly, the war on terrorism will be won through disciplined and targeted attacks that rely on the cooperation of US allies, not by aggressively and unilaterally overreacting.

Terrorists gain a military advantage not only by striking fear into a civilian population, but also by inducing their enemies to overreact. When the United States detains and tortures innocent people, or denies civil rights to its Muslim citizens, it makes it easier for al-Qaeda to frame the conflict as a war between the West and all Muslims. The same principle applies to the war in Iraq. Saddam Hussein had no operational links to al-Qaeda, and there was no reliable evidence that he was close to obtaining weapons of mass destruction. By illegally invading and occupying Iraq, the United States destabilized the Middle East, created new enemies in the Islamic world, lost the support of many of its key allies, withdrew its attention from al-Qaeda's main bases in Afghanistan, and increased its national debt. The United States violated the human rights of Iraqi citizens by failing to provide security after it deposed Hussein. The Bush Doctrine represented the overreach of a hegemonic state, and the war in Iraq proved to be counterproductive to the US fight against terrorism.

The United States is more than just a territory with a group of people living in it. The United States stands for a set of democratic values and ideals, and the protection of people's basic rights is central to these values. The United States has a long-term interest in the expansion of human rights around the world, and it cannot be a "city on a hill" for the rest of the world to follow if it does not practice what it preaches. For the United States to defend its national interests, it must not only protect its people and its territory, but also defend its core values. The war on terrorism is a threat to the identity of the United States, as much as terrorism is a threat to its citizens. This is why the protection of human rights in the fight against terrorism is absolutely necessary. Fighting terror with terror is not only ineffective and illegal, but also un-American.

* * *

Conclusion

Debates about US policies in the war on terrorism are highly emotional and politically charged. Many of the arguments explored here have been featured in political campaigns and in partisan debates in the US Congress. However, we should be careful not to frame the war on terrorism as exclusively a controversy between Republicans and Democrats, or between Bush and Obama. Some of the controversial policies of the Bush administration have been repudiated by members of both political parties, and other policies have received broad bipartisan sup-

> ### Think Again
>
> As explored throughout this book, realists, liberalists, and constructivists hold different theories about how international politics works. Can you identify each of the three theories within the specific arguments in this debate about restricting rights in the war on terrorism?

port even as they were condemned by human rights groups. For example, both major candidates in the 2008 US presidential election campaigned on a platform of ending the enhanced interrogation program. Republican presidential candidate John McCain was likely influenced by his own personal experience of torture as a prisoner of war in Vietnam in the 1960s. On the other hand, Republicans and Democrats have largely endorsed the expansion of the US government's surveillance power in the Patriot Act, and the use of military tribunals to keep terror suspects imprisoned.

President Obama campaigned on a platform of ending US human rights abuses in the war on terrorism and reviving the international reputation of the United States. Upon taking office in 2009, Obama immediately issued an executive order to end the enhanced interrogation and extraordinary rendition programs, and replaced them with the interrogation techniques listed in the US Army Field Manual. He began to draw down US troops in Iraq, and ultimately ended combat operations there in 2010. He also announced his intention to close the Guantanamo Bay prison and hold civilian trials for terror suspects on US soil, but this plan was blocked by members of both parties in Congress.

Although in some ways President Obama has upheld his promise to reverse the policies of the past decade, in other ways he has continued or even expanded previous programs. The Obama administration reauthorized the Patriot Act with most of its controversial provisions intact, and has not pursued any criminal investigations against Bush administration officials. Secret documents leaked by NSA contractor Edward Snowden in 2013 showed that Obama has continued the NSA's global surveillance program, which collects massive amounts of data from personal phone and internet records. Obama ordered a surge of troops in Afghanistan, and dramatically increased the use of unmanned drones to attack suspected terrorists in Pakistan and elsewhere (see Figure 8.1).[24] Obama's use of drones to execute targeted killings of suspected terrorists, and the inevitable civilian casualties that these bombings cause, have also been condemned by human rights organizations. While the Obama administration argues that these bombings are legal, narrowly targeted, and supported by US allies, the debate over their legality and effectiveness continues.

Ultimately, the debate over human rights in the war on terrorism raises the question of whether human rights are truly applicable during wartime and in cases of national emergencies. Some analysts say that human rights are effective in regulating a state's treatment of its own citizens, especially in peaceful and stable democracies. But these analysts claim that during war, the need for security is paramount, and that human rights may need to be temporarily sacrificed. This leads to a paradox: on the one hand, the norms of war such as the protection of civilians are universally shared; on the other hand, they are routinely violated on the grounds of military necessity.[25]

The war on terrorism is certainly not the first time that the United States has been accused of violating human rights during war. Recall, for example, the internment of Japanese Americans during World War II, the use of the atomic bomb against Japan, the spraying of Agent Orange in Vietnam, and US support for anticommunist dictators during the Cold War. This is just a small sample of controversial policies that the United States has implemented in the name of national security.

If human rights are to be truly meaningful in international relations, however, they must also be made to apply in the realm of national security. Exempting human rights in issues of national security creates a loophole that is far too large to restrain potential abusers. To the extent that national

Figure 8.1 Targeting Terror Suspects with Drones

Drones, or unmanned aerial vehicles, have become the Obama administration's most consistently used weapon for the targeted killing of terror suspects throughout the Middle East and Central Asia. There are some clear advantages associated with drones, for example, the improved targeting of enemies, enhanced collection of information, and better protection of soldiers and civilians.[26] However, the increasing use and importance of drones in fighting the war on terrorism has called into question their relation to international humanitarian law and their impact on human rights.

While drone strikes have sometimes proven effective in eliminating terrorist targets and reducing civilian casualties, it is difficult to determine the proportionality of these strikes. Are more lives saved by the use of drones than are taken? When drone strikes often occur in rural areas of the Middle East, the damage is difficult to measure, and government and NGO reports often vary widely. Another unsettling aspect of drone use lies in the complete authority of the US executive branch to determine who is a combatant and therefore subject to targeted killing.[27] Does the president have this legal authority? What mechanisms of judicial review are put in place to determine whom should be targeted? The idea that a high-ranking government official may sit alone as judge, jury, and executioner of a person halfway around the world is indeed disturbing.

Recently, the use of drones domestically has also caused concern among many citizens, activists, and organizations such as the **American Civil Liberties Union (ACLU)**. The biggest concerns are centered on the use of surveillance drones for the collection of information. Many believe that this represents a shift toward a "surveillance society" and the violation of privacy.[28] It has even been suggested in recent scandals that the United States might use weaponized drones to attack US citizens who are seen as threats, effectively denying them their right to habeas corpus and due process.

Despite these drawbacks, many drone supporters believe that these challenges can be overcome and that drones can be a highly effective tool of war and humanitarian intervention. New weapons and technologies are constantly being developed, spurring new laws and treaties defining and outlining their proper use and implementation. International humanitarian law and human rights law will adapt to accommodate the appropriate use of drones, and mechanisms for judicial review can be strengthened to ensure compliance with these laws. With policies in place to protect human rights, drones may very well be used to protect the personal security of civilians and armed forces. However, until the role and proper usage of drones are made clear by international and domestic law, the controversy will continue.

and international protections for human rights during wartime are still weak and embryonic, there is still much work for human rights activists to do.

Notes

1. Tom Cushman, *A Matter of Principle: Humanitarian Arguments for the War in Iraq* (Berkeley: University of California Press, 2005), p. 117.

2. For an economic estimate, see Daniel Trotta, "Iraq War Hits U.S. Economy: Nobel Winner," *Reuters,* March 2, 2008. For casualty estimates, see "U.S. and Coalition Casualties," *CNN,* http://www.cnn.com/SPECIALS/war.casualties/table .iraq.html, accessed July 9, 2012.

3. Ewen MacAskill, "Obama Releases Bush Torture Memos," *The Guardian,* April 16, 2009, http://www.guardian.co.uk/world/2009/apr/16/torture-memos-bush -administration.

4. James Risen and Eric Lichtblau, "Bush Lets U.S. Spy on Callers Without Courts," *New York Times,* December 16, 2005.

5. For arguments on both sides of the debate, see Richard Ashby Wilson, ed., *Human Rights in the War on Terror* (Cambridge: Cambridge University Press, 2005).

6. Pam Benson and Elaine Quijano, "Cheney Says Documents Show Interrogations Prevented Attacks," *CNN,* August 25, 2009, http://edition.cnn.com/2009 /POLITICS/08/25/terror.interrogations.

7. Andrew Malcolm, "Cheney Hints Waterboarding Prevented Terrorist Attack on Los Angeles; Should He Be Prosecuted?" *Los Angeles Times,* April 22, 2009, http://latimesblogs.latimes.com/washington/2009/04/la-terror-attack.html.

8. Stephen F. Hayes, "Miranda Rights for Terrorists," *Weekly Standard,* June 10, 2009, http://www.weeklystandard.com/weblogs/TWSFP/2009/06/miranda_rights _for_terrorists.asp.

9. Kathleen T. Rhem, "New Guantanamo Facility Safer for Guards, More Comfortable for Detainees," *American Forces Press Service,* January 11, 2007, http://www.defense.gov/news/newsarticle.aspx?id=2665.

10. Roza Pati, *Due Process and International Terrorism* (Leiden: Nijhoff, 2009), pp. 246–249.

11. "Vice President Tells West Point Cadets That 'Bush Doctrine' Is Serious," *American Forces Press Service,* June 2, 2003, http://www.defense.gov/news/news article.aspx?id=28921.

12. John Yoo, *The Powers of War and Peace: The Constitution and Foreign Affairs After 9/11* (Chicago: University of Chicago Press, 2006).

13. Bobby Ghosh, "A Top Interrogator Who's Against Torture," *Time,* April 24, 2009, http://www.time.com/time/nation/article/0,8599,1893679,00.html.

14. Andrea Stone, "Underwear Bomb Plot Foiled by Intelligence, Not TSA," *Huffington Post,* May 8, 2012, http://www.huffingtonpost.com/2012/05/08 /underwear-bomb-plot-al-qaeda_n_1500806.html.

15. Real Clear Politics, "Obama: Guantanamo Bay Is a Recruiting Tool for al Qaeda," September 10, 2010, http://www.realclearpolitics.com/video/2010/09/10 /obama_guantanamo_bay_is_a_recruiting_tool_for_al-qaeda.html.

16. "Report: 108 Died in U.S. Custody," *CBS News,* February 11, 2009, http://www.cbsnews.com/2100–224_162–680658.html.

17. Rosemary Foot, "Exceptionalism Again: The Bush Administration, the 'Global War on Terror,' and Human Rights," *Law and History Review* 26, no. 3 (2008): 707–725.

18. Dana Priest, "Wrongful Imprisonment: Anatomy of a CIA Mistake," *Washington Post,* December 4, 2005, http://www.washingtonpost.com/wp-dyn/content/article/2005/12/03/AR2005120301476.html.

19. Jane Mayer, "Annals of Justice: Outsourcing Torture," *New Yorker,* February 14, 2005.

20. Marjorie Cohn, "Under U.S. Law Torture Is Always Illegal," *CounterPunch,* May 8, 2008, http://www.counterpunch.org/2008/05/06/under-u-s-law-torture-is-always-illegal. For the Torture Statute, see 18 U.S.C. 113C.

21. Nat Hentoff, "President Reagan's Torture Advice to President Obama," Cato Institute, May 20, 2009, http://www.cato.org/publications/commentary/president-reagans-torture-advice-president-obama.

22. Human Rights Watch, *Getting Away with Torture: The Bush Administration and Treatment of Detainees* (New York, July 2011).

23. Eric Lichtblau and Scott Shane, "Report Faults Two Authors of Bush Terror Memos," *New York Times,* February 19, 2010.

24. Joseph Pugliese, "Prosthetics of Law and the Anomic Violence of Drones," *Griffith Law Review* 20, no. 4 (2011): 931–961.

25. Alex J. Bellamy, "Massacres and Morality: Mass Killing in an Age of Civilian Immunity," *Human Rights Quarterly* 34, no. 4 (2012): 927–958.

26. Kenneth Anderson, "The Case for Drones," *Commentary,* June 2013.

27. Milena Sterio, "The United States' Use of Drones in the War on Terror: The (Il)Legality of Targeted Killings Under International Law," *Case Western Reserve Journal of International Law* 45, nos. 1–2 (Fall 2012): 197–214.

28. Editorial, "The Dawning of Domestic Drones," *New York Times,* December 25, 2012, http://www.nytimes.com/2012/12/26/opinion/the-dawning-of-domestic-drones.html.

9

Are There Limits
to Freedom of Speech?

"God hates fags; God hates fag-enablers; therefore God hates America."[1] This is the message preached by the Westboro Baptist Church (WBC), a small independent church based in Topeka, Kansas. The group, led by its founder Fred Phelps, adopts a strict interpretation of selected biblical passages, which has led it to condemn virtually anyone who does not share its views, including Muslims, Jews, and Hindus, as well as Catholics and most Protestant Christians. The WBC apparently believes that God hates many things, including the media, Australia, Barack Obama, and Justin Bieber, but the main target of the WBC's anger is homosexuality. Although the WBC comprises only about forty members, it has gained national and international notoriety due to its "Thank God for dead soldiers" protest campaign. The WBC claims to have held more than 900 anti-gay, anti-American protests outside of military funerals and other public events since 1991.[2]

Most observers of the WBC certainly agree that the church's public protests are illogical, offensive, and hateful. The controversy revolves around whether the members of the WBC have the right to express their opinions in this particular manner. **Freedom of speech** is globally recognized as one of the most important human rights, foundational to the proper functioning of a democracy and to the exercise of many other rights. According to the Universal Declaration of Human Rights, Article 19, "everyone has the right to freedom of opinion and expression." The First Amendment to the US Constitution similarly protects freedom of religion, speech, and public protest. Yet both US and international law clearly recognize that free speech can be restricted by government to the extent that it infringes upon other people's rights. For example, no one is permitted to cause danger to the public by shouting "fire" in a crowded theater, or to gravely harm a person's reputation by spreading lies about them, or to use their speech to incite people to commit a violent crime.[3] In international law, the International Covenant on Civil and Political Rights acknowledges that free speech "carries with it special duties and responsibilities" and "may therefore be subject to certain restrictions, but these shall only be such as are provided by law and are necessary: a) For respect of the rights or reputations of others; or b) For the protection of national security or of public order, or of public health or morals."[4] The question is, at what point does free speech cross the threshold, from being merely disagreeable, into being truly harmful and therefore prohibited? Is there a clear line that can distinguish free speech from acts of slander, hate, and violence? If human rights are universal, should there be a universal standard, or should each society determine for itself what forms of expression can be banned?

The case of the WBC joins a long list of examples that have tested the boundaries of freedom of expression in the United States. For example, while citizens should clearly have the right to criticize their own government, the case of *Schenck v. United States* in 1919 determined that people are not permitted to encourage disloyalty and noncooperation among their fellow citizens if such speech creates a "clear and present danger" to national security. In that case, Charles Schenck, the leader of the Socialist Party, had planned to print leaflets calling on Americans to refuse to submit to the draft in World War I, which was equivalent to inciting illegal acts. Schenck's speech was not protected under the First Amendment. However, the Supreme Court has upheld the right to express antigovernment ideas, even those that refer to violence or revolution in broad terms, so long as they do not incite "imminent lawless action."[5] The boundaries of acceptable criticism of government have continued to be tested in recent cases of flag-burning at public protests. While the Supreme Court has protected this form of expression, the US Congress has made several failed attempts in recent years to pass a constitutional amendment banning the desecration of the US flag.

Other controversies about the limits of free speech revolve around the issue of obscenity. Does the government have the right to censor obscene language or visual content in order to protect public morals? The Supreme Court has ruled that the government can censor obscene or pornographic material if "the average person, applying contemporary community standards," would find the material to be "patently offensive," and if the material "lacks serious literary, artistic, political, or scientific value."[6] The legal standards for obscenity are therefore different even among different communities in the United States, as well as among different cultures around the world. One test of this standard came during a live televised broadcast of the Golden Globe Awards in 2003, when the musician Bono accepted an award by exclaiming, "This is really, really fucking brilliant!" The Federal Communications Commission initially determined that the television network could broadcast this statement without any penalty, because the speech was nonsexual in its meaning, and therefore not "indecent or profane." However, the commission later reversed this decision in 2009, and imposed fines on the broadcast of similar speech.[7] Therefore, the standards for free speech can change over time as well.

Do the WBC's protests cross these lines? Are they so obscene, disloyal, or otherwise harmful to society that they should be banned? Albert Snyder, the father of Matthew Snyder, a slain US soldier whose funeral was protested by the WBC in 2006, certainly thought so. He sued the WBC for defamation and the "intentional infliction of emotional distress," arguing that the church's protests should be legally prohibited. The case made its way to the Supreme Court in 2010.[8] Was Snyder correct, or was the WBC just expressing foolish and unpleasant ideas that are nevertheless protected under the First Amendment? It is to this debate that we now turn.

Argument 1
Freedom of speech can be legitimately restricted, especially in cases such as that of the Westboro Baptist Church.

Free speech is obviously an important right, but there are well-recognized limitations on this right when it infringes on the rights of others, violates community standards, and threatens public order. According to this argument, the WBC violates this right when it targets its hateful messages toward gay and lesbian people, and the families of dead US soldiers. The WBC has a right to express its religious beliefs and engage in political protests, but not in a manner that is outrageously offensive and harmful toward other individuals.

First, the WBC's protests violate free speech because they are defamatory; in other words, the WBC makes false claims that cause harm to other people and damage their reputations. The WBC has every opportunity to spread its message in a more respectful context, without targeting the families of dead soldiers. By specifically targeting soldiers' funerals, the WBC causes severe emotional distress to the families. By displaying signs with slogans such as "Fag soldier in hell" and "Thank God for dead soldiers," the WBC spreads lies that encourage disloyalty to the nation and damage the reputation of fallen soldiers. After the protest at Matthew Snyder's funeral, the WBC posted a poem on its website titled "The Burden of Marine Lance Cpl. Matthew Snyder," which accuses the Snyders of raising their son "for the devil."[9] This represents a deliberate and slanderous attack on the Snyder family that invades their privacy and causes severe emotional harm. As Albert Snyder said in his lawsuit against the WBC, "I [had] one chance to bury my son and they took the dignity away from it. I cannot re-bury my son. And for the rest of my life, I will remember what they did to me and it has tarnished the memory of my son's last hour on earth."[10] Similarly, Craig Roberts of the American Legion argued that by slandering US soldiers, the WBC's protests are a "bastardization of the right to free speech."[11] Although the Supreme Court ultimately ruled in favor of the WBC against Albert Snyder, Justice Samuel Alito provided the dissenting opinion, arguing that "our profound national commitment to free and open debate is not a license for the vicious and verbal assault that occurred in this case."[12]

Second, the WBC's protests are damaging not only to the families of slain soldiers, but also to lesbian and gay individuals. Because the WBC deliberately vilifies and intimidates homosexuals based on their sexual orientation, it has been classified as a "hate group" by the Southern Poverty Law Center.[13] Although **hate speech** is legally protected in the United States, speech becomes a **hate crime** when it incites violence or threatens or intimidates a group of people based on their identity. According to sociologist Evelyn Kallen, it is important to consider the social context when interpreting whether a message incites violence against a minority group.[14] For the lesbian, gay, bisexual, and transgender (LGBT) community, the social context involves an increased risk of suicide, discrimination, harassment, and acts of violence based on sexual orientation. In the case of the WBC, the continual use of the derogatory term "fag" for homosexuals constitutes harassment and intimidation. The clear implication of messages such as "God hates fags" and "Thank God for AIDS" is that homosexuals deserve death. This incites violence against LGBT individuals, and is akin to the Ku Klux Klan (KKK) burning crosses in African American communities. The Supreme Court has previously ruled that the KKK cannot engage in this kind of expression, to the extent that it is designed to intimidate people and encourage acts of violence.[15] The WBC's anti-gay messages could also be interpreted as "fighting words," which have also been ruled undeserving of constitutional protection. According to the Supreme Court, fighting words "are no essential part of any exposition of ideas, and are of such slight social value as a step to truth that any benefit that may be derived from them is clearly outweighed by the social interest in order and morality."[16]

Third, the WBC's protests violate free speech because they are obscene. The messages portrayed by the WBC are not merely unpatriotic and inflammatory; they are "so outrageous in character, and so extreme in degree, as to go beyond all possible bounds of decency."[17] The average person, applying normal standards of behavior, would find the WBC's messages to be indecent, profane, and deeply offensive. If the government has the right to censor obscene language and explicit sexual images, it should also have the right to censor the WBC's outrageous messages. The WBC would counter that although its beliefs may seem outrageous to most people, these beliefs should be protected under the First Amendment's freedom of religion clause. However, freedom of religion, like other First Amendment protections, can be exercised only to the extent that it does not violate other rights or basic community standards of decency.

Fourth, the WBC's protests at soldiers' funerals violate free speech because the WBC has ample opportunity to express its religious beliefs at alternate times and places. The government has the right to regulate the time, place, and manner of public protests (so-called **TPM restrictions**), as long as these regulations do not discriminate based on the content of the message expressed.[18] For example, the US Congress passed the Respect for America's Fallen Heroes Act in 2006, which prohibits all protests within 300 feet of a military cemetery within one hour of a funeral in progress. So-called free speech zones have also been implemented in the United States to legally prevent political demonstrations from occurring too close to a campaign event or official meeting. The government therefore has the right to prohibit WBC from protesting near soldiers' funerals. The WBC does not need to stand outside a cemetery in order to communicate its religious beliefs.

For these reasons, a jury agreed with Snyder's claims against the WBC, and awarded him with $10.9 million in compensatory and punitive damages. It is why members of Congress from both parties, and the attorneys general of forty-eight states, signed an amicus brief supporting Snyder's position in the Supreme Court case.[19] Although the Supreme Court ultimately ruled in favor of the WBC, in this case the Court was wrong, according to this argument. The WBC crossed the line.

Human rights are not determined by Supreme Court decisions in the United States, but by both national and international legal and moral standards. The egregious nature of the WBC's speech is demonstrated by the fact that Great Britain barred the group from entering the country in 2009. WBC members had planned to picket the production of a play about homophobia called *The Laramie Project,* but they were denied entry because their protests violated the United Kingdom's more restrictive laws on hate speech.[20] Indeed, the WBC's protests would be illegal in most other European and developed countries, which have overwhelmingly banned speech that degrades or insults people, or incites hatred and discrimination toward anyone based on their group identity.[21]

In sum, according to this argument, although it is vital that societies allow people the freedom to express their beliefs, even if those beliefs are disagreeable and foolish, people are not permitted to trample the rights of others, outrageously offend the moral conscience of their community, or disturb the public order. Free speech does not give people the right to say "whatever they want, whenever they want," as is commonly misunderstood. By violating these reasonable limitations on free speech, the WBC's protests and its hateful messages should not be protected by the law, and should have no place in a democratic society.

Argument 2
Freedom of speech should not be restricted, even in cases such as that of the Westboro Baptist Church.

The WBC may indeed be a group of religious extremists whose messages are ludicrous and difficult to defend. And clearly people like Albert Snyder deserve sympathy for the pain they have endured as a result of the WBC's protests at the funerals of their sons. Nevertheless, according to this argument, it is vital to protect the right to free speech precisely in cases like this, when the message is objectionable and offensive. Despite the distastefulness of the WBC's message, the church does have the right to express its beliefs in this manner. The protests may be an affront to the sensibilities of most people, but they do not infringe on anyone's rights or disturb the public order.

Support for this argument comes from the fact that the US Supreme Court ruled in favor of the WBC in *Snyder v. Phelps*—indeed, in a vote of 8 to 1, with only Justice Alito dissenting. Most US human rights groups also defended the WBC's right to protest in this manner. For example, the American Civil Liberties Union, one of the leading authorities on free speech in the United States, filed an amicus brief with the Court arguing that the WBC's protests were protected under the First Amendment.

Why do the WBC's protests qualify as free speech? First, they are not obscene or defamatory because the demonstrations are a form of political protest, and their messages do address "matters of public concern," according to the Supreme Court. US policies regarding sexual orientation, and use of the military, are legitimate public matters that can inspire a diversity of opinions. While messages like "God hates America" are certainly provocative and arguably unpatriotic, they do not incite illegal or revolutionary behavior against the government, and so they do not represent a "clear and present danger" to the nation. The Court concluded in *Snyder v. Phelps* that even though the statements were offensive and unpopular, the WBC had an opinion about a public issue that should not be quieted. Society has an interest in protecting these kinds of political protests, because of the abuses that governments can commit by limiting political speech. If a government is given the power to censor any speech it deems unpatriotic, then it can stifle all the political dissent that is central to a well-functioning democracy.

Second, the WBC is exercising free speech because its statements are not defamatory or slanderous toward any particular individuals. Although the WBC targeted Matthew Snyder's funeral and published a disparaging poem about him, its messages were "expressed solely through hyperbolic rhetoric" that did not purport to describe any private facts about Snyder as an individual. During the protest, the WBC did not target any signs solely at the Snyder family, or at any specific person. Since the church has held similar protests conveying the same message about the United States for over twenty years at various public events, there was no evidence in the *Snyder* case to imply that the protests were directed at the Snyder family in particular. According to the Supreme Court, "Westboro may have chosen the picket location to increase publicity for its views, and its speech may have been particularly hurtful to Snyder. That does not mean that its speech should be afforded less than full First Amendment protection under the circumstances of this case." Under US law, defamation involves the deliberate communication of false claims in order to cause harm to an individual. In this case, the Supreme Court judged that statements like "God hates fags" are not provably false,

> **Think Again**
>
> Do you think that hate speech should be illegal, as it is throughout most of Europe? Can you think of any reasons why European societies might consider racial or religious discrimination to be a greater threat to public order than the United States does? Does the theory of human rights allow for different laws in each society, or should there be a universal standard for freedom of speech?

and that the WBC appears to fully believe in their accuracy. Moreover, the Court ruled that although the protests caused the Snyder family emotional pain, free speech should be suppressed only when the emotional distress caused is "so severe that no reasonable [person] could be expected to endure it." Therefore, the WBC's protests do not qualify as slanderous toward slain US soldiers or their families.

Third, although the WBC's messages are hateful and discriminatory toward homosexuals, hate speech is protected by the First Amendment unless it is intended to incite specific acts of violence or threaten specific individuals. The church's followers believe that God hates virtually everyone who disagrees with them, but this is merely an opinion based on their religious beliefs, not a demand or encouragement for people to commit violence against LGBT individuals. A sign that reads "God hates fags" is hurtful and offensive, but it is substantively different than a sign reading "Buy a gun and kill a homosexual." The latter would obviously constitute fighting words, an incitement to violence, and a human rights violation. According to this argument, the United States is correct in allowing hateful groups like the KKK to hold regular demonstrations; in fact, even the burning of crosses has been deemed legal if it is not specifically intended to threaten or intimidate someone. The WBC's speech is hurtful and offensive to all of the groups whom it criticizes, but the United States "has chosen to protect even hurtful speech on public issues to ensure that public debate is not stifled."[22]

Finally, the WBC's protests are legal because they comply with all of the relevant TPM restrictions in the United States. The WBC was required to picket 1,000 feet away from the Snyder funeral in order to respect the grieving process of the Snyder family, which the church did. Albert Snyder testified that he was unable to view the WBC's signs from the funeral, and that he read the WBC's specific messages only through the media. Indeed, TPM restrictions and the free speech zones that they

> **Think Again**
>
> Freedom of expression means that the government cannot censor your speech, as long as you do not infringe on the rights of others. However, private entities can restrict speech, as long as they do so in a way that is not discriminatory. For example, a private business could fire employees who make public statements that interfere with their job performance. If you knew that the WBC was planning a protest in your town, how would you personally respond? What do you think is an effective way to counter the WBC's hateful language?

create have themselves been criticized by civil rights groups like the ACLU, because these restrictions can be easily abused in order to stifle political dissent.[23] Based on applicable precedents at the state level, it seems likely that TPM restrictions like the Respect for America's Fallen Heroes Act will be struck down by the Supreme Court in the future.

When people freely express their opinions, it can often cause disagreement, tension, and emotional pain. Yet it is critical that the government not be given the power to restrict speech when it merely offends or provokes. Freedom of speech must remain among the world's most cherished rights, because the right to hold personal beliefs and to freely participate in political discourse is central to a civilized society. It is central to human dignity. For free speech to have any meaning, it must be protected precisely when its content is unpopular or repulsive. As linguist Noam Chomsky has stated regarding Nazi propaganda minister Joseph Goebbels, "[He] was in favor of freedom of speech for views he liked. So was Stalin. If you're really in favor of free speech, then you're in favor of freedom of speech precisely for views you despise."[24]

★ ★ ★

Conclusion

Virtually all nations of the world recognize the importance of freedom of speech; the International Covenant on Civil and Political Rights has been ratified by 167 states.[25] Even among the states that are not party to the ICCPR, many have enshrined freedom of speech in their own national constitutions. For example, Article 35 of China's constitution declares that "citizens of the People's Republic of China enjoy freedom of speech." Why, then, are there so many restrictions on speech in China, as compared with the United States? If human rights are universal, and freedom of speech has gained a global consensus, why is there so much variation in the protection of this right around the world? Whatever position one takes on the WBC debate, we should recognize that freedom of speech is not absolute, and that it is not easy to determine the fine line that distinguishes free speech from a violation of rights.

Of course, part of the reason why the protection of free speech varies around the world is because authoritarian governments simply abuse their power in order to maintain their positions of authority. But another part of the answer lies in the fact that societies have different interpretations of what constitutes a reasonable restriction on free speech. As noted earlier, Article 19 of the ICCPR permits governments to restrict free speech when it threatens the "rights and reputations of others," "national security and public order," or "public health or morals." Governments are then able to justify censorship, and in some cases brutal crackdowns on free expression, in the name of national security or public morality. This produces wide variation in how societies treat free speech.

For example, defamation laws in the United Kingdom are more restrictive than those found in the United States. In the United States, people whose reputations have been harmed must prove that the statements made about them are false, and that the speaker deliberately lied in order to cause harm. In the United Kingdom, the speaker must prove that the statements are true, and the speaker can be sued for libel even if they did not intend to cause harm. Thus the United Kingdom recognizes the value of free speech, but shifts the balance in favor of the reputations of people who may be harmed by that speech.

In the defense of public order, some nations restrict speech that insults or criticizes the nation's rulers, regardless of the truth of the statements made. So-called **lese majeste laws**, which are common in constitutional monarchies such as Thailand and Morocco, criminalize speech that may offend the royal family. In 2011, a US citizen was convicted under Thailand's lese majeste laws and sentenced to more than two years in prison for publishing a book in the United States that was critical of the Thai king.[26] An eighteen-year-old soccer fan was similarly jailed in Morocco after writing "God, country, Barcelona" on his school chalkboard, rather than "God, country, king," which is the national motto.[27]

More authoritarian states systematically censor the media, prohibit public demonstrations, and imprison political dissidents, all in the name of national security. Despite the ostensible protection of free speech in the Chinese constitution, the Chinese government justifies its restrictions on free speech by claiming defense of state secrets. A Chinese law on state secrets was revised in 2010, allowing the government to censor virtually "any information the authorities deem as harmful to their political or economic interests."[28] Citizens of most Western countries would likely judge that China's policy vastly exceeds the reasonable restrictions permitted by freedom of speech. Yet China responds by claiming that outsiders are in no position to assess the balance between free speech and national security in China, and by claiming that Asian societies value political stability more than Westerners do.

The United States is arguably one of the world's strongest supporters of freedom of speech. The Supreme Court's strict interpretation of the First Amendment has allowed the US government to censor speech only in very limited circumstances. Yet we should also remember that freedom of speech also requires government to protect both free and equitable access to information and free and independent media. The United States ranks only forty-seventh in the world on the Press Freedom Index, which measures government transparency and the protection of journalists from harassment.[29] Likewise, in 2010 the Supreme Court ruled in *Citizens United v. FEC* that corporate entities can contribute unlimited amounts of money to political campaigns, equating monetary contributions to free speech. According to some analysts, this ruling threatens the free speech of individual citizens by weakening their ability to influence the political process.[30] Therefore, even the United States may have substantial room for improvement in the protection of free speech.

And so, despite the universal consensus that free speech is a basic right, there is still wide variation within and among countries in how they interpret that right over time and balance it with other political interests (see Figure 9.1). Because there is often such a fine line between free speech and the violation of human rights, it seems likely that debates over the boundaries of free speech will continue.

Figure 9.1 Free Speech or Religious Discrimination?

In 2011 the pastor of a small church in Florida named Terry Jones held a public protest in which he burned copies of the Quran, the Muslim holy book. Declaring that "Islam is of the Devil," the pastor used the demonstration to proclaim that Islam is a violent and false religion.[31] Although the protest was clearly odious and offensive, it was protected as legal under the First Amendment. The protest in the United States was reminiscent of earlier public assaults on Islam in Europe, where in 2005 a series of editorial cartoons was published in Danish newspapers that depicted the prophet Muhammad as violent and corrupt. The cartoons were reprinted in newspapers in over fifty countries around the world.

Desecrating the Quran is one of the most serious transgressions possible in the Muslim religion, as is any visual depiction of Muhammad. While these forms of expression were considered legal in the United States and Europe, they enraged Muslim communities throughout the world, sparking counterprotests that sometimes turned violent. In response to the publication of the cartoons, Danish embassies in Pakistan, Syria, Lebanon, and Iran were bombed and set afire by militants.[32] In response to the burning of the Quran, crowds in Afghanistan rioted, which resulted in the death of over a dozen people, including seven United Nations workers.[33]

Many Muslims and others argued that these Islamophobic expressions should be banned, particularly in Europe, as a form of hate speech against Muslims that is just as harmful as racial or sexual discrimination. By defaming a religion, Islamophobic expressions disparage an entire group of people

(continues)

Figure 9.1 continued

based on their identity. Indeed, in response to the cartoons published in the Danish newspapers, the **Organization of the Islamic Conference** supported a resolution condemning "defamation of religion" within the UN Human Rights Council (see Chapter 4). Many advocates of free speech and human rights, however, continue to defend people's right to make offensive statements, and voice concern about the defamation of religion resolution. They note that the defamation of religion laws that exist in most Islamic countries have frequently been used to silence critics of the governments, and to enforce a moral code that itself discriminates against minority religious groups in those states.

Ironically, as European states were defending their citizens' right to make public statements that offended Muslims, several states were simultaneously passing legislation that banned head-coverings such as the Muslim burqa from being worn in public.[34] In France, Belgium, and the Netherlands, a ban on wearing the burqa was implemented in the name of national security, and justified on the grounds that Muslim women did not truly have the freedom to choose this inherently oppressive style of clothing.[35] Critics, on the other hand, charged that the burqa ban violated women's freedom of religious expression found in Article 9 of the European Convention on Human Rights.[36] As these cases illustrate, the debate over the boundaries of free speech and religious expression is far from resolved.

Notes

1. See the Westboro Baptist Church website "God Hates Fags," http://www.godhatesfags.com.

2. Ibid.

3. See Justice Oliver Wendell Holmes's opinion in the Supreme Court case *Schenck v. United States,* 249 U.S. 47 (1919).

4. ICCPR, Article 19, Section 3.

5. See *Brandenburg v. Ohio,* 395 U.S. 444 (1969).

6. See *Miller v. California,* 413 U.S. 15 (1973).

7. Deborah Potter, "Indecent Oversight," *American Journalism Review* 26, no. 4 (September 2004): 80.

8. See *Snyder v. Phelps,* 562 U.S. ___ (2011).

9. "Church and Funeral Protest," *Gainesville Sun,* October 14, 2010, http://www.gainesville.com/article/20101014/GUARDIAN/101019767.

10. See *Snyder v. Phelps,* 580 F.3d 206, US Court of Appeals, Fourth Circuit (2009).

11. Tim Carpenter, "WBC: Court Case a 'No-Brainer,'" *Topeka Capital-Journal,* October 6, 2010.

12. *Snyder v. Phelps,* 562 U.S. ___ (2011).

13. Southern Poverty Law Center, "Westboro Baptist Church," http://www.splcenter.org/get-informed/intelligence-files/groups/westboro-baptist-church, accessed July 12, 2012.

14. Evelyn Kallen, "Hate on the Net: A Question of Rights/A Question of Power," *Electronic Journal of Sociology* (1998), http://www.sociology.org/content/vol003.002/kallen.html.

15. See *Virginia v. Black*, 53 U.S. 343 (2003).

16. See *Chaplinsky v. New Hampshire*, 315 U.S. 568 (1942).

17. *Snyder v. Phelps*, 562 U.S. ___ (2011).

18. See *Clark v. Community for Creative Non-Violence*, 468 U.S. 288 (1984).

19. Adam Cohen, "Why Spewing Hate at Funerals Is Still Free Speech," *Time*, September 29, 2010, http://www.time.com/time/nation/article/0,8599,2022220,00.html.

20. "Anti-Gay Preachers Banned from UK," *BBC News*, February 19, 2009, http://news.bbc.co.uk/2/hi/uk_news/england/hampshire/7898972.stm.

21. See, for example, the European Convention on Human Rights, Article 14.

22. *Snyder v. Phelps*.

23. American Civil Liberties Union, "Secret Service Ordered Local Police to Restrict Anti-Bush Protestors at Rallies, ACLU Charges in Unprecedented Nationwide Lawsuit," September 23, 2003, http://www.aclu.org/free-speech/secret-service-ordered-local-police-restrict-anti-bush-protesters-rallies-aclu-charges-u.

24. Mark Achbar and Peter Wintonick, *Manufacturing Consent: Noam Chomsky and the Media* (Zeitgeist Films, 2002).

25. United Nations, "International Covenant on Civil and Political Rights," *United Nations Treaty Collection*, http://treaties.un.org/Pages/ViewDetails.aspx?src=TREATY&mtdsg_no=IV-4&chapter=4&lang=en, accessed July 13, 2012.

26. Kocha Olarn, "American Gets 2.5 Years for Insulting Thai Monarchy," *CNN*, December 8, 2011, http://www.cnn.com/2011/12/08/world/asia/thailand-american-insults/index.html.

27. "Moroccan Jailed for King Insult," *BBC News*, October 27, 2008, http://news.bbc.co.uk/2/hi/africa/7693988.stm.

28. Isabella Bennett, "Media Censorship in China," Council on Foreign Relations, March 7, 2011, http://www.cfr.org/china/media-censorship-china/p11515.

29. Reporters Without Borders, "Press Freedom Index 2011/2012," January 25, 2012, http://en.rsf.org/press-freedom-index-2011-2012,1043.html.

30. *Citizens United v. FEC*, 558 U.S. 50 (2010). See also Floyd Abrams, "Citizens United and Its Critics," *Yale Law Journal Online*, September 29, 2010, http://yalelawjournal.org/the-yale-law-journal-pocket-part/constitutional-law/citizens-united-and-its-critics.

31. Kevin Sieff, "Florida Pastor Terry Jones's Koran Burning Has Far-Reaching Effect," *Washington Post*, April 2, 2011.

32. "Arson and Death Threats as Muhammad Caricature Controversy Escalates," *Spiegel Online*, February 4, 2006, http://www.spiegel.de/international/cartoon-violence-spreads-arson-and-death-threats-as-muhammad-caricature-controversy-escalates-a-399177.html.

33. Enayat Najafizada and Rod Nordland, "Afghans Avenge Florida Koran Burning, Killing 12," *New York Times*, April 2, 2011.

34. Geoffrey W. G. Leane, "Rights of Ethnic Minorities in Liberal Democracies: Has France Gone Too Far in Banning Muslim Women from Wearing the Burka?" *Human Rights Quarterly* 33, no. 4 (2011): 1032–1061.

35. Phyllis Chesler, "Ban the Burqa? The Argument in Favor," *Middle East Quarterly* 17, no. 4 (2010): 33–45.

36. Gerhard van der Schyff and Adriaan Overbeeke, "Exercising Religious Freedom in the Public Space: A Comparative and European Convention Analysis of General Burqa Bans," *European Constitutional Law Review* 7, no. 3 (2011): 424–452.

10

Do Women Have the Right to Choose Abortion?

In the United States, the controversy over abortion often gets played out on talk shows as a battle between "baby killers" and "woman haters." The abortion debate is one of the most highly charged political issues of our time, as the interests of pregnant women are pitted against the interests of unborn children. One side of the aisle describes their position as "pro-life" and their opponents as "pro-abortion"; the other side labels themselves "pro-choice" and their opponents "anti-abortion." When it comes to abortion, it seems that we cannot even agree on basic definitions. As Hillary Clinton once remarked, "I have met thousands and thousands of pro-choice men and women. I have never met anyone who is pro-abortion."[1]

There is ample reason why abortion stirs our collective emotions. The reproductive process is an intimate part of our humanity, and has historically been a central battleground in women's fight for equality. However, few things are more vulnerable than a fetus, and so the unborn child could potentially be deserving of protection even if this contradicts the interests of a pregnant woman. Since the landmark *Roe v. Wade* case of 1973, there have been an estimated 50 million abortions performed in the United States.[2] Roughly one out of every five pregnancies (excluding miscarriages) ends by induced abortion.[3] Abortion affects hundreds of millions of people around the world, and raises questions about the sanctity of life, basic health, freedom of choice, and bodily integrity.

Much of the abortion controversy revolves around its legality. In *Roe v. Wade*, the US Supreme Court concluded that the right to privacy, which is implied by the due process clause of the Fourteenth Amendment, is applicable to women's reproductive decisions. In a vote of 7 to 2, the Court decided that a woman's control over her own reproduction is a fundamental right, but that the woman's right extends only until the time of **viability** of the unborn child outside the mother's womb. In limiting reproductive rights in this way, the Court hoped to strike a delicate balance between the state's interests in the health of the mother and the potential life of the fetus.

In the period since the *Roe v. Wade* decision in the United States, there have been several restrictions on abortion passed at the national and state levels. In 1976 Congress passed the Hyde Amendment, which prohibits federal funding being used for abortions except in cases of rape, incest, or severe maternal health problems.[4] In 2003 Congress also passed the Partial-Birth Abortion Ban Act, which prohibits a specific medical procedure often performed in the second trimester of pregnancy, known as intact dilation and extraction. In *Planned Parenthood v. Casey* in 1992, the Supreme Court allowed the fifty states to place their own restrictions on abortion, as long as those measures did not contradict *Roe v. Wade* or place an undue burden on a woman's reproductive choice.[5] Many US states have since implemented their own limitations on abortion.[6] For example, forty-six states allow health care providers to refuse to participate in abortions. Nineteen states require women to undergo some form of counseling before receiving an abortion, and many of those states also mandate a waiting period before the procedure is performed. Thirty-seven states require some form of parental notification in a minor's decision to have an abortion.

A great deal of the abortion debate also revolves around religious belief. In national polls, opposition to abortion is highest among evangelical Protestants and Catholics, while people who profess no religion are more likely to support reproductive rights for women.[7] Likewise, countries with strong ties to the Roman Catholic Church, such as Ireland and El Salvador, tend to have some of the strictest anti-abortion laws, while secular, Western states, such as Germany and France, tend to have more permissive laws on abortion.[8] In 2013, the Supreme Court of El Salvador even rejected the abortion plea of a woman with major medical problems whose life was in danger due to her pregnancy. Although the woman survived the birth, the baby died shortly thereafter due to a known birth defect.[9] Pro-life activists often cite biblical passages to justify the notion that human life begins at the point of conception, while pro-choice activists interpret a different meaning from the same religious texts. The Roman Catholic Church recently charged the Obama administration with conducting a "war on religion" by requiring private health care providers to offer contraceptive and reproductive services, including the removal of age restrictions for the controversial form of emergency contraception often referred to as the "morning after" pill.[10]

It is important to note, however, that a human rights perspective on abortion is unique. Human rights activists cannot merely concern themselves with whether abortion is legal, or whether it is approved by God. While partly drawing from both legal and religious arguments, a human rights–based argument must address whether abortion violates basic human dignity and, conversely, whether a ban on abortion would violate a woman's dignity? In order to answer these questions, some vexing philosophical issues must be addressed: Who counts as "human," and when does human life begin? When people's basic rights conflict with each other, whose rights should take priority? Which rights are more basic for the protection of human dignity?

Although a human rights perspective has much to offer to the abortion debate, arguments drawn explicitly from a human rights perspective have not featured prominently in abortion debates in the United States. The language of human rights is touched upon occasionally by the pro-life movement, as illustrated by the National Right to Life campaign and the **personhood amendments** on the ballot in several states; yet the pro-life movement is more likely to use broader ethical or religious language to justify its position. Similarly, many progressive human rights organizations in the United States deploy the language of reproductive rights and women's rights, but fail to analyze the issues in terms of any rights that may belong to the fetus. Amnesty International, the world's largest human rights organization, had adopted a neutral stance on abortion for most of its history, but in 2007 changed its policy, supporting the legal provision of abortion services worldwide in cases of rape, incest, violence against women, or threats to the mother's health. This decision sparked controversy within and outside Amnesty International, and many of its faith-based members threatened to withdraw their support from the organization.[11]

It is therefore important to analyze the abortion debate from a human rights perspective. The first argument is that abortion should remain a legal and accessible option for women until the point that the life of the fetus is viable outside the mother's womb. Before that point, according to this argument, the fetus is not human and therefore does not possess any rights that would supersede those of the mother. The second argument is that a fetus should be considered a human being at (or near) the time of conception. Thus the right to life of an unborn child would take precedence over the convenience, physical integrity, and even the health of the mother.

Argument 1
Women should have the right to choose abortion.

According to this argument, human rights must be reserved for humans if they are to have any meaning. Because a fetus is not yet human, it does not have any rights that can be weighed against the rights of the mother. Until the time of viability, the fetus is an indistinguishable element of the woman's body, and women clearly should have the right to choose what happens to their bodies.

Abortion is legal in the United States, and in countries as diverse as France, Turkey, Russia, China, and India. Approximately two-thirds of all women live in countries where abortion can be legally obtained for a broad range of reasons.[12] The main reason why abortion is legal is because, under the law, a fetus is not considered a person. The US Supreme Court explicitly stated in *Roe v. Wade* that legal personhood begins at birth, not at conception.[13] While the government does have an interest in protecting the potential lives of unborn children, so as to maintain its population over time, it cannot violate the privacy and bodily integrity of women in order to achieve that interest. A woman's privacy and control over her own body are a fundamental right, and regulating the reproductive process would represent a massive overstep of governmental power. The government can regulate a woman's body only when the state's interests are so compelling that they would outweigh this fundamental right to privacy.

From a human rights perspective, if a fetus is fully human, then it would inherently possess the right to life. The justices in *Roe v. Wade* acknowledged this. However, a fetus is not considered human until it can viably survive outside the mother's womb. The Supreme Court defined this point as being approximately seven months into the pregnancy; however, medical advances since the 1970s have pushed that point earlier into the pregnancy. Until the point of viability, a fetus is inseparable from the mother and is fully dependent on her for life, so a fetus cannot be an autonomous human being until reaching viability. Before that point, a fetus has not acquired the characteristics that define humans as a unique species, such as self-consciousness, the (potential) ability to reason, and the ability to suffer pain. The brain and neurological system of a fetus have simply not developed these capabilities. Because in actuality the life of the fetus is derived from the life of its mother, so the rights of the fetus are derived from the choices of its mother.

It would be irrational to define the beginning of life as occurring before the point of viability. If life began at the point of conception, then nature (or God) would be responsible for roughly 100 million "deaths" each year, because up to 70 percent of fertilized eggs never implant in the uterine wall. Even after conception results in implantation of the egg in the uterus, an estimated 30 percent of these early pregnancies result in miscarriage due to natural causes.[14] Defining the beginning of life at the point of conception would also classify a common form of birth control as a human rights violation, since most oral contraceptives include a chemical that prevents fertilized eggs from implanting in the uterus. It would be a cruel world, indeed, if personhood did begin at the moment of conception.

Society cannot afford to treat the reproductive rights of women with disrespect. Not only are reproductive rights intrinsically important for women, but they are also important because they are connected to the protection of so many other rights. When women lose the right to control their own bodies, they also lose social equality within the family, the ability to freely make economic choices, and the ability to fully participate in political processes. A woman typically cannot climb the corporate ladder or run for political office if she cannot even make decisions about when and whether to have children. Not only this, but in countries where abortion is illegal, women often turn to unsafe and underground clinics out of desperation in order to have the procedure done, which threatens their basic health. For these reasons, reproductive rights have stood as the centerpiece of many struggles for women's rights in recent history (see Figure 10.1).

Women's unique biological role in birthing children also makes them uniquely vulnerable to certain kinds of human rights violations. Women

Figure 10.1 Do Women's Rights Deserve Special Protection?

Because women perform a unique biological and social role in society, some argue that their rights are worthy of special protection. This position is drawn from difference feminism, which focuses on inherent differences between men and women. Does the idea of special protection contradict the idea of human rights, which prescribes a set of universal norms applicable to all people equally? Not exactly, because the same reproductive rights could also be justified through liberal feminism, which focuses on the inherent equality of men and women. According to liberal feminists, everyone has a right to privacy and bodily integrity. Just as the government cannot force men to undergo medical experiments for the interests of the state, as it did in the Tuskegee experiments, in which the US Public Health Services infected hundreds of black men with syphilis without their consent, it cannot force women to carry a fetus to term. Thus, the idea of universal rights is consistent with the idea that certain groups of people (for example, women, children, and indigenous people) may be particularly vulnerable to abuses in specific situations, and therefore deserving of special protection.

are more likely than men to be threatened by domestic violence and abuse within their own homes. Women earn lower wages than men for performing similar tasks in the workplace, and women hold fewer positions in government than men. Women are more likely than men to be the victims of **human trafficking**. In the context of war, combatants sometimes commit widespread rape against women in order to terrorize a population or "infect" an ethnic group with the children of the enemy. Therefore, when a woman loses the agency to make decisions about her own body, she is put at a greater risk for the degradation of other rights. This is why international law recognizes the importance of gender equality and calls for an end to discrimination against women. The **Convention on the Elimination of All Forms of Discrimination Against Women (CEDAW)** is an international treaty ratified by 187 countries that prohibits all forms of discrimination against women, including the violation of reproductive rights.[15] Article 16 of CEDAW recognizes women's right to "decide freely and responsibly on the number and spacing of their children," and Article 10 acknowledges the right to have access to family planning.[16]

According to this argument, until the point that a fetus develops into a viable human being, women have the right to control their own fertility and make autonomous decisions about reproduction. Men have no right to tell women what to do with their bodies, since they do not experience pregnancy and cannot fully understand the choices involved in the reproductive process. As the rapper Tupac Shakur famously claimed, "Since a man can't make one, / He has no right to tell a woman when and where to create one."[17] It is therefore ironic that most of the intrusive government regulations over women's reproductive process have been passed by legislatures dominated by men.

If human rights are designed to protect individual choice, then reproductive choices must be included as a fundamental right. A fetus is not a person, as it has not yet had the time to develop the physical capacity to think, suffer, and make choices of its own. As a result, the fundamental rights of the woman must take precedence over the state's interests in protecting the potential life of the fetus.

Argument 2
Women should not have the right to choose abortion.

The right to choose abortion hinges on whether a fetus is considered a human being. According to this second argument, a fetus should indeed be considered human, the right to life takes precedence over reproductive choice, and women do not have the sole authority to determine what happens inside their own bodies.

Is a fetus really a human being? There is actually no empirical or scientific boundary that unequivocally determines the beginning of life. Personhood is a philosophical and subjective category, not a scientific one. The Supreme Court in *Roe v. Wade* acknowledged as much, as Justice Harry Blackmun wrote in a series of internal memos to the Court. When determining the point at which the state could interfere with a woman's right to privacy, the Court initially designated this as the end of the first trimester, or thirteen weeks. Blackmun wrote, "This is arbitrary. . . . But perhaps any other selected point, such as quickening or the viability of the fetus, is equally arbitrary."[18] The Court eventually settled on using the criterion of viability, but even that is ambiguous and highly subject to changes in technology over time. With modern medical advances, it is certainly conceivable in the near future that a fetus could be taken from fertilization to birth completely outside the mother's womb. In that case, when would the life of the fetus be considered viable? Personhood does not appear at some predetermined point of fetal development; it is a status that society chooses to assign to an individual.

Although it is possible to identify some common physical and mental features that seem to make humans unique, the problem is that not all humans share these characteristics, and some nonhumans also possess them. If personhood is dependent on self-consciousness and the ability to reason, then people with certain kinds of mental illnesses or other deficiencies must not count as fully human. Even newborn babies, who are universally recognized as human, have not fully developed these "human" capacities. If personhood depends on the ability to suffer, would animals not also count as human? Indeed, there is some evidence that fetuses seem to show some signs of suffering several weeks before the legal age of viability.[19] Human rights gained strength in Western civilization because of the prevailing belief that humans possess a soul with inherent rights attached to it. How do we know that fetuses and even embryos do not also possess a soul, infused with all of the potential for human development that a newborn baby has? Ultimately, deciding what constitutes a human being is a philosophical and political choice, rather than a scientific conclusion.

Thus, lacking an objective definition of personhood, and given the changes that medical technology can generate, society should err on the side of caution and inclusiveness in deciding who is human. In other words, because we cannot know with any certainty, and because the potential life of a child is at stake, we should give the fetus the benefit of the doubt. Just a few centuries ago, the legal definition of personhood extended only to landowners, citizens of particular states, and white males. Over time, the political struggle for human rights has expanded the definition of personhood to include women, former slaves, and foreign nationals. All of these populations were at one time relatively voiceless and vulnerable to abuse, as they were not considered equal persons under the law. Why not extend this definition of personhood to include fetuses, who are some of the most vulnerable and voiceless members of society imaginable? When in doubt, the most inclusive, compassionate, and reasonable option is to decide that life begins at the point of conception.

If this is the case, then it certainly follows that the fetus's right to life takes precedence over the mother's right to privacy. Some human rights are more fundamental to human dignity than others, and the right to life is among the most basic.[20] In cases like abortion, in which the rights of the fetus must be weighed against the rights of the mother, more basic rights must be given priority. This means that abortion is not an acceptable option unless the mother's life is itself at stake. Even in extreme cases of rape or incest, the ethical trade-off should favor the life of the child over the physical and emotional pain of the mother. There are reasonable ways to protect the rights of the mother while she carries the baby to term, at which point she would be able to put the baby up for adoption or explore other options that she deems necessary.

Thus, the legal balance that the Supreme Court struck regarding reproductive rights is incorrect if we accept the personhood of the fetus. Indeed, many liberal and conservative legal analysts have found fault with the Court's reasoning in granting pregnant women any fundamental right to privacy in the first place. As Justice Byron White wrote in a dissenting opinion in another important abortion case, *Doe v. Bolton,* "I find nothing in the language or history of the Constitution to support the Court's judgment. The Court simply fashions and announces a new constitutional right for pregnant women and, with scarcely any reason or authority for its action, invests that right with sufficient substance to override most state abortion statutes. . . . [The] judgment is an improvident and extravagant exercise of the power of judicial review."[21]

Indeed, the same case is made in regard to international law. While pro-choice activists often cite international treaties such as CEDAW, Article 16, as evidence of the right to choose abortion, this is clearly a manipulation of a vaguely worded law.[22] Because the right to choose abortion is never explicitly stated in international law, it can be asserted that this right does not exist and is in actuality a human rights violation. In 2011 the

"San Jose Articles," arising from this viewpoint, were launched by a group of pro-life human rights activists at UN headquarters in New York. They proclaimed that "no UN treaty can accurately be cited as establishing or recognizing a right to abortion. . . . Accordingly any such body that interprets a treaty to include a right to abortion acts beyond its authority and contrary to its mandate."[23] Other scholars have argued that international treaties such as the International Covenant on Civil and Political Rights and the Convention on the Rights of the Child implicitly protect the right to life of the fetus, even though these instruments do not mention abortion explicitly.[24]

Clearly reproductive rights have played a long historical role in the broader struggle for women's rights, and clearly gender equality is vital to human rights. However, according to this argument, modern societies can protect women's rights, and even reproductive rights, without permitting abortion. With proper forms of birth control, women can be empowered to decide when to have children and how many children they want to have. Women can still exercise their right to own property, to be free from violence, and to participate in political life. Although women are endowed with the unique biological capacity to have children, this does not permit women to infringe on the rights of their unborn children. Indeed, many feminist pro-life activists have argued that restricting abortion can have positive effects on women's psychological health and political empowerment.[25]

Last, according to this argument, the idea that only women should have the authority to decide what happens to their bodies is inconsistent with the human rights framework. The claim that men have no legitimacy to speak about reproductive rights is analogous to cultural relativism, the argument that one cannot judge violations of rights in cultures outside one's own (such as Westerners condemning the practice of female circumcision in Africa). The theory of human rights explicitly rejects this argument, because human rights are universal claims that are supposed to be equally applicable to everyone. Either fetuses have human rights, or they do not. Regardless, in public opinion polls taken in the United States, the proportions of men and women who support the right to choose abortion are roughly equivalent, but a greater proportion of men than of women support the right to partial-birth abortion, or to abortion performed during the third trimester.[26] Thus, even if men are considered not to have the authority to speak about abortion, the arguments in favor or against the right to choose abortion would be largely the same.

In sum, according to this argument a human rights perspective on abortion should recognize that personhood is a socially constructed category that does not represent a scientific truth. The precautionary principle, combined with basic human compassion, calls us to extend personhood to include unborn children. If a fetus is a person, then the more basic rights of the fetus should take priority over the less basic rights of the mother.

* * *

Conclusion

Many human rights advocates claim that the main power of human rights lies in their ability to serve as political or legal "trump cards" that end further debate on an issue. In other words, once a person claims that a fundamental right has been violated, then the violator must end the practice and provide a remedy. However, the abortion controversy is a good illustration of the fact that human rights do not end the debate on an issue, but rather serve as a specific arena where that debate can take place. In the arena of human rights, the debate about abortion is not about religion versus law. The debate is about whether a fetus is a human being, and whether its rights must therefore be balanced against the rights of the mother. As we have seen, the human rights framework does not provide conclusive answers to these questions, but it does point toward specific avenues in the search for answers.

Even if abortion were to be deemed to be a human rights violation, we should recognize that there may be many different ways to stop the practice, with varying degrees of effectiveness. As with the case of female circumcision (see Chapter 11), implementing a legal ban on abortion is only one method, and it may not be effective in reducing the actual number of abortions performed. Abortion laws vary widely across the world. Many European and Asian countries have joined the United States in making abortion legal, but most other countries permit abortion only under limited circumstances. For example, most Latin American and African states allow abortion only in cases of rape, or if carrying a fetus to term would threaten the life and health of the mother.[27] At the other end of the spectrum, some countries, such as Sweden, not only permit women to choose abortion, but also provide financial support and health care coverage to women who choose abortion.[28] Laws permitting abortion in European countries, such as France, Britain, and the Netherlands, have been held up in European courts, which define personhood as beginning at birth.[29]

According to a study by the **World Health Organization (WHO)**, abortion rates in countries that outlaw abortion are roughly equivalent to abortion rates in countries that permit abortion.[30] This is because safe contraception is not widely accessible in many of the countries where abortion is prohibited, and thus more unwanted pregnancies occur in those countries. When a woman has an unwanted pregnancy, the law typically does not deter her from having an abortion. Instead, out of desperation, many women seek abortions from underground clinics, which present a greater risk to their health. As a result, the WHO has published guidelines on abortion policies worldwide, recommending that, at a minimum, the legalization of abortion in cases of rape or incest, or when a woman's life or health is in danger.[31] This is based on a regional human rights treaty, the Protocol to the African Charter on Human and People's Rights, which uses similar language.[32]

Thus, in order to reduce the number of abortions worldwide, perhaps we should focus less attention on the legality of abortion, and more attention on the root causes of unwanted pregnancies.[33] Many of these root causes are directly related to the rights that Amnesty International and other human rights groups advocate for every day—that all women should have access to safe and culturally appropriate forms of birth control, be educated and empowered to control their own sexual lives prior to pregnancy, be protected from physical and sexual violence, and be economically and politically empowered so that motherhood is not their only option for survival. These kinds of policies can significantly reduce the number of unwanted pregnancies, and consequently the number of abortions performed.

Notes

1. Hillary Clinton, remarks at a meeting of the National Association for the Repeal of Abortion Laws (NARAL), Washington, DC, January 22, 1999, http://www.ontheissues.org/senate/hillary_clinton_abortion.htm.

2. *Roe v. Wade,* 410 U.S. 113 (1973).

3. Rachel K. Jones and Kathryn Kooistra, "Abortion Incidence and Access to Services in the United States, 2008," *Perspectives on Sexual and Reproductive Health* 43, no. 1 (March 2011): 41–50.

4. See National Abortion Federation, "History of Abortion," http://www.pro choice.org/about_abortion/history_abortion.html, accessed July 16, 2012. Note that the Hyde Amendment is a rider to appropriations bills in Congress, not an amendment to the US Constitution. It must therefore be renewed annually in order to remain in effect.

5. *Planned Parenthood v. Casey,* 505 U.S. 833 (1992).

6. Guttmacher Institute, "State Policies in Brief: An Overview of Abortion Laws," July 1, 2002, http://www.guttmacher.org/statecenter/spibs/spib_OAL.pdf.

7. Dalia Sussman, "Poll: Abortion Support Conditional," *ABC News,* January 22, 2003, http://abcnews.go.com/US/story?id=90413&page=1.

8. Michael Minkenberg, "Religion and Public Policy: Institutional, Cultural, and Political Impact on the Shaping of Abortion Policies in Western Democracies," *Comparative Political Studies* 35, no. 2 (2002): 221–247.

9. Karla Zabludovsky, "Woman Who Sought Abortion in El Salvador Delivers Baby," *New York Times*, June 4, 2013, http://www.nytimes.com/2013/06/05/world /americas/woman-who-sought-abortion-in-el-salvador-delivers-baby.html.

10. Huma Khan, "Catholic Church vs. Obama in Election Year Showdown," *ABC News*, January 30, 2012, http://abcnews.go.com/blogs/politics/2012/01/catholic -church-vs-obama-in-election-year-showdown.

11. Robert Pigott, "Amnesty Ends Abortion Neutrality," *BBC News*, August 18, 2007, http://news.bbc.co.uk/2/hi/americas/6952558.stm.

12. United Nations Department of Economic and Social Affairs, "World Abortion Policies 2007" (New York, April 2007).

13. *Roe v. Wade*, Section 9.

14. Linda J. Heffner, "Advanced Maternal Age: How Old Is Too Old?" *New England Journal of Medicine* 351 (November 2004): 1927–1929.

15. United Nations, "Convention on the Elimination of All Forms of Discrimination Against Women," *United Nations Treaty Collection*, http://treaties.un.org /Pages/ViewDetails.aspx?src=TREATY&mtdsg_no=IV-8&chapter=4&lang=en, accessed July 17, 2012.

16. Carmel Shalev, "Rights to Sexual and Reproductive Health: The ICPD and the Convention on the Elimination of All Forms of Discrimination Against Women," *Health and Human Rights* 4, no. 2 (2000): 38–66.

17. From the 2Pac song "Keep Ya Head Up," 1993.

18. See Bob Woodward, "The Abortion Papers," *Washington Post*, January 22, 1989.

19. Susan J. Lee et al., "Fetal Pain: A Systematic Multidisciplinary Review of the Evidence," *Journal of the American Medical Association* 294, no. 8 (August 2005): 947–954.

20. Henry Shue, *Basic Rights* (Princeton: Princeton University Press, 1996).

21. *Doe v. Bolton*, 410 U.S. 179 (1973). This case was similar in substance to *Roe v. Wade*, and the Supreme Court verdict was rendered on the same day.

22. Shalev, "Rights to Sexual and Reproductive Health."

23. European Dignity Watch, "No Right to Abortion Under International Law," October 6, 2011, http://www.europeandignitywatch.org/de/day-to-day/detail /article/no-right-to-abortion-under-international-law.html.

24. Rita Joseph, *Human Rights and the Unborn Child* (Leiden: Nijhoff, 2009).

25. Wendy Guns, "The Influence of the Feminist Anti-Abortion NGOs as Norm Setters at the Level of the UN," *Human Rights Quarterly* 35, no. 3 (2013): 673–700.

26. According to a January 16–20, 2004, national telephone poll conducted jointly by *ABC News* and the *Washington Post* with a random sample of 1,133 adults, 54 percent of men supported the right to abortion, compared to 58 percent of women; 28 percent of men supported the right to partial-birth abortion, compared to 19 percent of women; and 15 percent of men supported the right to third-trimester abortion, compared to 8 percent of women.

27. United Nations Department of Economic and Social Affairs, "World Abortion Policies 2007."

28. Minkenberg, "Religion and Public Policy," p. 227.

29. Rebecca J. Cook and Bernard M. Dickens, "Human Rights Dynamics of Abortion Law Reform," *Human Rights Quarterly* 25, no. 1 (2003): 1–59.

30. Elisabeth Rosenthal, "Legal or Not, Abortion Rates Compare," *New York Times,* October 12, 2007.

31. Joanna N. Erdman, Teresa DePineres, and Eszter Kismodi, "Updated WHO Guidance on Safe Abortion: Health and Human Rights," *International Journal of Gynecology and Obstetrics* 120 (2003): 202.

32. Charles G. Ngwena, "Inscribing Abortion as a Human Right: Significance of the Protocol on the Rights of Women in Africa," *Human Rights Quarterly* 32, no. 4 (2010): 783–864. See Article 14(2)(c).

33. Stanley K. Henshaw, Susheela Singh, and Taylor Haas, "The Incidence of Abortion Worldwide," *Family Planning Perspectives* 25, supplement (1999): S30–38.

11

Is Female Circumcision
a Violation of Human Rights?

Fauziya Kassindja was seventeen years old when she applied for **asylum** in the United States from her home country of Togo in West Africa. This was unusual, because Togo was not experiencing a civil war or major political repression, the typical reasons why refugees would seek asylum. Yet in 1996 the US Board of Immigration Appeals granted Kassindja asylum and the right to stay permanently in the United States, on the basis of her "well-founded fear of persecution" in Togo.[1] According to the immigration judges, the persecution that Kassindja faced was the prospect of soon becoming circumcised and being forced to marry against her will. Kassindja's legal claim became the first case in which the United States granted asylum to a refugee fleeing her country as a result of female circumcision.

Female circumcision is a childhood rite of passage practiced widely in sub-Saharan Africa and the Middle East. Although the procedure varies widely by location, it involves the "partial or total removal of the external female genitalia, or other injury to the female genital organs for non-medical reasons," according to the World Health Organization.[2] It is performed on girls ranging in age from only a few days old in some cases, through puberty. On some occasions the procedure is done in a hospital, but more commonly it is performed without anesthesia by a traditional circumciser, using a knife, razor, or scissors. The WHO estimates that female circumcision has been performed on roughly 140 million girls and young women across the world.[3] Human rights activists also often refer to it as female genital mutilation or female genital cutting, which perhaps better convey the physical pain caused by the procedure and tilt the debate toward their position.

Many human rights organizations and medical professionals have called for an end to female circumcision, arguing that it unnecessarily harms young women like Fauziya Kassindja. They say that female circumcision is tantamount to torture, and because every person has the right to be free from torture, female circumcision should be banned everywhere. These advocates base their argument on the philosophy of universalism—that is, the idea that human rights apply equally to everyone.

However, human rights activists have encountered strong resistance from religious and cultural leaders from within the regions that practice female circumcision. These leaders argue that female circumcision is misunderstood by Western activists, and that female circumcision actually provides many benefits to the individuals and the societies that practice it. They accuse human rights activists of trying to force traditional societies to accept Western values that are incompatible with their way of life. Defenders of female circumcision draw on the notion of cultural relativism, which contends that there are no universal principles that apply to everyone. Instead, moral values and beliefs are created within the context of a particular society, and they should apply only within that society. Therefore, Western activists have no authority to criticize the practices of other societies, because the values they hold may not be accepted within other cultures.

The issue of female circumcision also raises questions over women's rights, children's rights, and the notion of free choice.[4] Are women and girls particularly vulnerable to certain human rights abuses, and therefore deserving of special protection? At what stage in life should children be able to decide what happens to their bodies? Do individuals have any obligation to uphold and perpetuate the cultural practices that are important to their community? And ultimately, do human rights provide a sufficient basis for activists to criticize behavior that is widely accepted in other cultures?

Argument 1
Female circumcision is a violation of human rights.

According to this argument, female circumcision is a violation of human rights because it amounts to torture, and torture, regardless of where it is practiced, or the justifications for its existence, is a violation of human rights. No cultural or religious tradition is an adequate excuse to injure and oppress young women.

The United Nations Convention Against Torture defines torture as "any act by which severe pain or suffering, whether physical or mental, is intentionally inflicted on a person . . . for any reason based on discrimination of any kind."[5] There is no question that female circumcision often causes severe pain and long-term injury that is cruel, inhuman, degrading, and discriminatory, which would be prohibited under the convention. The procedure, especially when performed in a nonsterile environment, can cause fatal infections. By removing healthy tissue, the more complete forms of female circumcision permanently interfere with a woman's ability to experience sexual pleasure. The most extreme form of female circumcision involves "infibulation," or the "narrowing of the vaginal opening through the creation of a covering seal" by stitching the skin or tying the legs together.[6] Other complications from the procedure can include shock, hemorrhaging, recurrent urinary-tract infections, cysts, infertility, and an increased risk of childbirth complications.[7] Female circumcision is different from male circumcision, in that it permanently damages the natural functioning of a woman's body. While male circumcision has some demonstrable health benefits, such as reducing the risk of HIV infection, female circumcision has no known health benefits. The real justification for female circumcision is entirely cultural and religious, rather than medical.

This is why the WHO has described female circumcision as an "extreme form of discrimination against women."[8] Western activists are not alone in condemning this practice; the whole world has declared that female circumcision is an abuse of women's human rights that should be ended immediately. At the International Conference on Population and Development in Cairo in 1994, all the world's nations adopted an action program that described female circumcision as a "basic rights violation" and urged governments to "protect women and girls from all similar unnecessary and dangerous practices."[9] Likewise, in the fourth World Conference on Women in Beijing in 1995, all countries adopted the platform that listed female circumcision as a case of violence against women.[10] It was African human rights activists who led the effort to include language condemning female circumcision in the Beijing statement, and African NGOs continue to work to end female circumcision throughout the continent.[11]

Supporters of female circumcision argue that the practice preserves important cultural and religious traditions. But although the human rights perspective allows for diverse cultural practices, when those practices violate universal, minimum standards of decency, then the tradition must be declared wrong and ended. Religion has been misunderstood and manipulated throughout history to attempt to justify mass atrocities, but respect for culture and tradition can never serve as an excuse to violate human rights. Some of the ideas that perpetuate female circumcision are simply false and misogynistic, and human rights activists must call them for what they are. In some societies, uncircumcised women are considered too "dirty" to handle food; in others, the clitoris is believed to be lethally dangerous, capable of killing upon contact.[12] These beliefs should be denounced when they exist in non-Western societies, just as similar beliefs were denounced when they pervaded Western societies in the nineteenth century.[13]

Female circumcision is justified by destructive stereotypes of women, which are made possible by patriarchal social structures. Studies have found that women with higher levels of education and wealth are less likely to consent to circumcision for themselves or their daughters.[14] Young women do receive some economic and social benefits from circumcision, but only the limited benefits available to them within a patriarchal society. Most circumcised women still cannot own property of their own, or control decisions about whether to have children. Therefore, the "choice" that many girls and their mothers make to undergo female circumcision is a coerced choice at best, performed under immense social pressure and often in the midst of economic deprivation. In this context, female circumcision is a particularly sadistic way of perpetuating male dominance.

At a fundamental level, human rights protect the freedom to choose one's path in life. This is what makes the experience of female circumcision different than plastic surgery or body piercing, the latter of which a woman is free to choose. Some may find these medical procedures distasteful, but a woman has the right to decide how to treat her own body. However, even if Westerners are acting hypocritically in their condemnation of female circumcision, hypocrisy alone does not alter the fact that female circumcision is a gross human rights violation because it violates free choice by forcing an objectively harmful experience upon girls who are too young to decide for themselves. Although parents should have the ability and the right to make critical decisions for their children, they should not have the right to violate their children's bodies and their physical security. They have a duty to make decisions that are in the best interests of their children.

Furthermore, the contention that female circumcision, when done with proper sterilization and medical care, is ultimately benign, is not ac-

> **Think Again**
>
> At what stage of development do you think children should be empowered to make critical decisions about their own lives? Should such empowerment be based on age, or other criteria? Should the criteria be different for every culture, or is it possible to devise a set of universal criteria?

curate. There are inherent risks involved with all medical procedures, making female circumcision dangerous in even the most controlled environments. In 2013 a thirteen-year-old Egyptian girl died while undergoing circumcision due to complications from anesthesia.[15] Despite the fact that the procedure was done by a trained medical professional in proper medical facilities, the young girl died. The high risks involved in female circumcision therefore drastically outweigh any possible social or cultural benefits that circumcised women may receive.

In sum, according to this argument universal standards of human rights give anyone reasonable grounds to condemn practices that do not conform to those standards. The idea of human rights renders cultural relativism invalid, because all people belong to the same human society, regardless of our differing ideas and traditions. We all share the same basic moral code, because we are all human. Although African and Middle Eastern societies have good reason to reject criticism from Westerners, given their experience with colonialism, many people within societies that practice female circumcision are speaking out against female circumcision as well. While female circumcision is often justified by referencing Islamic tradition, many Islamic scholars have noted that there is nothing in the Quran that requires female circumcision.[16] Many religious leaders in Africa and the Middle East have issued decrees calling for their followers to end female circumcision. Other African activists, such as Nahid Toubia, Sudan's first female surgeon, have led the charge to bring attention to the problem and undertake a range of holistic solutions.[17]

Argument 2
Female circumcision is not a violation of human rights.

According to this argument, Western human rights activists, who generate most of the criticism of female circumcision, have no basis for condemning cultural traditions that they do not fully understand. Female circumcision promotes important cultural values and binds communities together in Africa and the Middle East. Western activists who criticize female circumcision are practicing cultural imperialism and ultimately doing more harm than good.

This rite of passage plays a central role in many African cultures. From the outside, it may seem like a misogynistic practice that injures and subjugates women. The activists who call for an end to female circumcision believe that they are speaking up for the benefit of women and girls. But in fact, women in these cultures support and perpetuate this practice because it fulfills a religious duty and provides important social benefits for the girls who become circumcised. In national surveys conducted in six African countries, a majority of women in five of the six supported the continuation of female circumcision. Indeed, women supported female circumcision at a higher rate than did men.[18]

According to this argument, Western societies value an extreme form of individualism that is devoid of social responsibility, while many non-Western cultures value a more central role for the family. Mothers and grandmothers are proud to have their daughters circumcised, and this ritual helps to reinforce proper gender relations and social roles. Although painful for a short period of time, the ritual is performed in the context of a joyful community event that praises the family for fulfilling its duties. Girls who are circumcised are deemed by the community to be virtuous and ready to start families of their own. Since circumcision is a prerequisite to marriage, the girls who are circumcised receive substantial social and economic benefits from the procedure, including housing, financial support, and the opportunity to have children. As a female doctor from Sierra Leone has stated, "It is difficult for me—considering the number of ceremonies I have observed, including my own—to accept that what appears to be expressions of joy and ecstatic celebrations of womanhood in actuality disguise hidden experiences of coercion and subjugation. Indeed, I offer that the bulk of Kono women who uphold these rituals do so because they want to."[19] Attempting to stop this ritual can therefore disempower women and girls by alienating them from their family and community, their main sources of emotional and financial support.

According to the World Health Organization, female circumcision can cause permanent physical and emotional damage to young women.[20] However, other medical professionals have found no significant differences in health outcomes between women who have undergone circumcision and those who have not. Women who have been circumcised report that their reproductive systems are just as healthy, and their sexual lives just as satisfying, as those who have not been circumcised.[21] Although there are cases in which the procedure is performed carelessly, causing unintended damage, the best way to remedy these cases is to ensure that traditional practitioners are trained and provided with sterilized instruments. When human rights activists condemn the entire ritual, and attempt to get it legally banned, this causes communities to turn to more informal, unregulated, and unsafe procedures, resulting in fewer girls undergoing the procedure in hospitals or under the care of well-trained practitioners. Thus human rights activists may have caused more harm than good. If we truly care about the young women who are being circumcised, we should be making it safer by supporting the communities who practice female circumcision, rather than trying to eliminate the practice altogether.

In addition, Western activists have deliberately described this ritual using the harshest possible labels in order to stigmatize it. This also harms women rather than helping them. As a cultural anthropologist notes, "'Female genital mutilation' is an invidious and essentially debate-subverting label. . . . African women object to naming a practice that they describe in local terms as 'the celebration' or the 'purification' or the 'cleansing' or the 'beautification' as 'mutilation.'"[22] By transforming something perceived to be a beautiful ritual into a form of child abuse, human rights activists threaten the psychological health of girls who have been circumcised. This labeling might harm a young woman's image of herself, when she learns that her body has been "mutilated." As one woman who works in the United States with African immigrants explains, "The pain of hearing yourself described [as mutilated] is more painful than being cut."[23]

According to this argument, Western criticism of female circumcision is not only uninformed, but also hypocritical and inconsistent. Western societies engage in the ritual of male circumcision without any criticism from human rights activists. Perhaps this is because male circumcision is traditional in Christian and Jewish societies, while female circumcision is more common in Muslim communities. Although supporters of male circumcision argue that there are health benefits to the practice, in fact there are both benefits and risks, and the ritual survived for centuries before any health benefits were ever discovered to justify it.[24] Young women in Western societies are likewise pressured to alter their bodies in order to conform to social norms and appeal to potential romantic partners. Breast augmentation, facial reconstructive surgery, liposuction, body piercing, tattoos, and even "vaginal rejuvenation" are all commonly practiced in the same societies that condemn female circumcision. These cosmetic procedures provide no health benefits and carry some significant health risks. Western activists may respond that, in all of these cases, the individual has the freedom to choose whether or not to undergo the procedure. Yet given the immense cultural pressure in Western societies for women to fit into an ideal physical type, how free is this choice? Are Western women, who freely choose to undergo elective and cosmetic surgeries, any more empowered than the young women in sub-Saharan Africa and the Middle East? At least female circumcision can be seen as providing tangible benefits such as fulfilling a religious duty, building a family, and joining together a community.

Clearly free choice is an important element of human rights. Having a right implies having the freedom to choose whether or not to exercise that right. If a woman chooses to mutilate herself, it is qualitatively different than if she is injured against her will. However, parents have the duty to make choices for their children until their children achieve the developmental capacity to think independently, to reason, to evaluate alternatives and weigh possible consequences. Thus, decisions affecting children's bodies, possessions, experiences, and futures fall upon their parents. There is no universal age at which children are considered to have acquired the capability to make free choices for themselves. Rather, the transition to adulthood is determined by the culture in which the child lives. Therefore, it is the parents who are best able to make decisions about their own children, regardless of proclamations of universal rights from Western activists. While female circumcision may seem brutal or revolting to Westerners, there are many Western practices that seem equally revolting to non-Westerners. Personal preference is not sufficient grounds for moral condemnation.

In sum, according to this argument, although human rights are a helpful guideline for thinking about how to preserve human dignity and protect free choice, they cannot be used to condemn cultural and religious traditions from the outside. Societies should be free to choose their own rituals, because they know best how to interpret and apply human rights in their own local environment, according to their own local values. Some societies may decide to end the practice of female circumcision, but the decision should be entirely up to those families, not human rights activists from the West. When human rights activists criticize cultural traditions in Africa, it rings of colonialism and the "white man's burden." White Europeans have always proclaimed to know what is best for the people of Africa, but they have rarely succeeded in persuading the colonized that they are correct. It is therefore no surprise that Western attempts to ban female circumcision have often met with protest from the African societies themselves, and have sometimes increased the resolve of these societies to continue the practice as a way of resisting cultural imperialism.[25]

* * *

Conclusion

Is female circumcision a human rights violation? For cultural relativists, only members of societies who practice female circumcision can answer that question for themselves, because they are the only ones who understand the relevant cultural context and share a similar moral code. For universalists, human rights provide everyone with the same moral code, and female circumcision violates that code because no woman would rationally accept female circumcision if she were truly free to decide.

It is important to note that the question of whether female circumcision is a human rights violation is distinct from the question of *how* to end female circumcision effectively. Human rights activists may have sufficient grounds to condemn female circumcision, but they may find it unwise or unhelpful to condemn certain religious traditions from the outside. There is a difference between cultural relativism and cultural sensitivity. Even when human rights activists are convinced that a violation must end, they must be sensitive to the unique features of a particular culture, so that they will know how to end that practice effectively. Fortunately, there are many options available for strategically promoting and implementing human rights. Many different actors exist, and what may work for one actor may not work for another. For example, an NGO like Amnesty International could start a media campaign condemning female circumcision, or it might financially support an African NGO that promotes alternatives to female circumcision.[26] It could bring a country practicing female circumcision before the UN Human Rights Council to be investigated, or it could sponsor a religious dialogue among progressive Islamic scholars. These strategies would likely produce very different results in terms of actual improvements on the ground. Likewise, a government could place economic sanctions on a country practicing female circumcision, or it could donate funds for primary education for girls in that country. It could enforce a "zero tolerance" policy on female circumcision, or it could work with other governments to make female circumcision procedures more sanitary and less harmful. It could focus exclusively on the violations of other states, or it could strive to improve its own human rights record. Many of the important debates in human rights revolve around these kinds of policy decisions.

One option for ending female circumcision is to impose a legal ban on the procedure, which several African countries have already done. However, as Figure 11.1 shows, the practice of female circumcision continues to thrive even in many of the countries that have made it illegal. This illustrates the fact that laws protecting human rights are unlikely to be effective in places where there is strong cultural resistance to the law. In fact, some have argued that laws criminalizing female circumcision have had the unintended consequence of harming young women, as more women in these countries are now circumcised by untrained practitioners operating outside the law. A different approach could involve making female circumcision less harmful to

Figure 11.1 Female Circumcision and the Law

Countries Where Female Circumcision Is Legally Banned	Percentage of Females Circumcised
Benin	50
Burkina Faso	72
Central African Republic	43
Chad	60
Côte d'Ivoire	43
Djibouti	98
Egypt	97
Eritrea	95
Ethiopia	85
Ghana	80
Guinea	99
Kenya	38
Mauritania	25
Niger	5
Senegal	20
Tanzania	18
Togo	12

Sources: Center for Reproductive Rights, "Female Genital Mutilation (FGM): Legal Prohibitions Worldwide," December 11, 2008, http://reproductiverights.org/en/document/female-genital-mutilation-fgm-legal-prohibitions-worldwide; Comfort Momoh, ed., Female Genital Mutilation (Abingdon: Radcliffe, 2005), p. 6.

young women by promoting and educating women about less invasive versions of the procedure. For example, a group of physicians in the United States has recommended that doctors be allowed to perform a ceremonial pinprick or "nick" in order to circumcise girls without causing long-term damage.[27] If we want to protect human rights, our efforts outside the law are just as important as legislation and judicial action.

Ultimately, it is important to remember that the notion of human rights is an inescapably universalist idea. We may want to respect cultural differences, but if we believe in human rights, then that respect has limits. At the point where cultural traditions violate basic rights, then those traditions are in need of reform. Universalism, however, inherently presents some philosophical and practical problems. First, who has the authority to determine what the universal standards are, and to interpret when behavior does not meet those standards? Human rights activists often hope that a global consensus embodied in international law can be the source of these universal standards. After all, it is the Universal Declaration of Human Rights that everyone has agreed to follow. The problem is that the consensus is not truly shared by everyone. There is persistent disagreement about which rights should take priority, which situations should require restriction of rights, and which actors should be responsible for implementing rights. International law is vaguely worded, while international politics is extremely complex. This leaves tremendous space for contrasting interpretations of rights and conflicting approaches to implementing them.

Second, universalism is plagued by the problem of power. In an ideal world, human rights violators can be taught, persuaded, or encouraged to improve their protection of rights. Occasionally, however, the implementation of human rights requires threats, coercion, and punishment. Without a singular authority to determine and enforce the universal standards, the enforcement of human rights falls to the most powerful states. These states often pursue their own interests, and so the implementation of supposedly universal standards becomes uneven and inconsistent. It is easy to see how this kind of uneven enforcement of human rights standards begins to look like Western imperialism from the perspective of the actors being coerced. Even if human rights are universal in theory, their implementation by the powerful is often (and perhaps fairly) perceived as cultural imperialism. This is evident in the debate over female circumcision, as those claiming that it is a human rights violation are not necessarily the same people as those experiencing female circumcision. It is no surprise that societies with less power to determine the rules often use cultural relativism to claim that the rules do not apply to them.

> ### What Would You Do?
>
> Imagine that you are a government minister in the Gambia, where female circumcision is widely practiced. You believe that female circumcision does harm to millions of women, but that it also serves a valuable role in keeping communities together and preventing some of the problems common in the West (for example, HIV/AIDS, unwed mothers, and sexual promiscuity). Many of your citizens support female circumcision, but a growing number of women are voicing their opposition and taking action to stop it. What policies would you recommend that the Gambian government take to stop female circumcision? Would you impose a legal ban against female circumcision?

The philosophy of cultural relativism, though, presents problems of its own. For example, the boundaries that people draw between cultural "insiders" and "outsiders" are inherently arbitrary and often changing. Cultural relativism assumes that distinct societies exist, each with its own unique and homogeneous set of values and traditions. But we know, especially in the age of globalization, that societies intermingle, ideas are exchanged, and traditions change. Each society represents a diverse and dynamic mix of cultural values (see Figure 11.2). Cultural relativism gives no guidance about which of these values should be dominant and thus be protected from "outside" influence. As a result, the notion of cultural relativism can easily become an excuse for dominant members *within* a society to extend their

---

Figure 11.2 Cultural Relativism and "Asian Values"

The tension between universalism and cultural relativism is manifested in other global human rights controversies, such as the debate over **Asian values**. In the 1990s, as human rights activists pushed for greater respect of civil and political rights around the world, Asian leaders like Lee Kwan Yew of Singapore and Mahathir Mohamad of Malaysia declared that these rights did not apply in Asian societies. These leaders argued that Eastern cultures valued **collectivism** over **individualism**—in other words, that Asian people gained their identity through their duties to the community, not by claiming rights for themselves. They also argued that Asian societies, which were less economically developed than Western societies, were more interested in putting food on their tables and roofs over their heads than in having the right to vote or criticize their government. They claimed that the attainment of economic and social rights in Asian societies relied on political stability, which sometimes required a strong central government and the restriction of civil and political rights. Although they did not dispute the existence of universal rights, they argued that different societies march on different pathways toward their attainment. For them, achieving economic well-being was a necessary first step toward instituting democratic rights. This sentiment was expressed most clearly in the 1993 **Bangkok Declaration**, in which Asian countries agreed on a common statement emphasizing the importance of Asian values and the principle of national sovereignty.

Indeed, these Asian leaders seemed to have a point, as they presided over a period of dramatic economic growth in the latter part of the twentieth century that pulled millions of their people out of extreme deprivation. Most Asian leaders have remained relatively popular even as they operate single-party, authoritarian states. Nevertheless, internal pressure for democratic reform continues, as activists from China to Singapore claim the mantle of universal human rights. As Nobel Prize–winning economist Amartya Sen has argued, Asian people value the right to speak as much as they value the right to eat, and these two things need not be traded against each other in national policy. According to Sen, societies that protect civil and political rights are also the ones that are best able to protect economic and social rights.[28] These rights should therefore be viewed as interdependent and equally deserving of protection.

authority and control. This is also evident in the debate over female circumcision, as people interested in maintaining their position of authority in a patriarchal society seek to defend the values and traditions underlying this practice. Cultural relativism gives people no justification to fight against inhuman practices or change the cultural status quo.

In the end, either human rights universally apply to all societies and cultures, or they do not. At some level, universalism is incompatible with cultural relativism. Yet there are ways to make human rights compatible with some cultural diversity and differences in values. We can think of human rights as prescribing a set of core obligations, setting a minimum threshold for behavior that absolutely everyone must comply with. No one is allowed to commit mass atrocities or violate a person's basic dignity. Beyond that minimum threshold, however, human rights standards may allow for tremendous diversity in behaviors and traditions. Similarly, we can also think of human rights as prescribing a strict set of goals or outcomes that must guide policymaking processes. However, there may be multiple pathways to reaching these goals that are still consistent with human rights standards. This is why, even if universal human rights were strengthened across the world, we might still expect to see a wide range of policies that apply these standards within a particular cultural context.

Notes

1. Center for Gender and Refugee Studies, "Fauziya Kassindja and the Struggle for Gender Asylum," http://cgrs.uchastings.edu/about/kasinga.php, accessed June 28, 2012.

2. World Health Organization, "Female Genital Mutilation," Fact Sheet no. 241, February 2012, http://female circumcision.who.int/mediacentre/factsheets/fs 241/en/index.html.

3. Ibid.

4. For a detailed overview of the arguments on both sides, see Alison T. Slack, "Female Circumcision: A Critical Appraisal," *Human Rights Quarterly* 10, no. 4 (1988): 437–486.

5. United Nations Convention Against Torture, Article 1. Signed December 10, 1984; entered into force June 26, 1987.

6. World Health Organization, "Female Genital Mutilation."

7. Ibid.

8. Ibid.

9. United Nations International Conference on Population and Development, "Summary of the Programme of Action," Cairo, March 1995.

10. United Nations Fourth World Conference on Women, "Platform for Action," Beijing, September 1995, para. 113.

11. Frances A. Althaus, "Female Circumcision: Rite of Passage or Violation of Rights?" *International Family Planning Perspectives* 23, no. 3 (September 1997): 130.

12. Amnesty International, "What Is Female Genital Mutilation?" September 30, 1997, http://www.amnesty.org/en/library/info/ACT77/006/1997.

13. Comfort Momoh, ed., *Female Genital Mutilation* (Abingdon: Radcliffe, 2005), p. 5.

14. Nahid Toubia, *Female Genital Mutilation: A Global Call to Action* (Berkeley: Women Ink, 1993).

15. Sara C. Nelson, "Soher Ebrahim Egyptian Girl, 13, Dies After Illegal Female Genital Mutilation (FGM)," *Huffington Post,* June 6, 2013, http://www.huffingtonpost.co.uk/2013/06/10/soher-ebrahim-egyptian-girl-13-dies-illegal-female-genital-mutilation_n_3417398.html.

16. Momoh, *Female Genital Mutilation,* p. 1.

17. See the Research Action and Information Network for the Bodily Integrity of Women (RAINBO) website, at http://www.rainbo.org, accessed July 3, 2012.

18. Althaus, "Female Circumcision." Only in the Central African Republic did a majority of women not support the continuation of female circumcision.

19. John Tierney, "A New Debate on Female Circumcision," *New York Times,* November 30, 2007.

20. World Health Organization, "Female Genital Mutilation."

21. Linda Morison et al., "The Long Term Reproductive Health Consequences of Female Genital Cutting in Rural Gambia: A Community Based Survey," *Tropical Medicine and International Health* 6, no. 8 (August 2001): 643–653.

22. John Tierney, "'Circumcision' or 'Mutilation'? And Other Questions About a Rite in Africa," *New York Times,* December 5, 2007.

23. Ibid.

24. Mark C. Alanis and Richard S. Lucidi, "Neonatal Circumcision: A Review of the World's Oldest and Most Controversial Operation," *Obstetrical and Gynecological Survey* 59, no. 5 (May 2004): 379–395.

25. Althaus, "Female Circumcision."

26. Linda A. Williams, "Eradicating Female Circumcision: Human Rights and Cultural Values," *Health Care Analysis* 6 (1998): 33–35.

27. Pam Belluck, "Group Backs Ritual 'Nick' as Female Circumcision Option," *New York Times,* May 6, 2010.

28. Amartya Sen, *Development as Freedom* (New York: Knopf, 1999).

Part 3

Economic and Social Rights

12

Are Food, Housing, and Health Care Valid Human Rights?

The Cold War embodied an enormous ideological divide over the legitimacy of civil and political rights, as opposed to economic, social, and cultural rights. Why was the supposedly indivisible set of human rights divided into these two subsets, and why do some policymakers continue to reject the validity of some of the rights laid out in the Universal Declaration of Human Rights? While the UDHR was written in 1948 as an all-encompassing, indivisible set of rights, the political polarization of the Cold War era led to an ideological polarization in the field of human rights.[1] From this divide was born the International Covenant on Civil and Political Rights, which was largely supported by Western countries, and the International Covenant on Economic, Social, and Cultural Rights, which drew its support from the Eastern Soviet bloc of countries. Each group of countries claimed that their set of rights constituted "real" human rights, while asserting that the opposing set of rights were not real rights but merely privileges that were not necessary to the achievement of human dignity.

Though the Soviet Union no longer exists, the debate surrounding the legitimacy of economic, social, and cultural rights continues today. Central to this debate are the rights to food, housing, and health care. Not only do these rights clearly fall under the category of economic, social, and cultural rights, but they are also specifically outlined in Article 25 of the UDHR.[2] Although food, housing, and health care are widely recognized as some of the basic necessities required for human survival, there is still a great deal of skepticism, especially from supporters of free market capitalism, over whether these necessities should be viewed as universal human rights. Although food, housing, and health care are not the only controversial rights, because of the magnitude of their importance to both human survival and geopolitical interests they are the subject of this chapter's debate.

The first argument claims that food, housing, and health care are valid human rights, and their existence is the only way to achieve both economic, social, and cultural rights, and civil and political rights. While it can be difficult to define and protect economic, social, and cultural rights, this is not really any different than defining and protecting civil and political rights. Many countries have already proven that it is possible to protect both sets of human rights without sacrificing personal freedom or economic growth.

The second argument claims that food, housing, and health care, though necessary for human survival, are not valid human rights. It claims that the best way for these economic goods to be acquired is for governments to vigorously enforce civil and political rights. Indeed, it is argued that if governments try to enforce economic, social, and cultural rights, this will prove devastating to both those rights as well as civil and political rights.

Argument 1
Food, housing, and health care are valid human rights.

No one denies that food, housing, and health care are essential to human survival; as such, they are basic human needs. Human rights are not merely legal entitlements granted by the state; they are also moral and political claims that arise from basic human needs. According to this argument, because economic, social, and cultural rights represent human needs that people have good reason to lay claim to, they are valid human rights. Indeed, states should deliberately protect economic, social, and cultural rights in their legal systems and in their economic policies. For the full flourishing of human dignity, it is necessary to ensure that every human being has access to adequate food, housing, and health care, as well as to ensure that every human being can have a voice in the political system.

Perhaps it is true that not all rights are indivisible and equal. However, if this is the case, then the important distinction is not between civil and political rights on the one hand, and economic, social, and cultural rights on the other, but between **basic rights** and secondary rights. Basic rights, according to philosopher Henry Shue, are rights that not only are important for their own sake, but also serve as the necessary foundation for all other rights.[3] Food, housing, and health care are therefore basic rights, because a person obviously cannot meaningfully exercise their right to vote or speak freely if they are dying of malnutrition or malaria. For Shue, basic rights include both material subsistence (an economic, social, and cultural right) and physical security (a civil and political right). Because these are basic rights, states should prioritize them in their policy-making, and guarantee them for all people to the greatest extent possible.

We should also remember that there are roughly a billion people in the world today who lack access to these basic material needs.[4] One out of every seven people in the world lacks sufficient food, housing, and health care. Over 20,000 people die every day from malnutrition or a preventable illness, primarily in the global South. If human rights are meant to apply to all humans, they must be relevant to the most pressing concerns of the global South, which clearly involve access to food, housing, and health care. As the former **United Nations High Commissioner for Human Rights**, Mary Robinson, has said, "When I am asked to identify the most serious human rights violation in the world today, my reply is consistent: extreme poverty."[5] Since Western human rights activists ignored these rights for decades, it is no surprise that many people in the rest of the world became cynical of the international human rights regime as a biased institution that didn't address their main concerns.[6]

The argument that food, housing, and health care are *not* valid human rights is based on the claim that these are legally unenforceable because they are **positive rights**—in other words, that these rights require active government intervention in order to be realized. But this claim is misguided, for several reasons. First, human rights scholars are increasingly recognizing that Isaiah Berlin's classical distinction (civil and political rights as **negative rights**—those, like freedom of speech, that are protected by the absence of actions by others—versus economic, social, and cultural rights as positive rights) does not hold up in practice.[7] In reality, both sets of rights are interdependent; in other words, it is difficult to actually guarantee access to material needs if the population is uneducated or unable to participate in government, and vice versa.[8] Likewise, both sets of rights impose both positive and negative duties on other actors. For example, the right to due process (a traditional civil and political right) requires the state to spend money on courts, judges, and public defenders. Freedom from cruel and unusual punishment, a supposedly negative right, requires the state to take a proactive role in building humane prisons, providing food and health care for prisoners, and training prison guards in proper treatment.[9]

Thus, rather than categorizing rights as either negative or positive, it is better to think of *all* rights as conferring both negative and positive duties on the state and other actors.[10] All rights involve the negative duty to respect; that is, the state must refrain from actively violating the right itself. In other words, the government must not actively torture a person or burn down their home. Many economic, social, and cultural rights are lost because governments actively violate this negative duty to respect these rights. They seize poor people's land, forcibly evict the poor from their homes, and destroy the environments that the poor depend on. All rights also involve a duty to protect; that is, the state must try to ensure that private actors do not violate people's rights, and it must provide a remedy in case of a violation. In other words, the government must arrest and prosecute the offender who commits domestic violence or robs someone's home. Finally, all rights involve the positive duty to fulfill, which means proactively creating the conditions in which the right will be protected. In other words, the government must spend money to train police officers or provide loans for affordable housing.

Therefore, there is no inherent or natural distinction between civil and political rights on the one hand, and economic, social, and cultural rights on the other. When a right is violated, it is sometimes difficult to assign responsibility when the causes are complex and structural. However, this is no different for civil and political rights than it is for economic, social, and cultural rights. If a suspect accused of a crime receives an incompetent public defender, a corrupt judge, and a racist jury, whose responsibility is it to remedy this violation of the suspect's right to due process? Precise duties may be difficult to assign in each case, but this does not damage the validity of the underlying human right.

While there is no natural distinction between civil and political rights, and economic, social, and cultural rights, there is in fact a historical difference in practice. The West has simply devoted attention and protection to civil and political rights for two centuries, while largely ignoring economic, social, and cultural rights. As a result, civil and political rights evolved gradually from vague, amorphous claims into relatively precise and strong legal instruments in the West. This is reflected in differences in the international treaties, between the explicit language of the ICCPR and the vague language of the ICESCR. But this is no reason to decry the "unenforceability" of economic, social, and cultural rights; rather, this is a clarion call to more clearly define these rights and strengthen their enforcement.

This is exactly what is happening around the world at an increasing pace.[11] Many states have decided that economic, social, and cultural rights are important enough to write them into their national constitutions.[12] Human rights activists have used these laws to pressure their governments to fulfill their legal obligations to protect economic, social, and cultural rights. Individuals and NGOs have pursued legal action in the courts, and the courts have at times forced the state to increase access to food, housing, and health care for its most vulnerable citizens. One example (among many) is the Treatment Action Campaign, a South African NGO that sued its government in 2001 to provide the drug Nevirapine to all HIV-infected pregnant mothers, in order to prevent transmission of HIV to their children. The Treatment Action Campaign won its lawsuit before the South African Constitutional court, forcing the government to implement a nationwide HIV prevention plan. Rather than dictating to the state exactly how it should spend its limited budget, the Court simply required the state to have a "reasonable" policy that prioritizes the most vulnerable people. This legal standard is common throughout the world. Therefore, counter to the claim that economic, social, and cultural rights are legally unenforceable, in fact these rights are being enforced. In cases where legal enforcement fails, it is not because these rights are unenforceable, but because some societies are biased against economic, social, and cultural rights.

Human rights are not just legal instruments, but also moral claims that inspire people to change their government's policies. Economic, social, and cultural rights empower impoverished communities to stand up and demand their basic rights to food, housing, and health care, as they are doing throughout the world. Poor people have successfully opposed the privatization of their water systems, prevented the seizure of their land and housing, and pressured their governments to prioritize social needs in their budgets.[13] For example, the Brazilian workers' movement that elected President Luiz Inácio Lula da Silva in 2002 led him to implement a "zero hunger" program for the whole country and redirect state resources to achieve this goal.

The claim that these redistributive policies stifle growth and are ultimately counterproductive to meeting the needs of the poor is ultimately not true.[14] In fact, when the government enacts policies that support the poor, it allows poor people to start small businesses, save money, and buy more consumer goods, which actually stimulates economic growth. This is called pro-poor growth, as opposed to policies that favor private corporations and investors. In Brazil, the "zero hunger" program has dramatically reduced hunger and inequality, cutting extreme poverty in half in only five years; meanwhile, Brazil's GDP has simultaneously grown at over 5 percent annually.[15] Indeed, most of the developed countries in the world have been able to build a strong social safety net (in other words, policies that ensure near-universal access to food, housing, and health care) without sacrificing economic growth or their democratic institutions. The social democracies of Europe have increased their wealth and competed successfully in the global economy while maintaining a far lower rate of poverty than exists in the United States, with its economic policies born of **neoliberalism**. Of course, Europeans do pay higher taxes and are subject to more government regulation than are Americans, but Europeans have accepted that this trade-off is preferable in order to ensure equitable growth and fulfill their social responsibility to their most vulnerable compatriots.

What about countries mired in extreme poverty, which simply do not have the resources to spend on food, housing, and health care? Is it fair to blame these states for "violations" of their duty to protect economic, social, and cultural rights—or for that matter, to blame wealthy states for not helping the poor states? International law does indeed provide guidance to resolve this problem. The ICESCR requires each state, whether wealthy or poor, to "take steps, individually and through international assistance and co-operation, especially economic and technical, to the maximum of its available resources, with a view to achieving progressively the full realization of [these] rights." In other words, even if a state is unable to meet all of its population's basic needs, it must be taking deliberate steps to reach that goal through prioritizing policies that support the poor. If a state is taking all possible steps to end poverty, and still lacks the necessary resources, then wealthy states are obligated to provide international assistance. Even though international law doesn't identify exactly which states have this obligation, and though it is impossible to force wealthy states to provide foreign aid, this duty at least puts some political pressure on the wealthiest states to help end extreme poverty on a global level. Critics may object that if the United States or Europe tried to take responsibility for the world's poverty, then this would bankrupt their already weak and indebted economies. However, economists have noted that the amount of foreign aid required to eliminate extreme poverty is not overwhelming—perhaps $100–200 billion total, if it is well targeted.[16] While this amount sounds large, it is actually less than the 0.7 percent of GDP that wealthy countries have already promised repeatedly in international assistance, but have yet to deliver. Even in the midst of economic recessions and budget crises, wealthy states can afford to sacrifice 70 cents out of every $100 to increase global access to basic material needs.

In sum, this argument claims that food, housing, and health care are not only valid human rights, but also among the most important rights that humans can claim. The West has ignored these rights for too long. While there are challenges to the legal enforcement of economic, social, and cultural rights, they are not qualitatively different than the challenges involved in enforcing civil and political rights. Civil and political rights have simply benefited from a two-century head start. When proper attention is given to economic, social, and cultural rights, they can become legally enforceable entitlements for poor individuals. They can also become effective guidelines to help states develop policies that eliminate extreme poverty and severe deprivation. Insofar as human rights activists claim to speak for the global community, they must advocate for the basic rights that 1 billion of their fellow humans currently lack.

Argument 2
Food, housing, and health care are not valid human rights.

Clearly food, housing, and health care are essential to human survival, and should be pursued with every available effort. However, there is a difference between a human need and a human right. Rights are individual entitlements that place legal duties upon states, and states should be required to enforce only those rights that they can be reasonably expected to enforce. It is not reasonable to require the state to provide goods that it should not and cannot provide. The state should not and cannot be required to provide these economic goods to individuals, and thus food, housing, and health care are not valid human rights.

For this reason, in 1951 the US ambassador to the United Nations, Walter Kotschnig, argued that

> civil and political rights were of such a nature as to be given legal effect promptly by the adoption of such legislation or other measures as might be necessary. The economic, social and cultural rights while spoken of as "rights" were, however, to be treated as *objectives* toward which States adhering to the [proposed] Covenant would within their resources undertake to strive, by the creation of conditions which would be conducive to the exercise of private as well as public action, for their progressive achievement.[17]

In other words, food, housing, and health care are important objectives to aspire to, but not really rights. This has been the official position of every US administration since 1948. Why? According to philosopher Isaiah Berlin, food, housing, and health care are positive rights.[18] Positive rights, typically considered entitlements to something, are those that require governments and other actors to take an active role in providing goods for people. Positive rights require the state to spend money and resources on their implementation. In contrast, negative rights, usually considered protection from something, simply require governments and individual people to abstain from taking action. If we want to be free from torture, then the state must simply refrain from torturing; if we have a right to open political participation, then the state must simply not interfere in elections. Thus, economic, social, and cultural rights are positive rights, whereas civil and political rights like protection from torture and the right to political participation are negative rights. The problem is that positive rights are not legally enforceable, whereas negative rights are. This is why civil and political rights have been declared in the US Constitution and enforced for two centuries, and why economic, social, and cultural rights have not.

The claim that there is no distinction between positive and negative rights simply makes no sense if one cannot identify the duty-holder who is responsible for protecting a right, and if there is no legal remedy when the duty-holder fails. When negative rights are violated, we know which duty-holder failed (for example, the torturer), and we have access to a remedy to hold that violator accountable (for example, by prosecuting them in court). Conversely, when positive rights are violated, there is no comparable mechanism that can keep duty-holders accountable. If an individual is hungry or homeless, whose responsibility is it to provide a solution? Should that individual be able to sue the government for failing to provide their right to food or housing? If such a lawsuit is brought before the courts, should the courts have the ability to force the government to spend more of its limited resources on food and housing, as opposed to, say, national defense? No. Because positive rights involve the distribution of scarce resources, which require difficult trade-offs between important societal goals, and therefore courts cannot and should not order legislatures to allocate their budgets in a certain way. As a result, without any access to a legal remedy, economic, social, and cultural rights are not really rights. One of the foremost human rights activists in the United States put it this way:

> I think of rights as only having meaning if it is possible to enforce them. I don't think rights are an abstract concept—I think they are a contract between the citizen and the state or community, and the citizen has to be able to enforce his or her side of that contract. Enforcing that contract means that there must be some mechanism of enforcement, and judicial enforcement seems to be the mechanism that we have hit upon in order to enforce rights. Therefore, from my standpoint, if one is to talk meaningfully of rights, one has to discuss what can be enforced through the judicial process. . . . The concern I have about economic and social rights is when

there are broad assertions which broadly speak of the right to shelter, education, social security, jobs, health care . . . then I think we get into territory that is unmanageable through the rights process or the judicial process. . . . So I think it's dangerous to the idea of civil and political rights to allow this idea of economic and social rights to flourish.[19]

Indeed, economic, social, and cultural rights are impossible to enforce not only because of the lack of a legal remedy, but also because it is impossible to determine when a violation has occurred, or who is responsible for it. Does the mere existence of hunger, homelessness, or sickness constitute a human rights violation? Some human rights activists have gone so far as to say that, yes, extreme poverty is itself a human rights violation.[20] In this case, who is the violator? Poverty can be influenced by an individual's own efforts, the actions of private businesses, the policies of local and national governments, the assistance of wealthy external donors, and even broader structural factors (such as the price of bread, the amount of air pollution, or the existence of violent conflict) that are outside the control of any of these actors. Because food, housing, and health care are subject to such complex structural causes, it is misguided to try to place blame on the state when these goods are lacking. Perhaps the poor person's government, like many in the developing world, lacks sufficient resources to guarantee access to food, housing, and health care for its poorest citizens. In this case, do wealthier countries like the United States then have the obligation to provide aid to all of these developing states? And which wealthy countries should share this burden? Given the economic problems and debt that most wealthy states face, it is unrealistic to assign them the duty to protect economic, social, and cultural rights throughout the rest of the world. Whereas we already have clearly elaborated norms, precise duties, and strong legal mechanisms to protect civil and political rights, we have none of these for economic, social, and cultural rights. As a result, while food, housing, and health care might be useful as policy guidelines, they cannot be conceived of as individual entitlements or rights.

In terms of policy guidelines, it is far more effective to focus on the protection of traditional civil and political rights like freedom of speech, rather than have the government get involved in providing economic goods. Food, housing, and health care are most easily acquired when the overall economy is growing, and economic growth is best facilitated by the free operation of private markets rather than by government interference in the economy. According to classical economic theory, whereas private markets distribute goods and set prices efficiently through the forces of supply and demand, state-run economies tend to stifle growth through their inefficiencies and opportunities for corruption. In order for the government to get directly involved in providing food, housing, and health care to all of its citizens, it must enact extremely high taxes, re-strictive regulations on business, and other interventions that end up being counterproductive to actually achieving access to these goods. This is why economic, social, and cultural rights have been described as a "So-viet, Third World creation" that "encourages unlimited government med-dling of the sort on which dictatorships thrive."[21] As much as we might want to guarantee access to food, housing, and health care, when govern-ments become the primary actor in providing these goods, it "entrench[es] the very problem it purports to address."[22] Not only does it stifle eco-nomic growth, but it also threatens the exercise of civil and political rights by expanding government and encouraging corruption. As the bru-tality and ultimate collapse of dozens of Marxist governments have shown, when governments expand their power into the economic sphere, they often justify restricting political freedoms in order to protect their economic power. It is a lose-lose scenario.

In sum, according to this argument, although humans do need food, housing, and health care in order to survive, such economic, social, and cul-tural rights are best conceived of as ideal goals and aspirations rather than human rights. As individual legal entitlements, only negative rights (such as freedom of speech, assembly, due process, and religion) can be protected within the judicial system. No legal remedy is available when someone is simply too poor to acquire food, housing, or health care. Positive rights are therefore not really rights at all. Even in the policy arena, food, housing, and health care are better provided when the state loosens its control over the economy and allows private market forces to distribute goods effi-ciently. Since economic, social, and cultural rights are ultimately counter-productive, priority should be given to the two-century history of traditional civil and political rights found in the US Constitution. In the end, human rights activists would be better off using their limited resources to protect rights that have gained a solid legal foundation and social consensus.

* * *

Conclusion

The debate about food, housing, and health care touches on a number of important philosophical, political, and economic questions. For example, are some of the rights listed in the Universal Declaration of Human Rights more important than others, or are all human rights indivisible? Interestingly, both sides in this debate question the notion of indivisibility, but they point to different rights as being more important than others.

Do human rights require legal enforcement in order to be considered valid (as legal positivists would suggest), or are human rights equally valuable as moral claims that inspire political action? Is legal enforcement possible in the absence of clearly defined duties to protect rights? Skepticism about the possibility

> **Think Again**
>
> In your opinion, which side of this debate made the better argument? Do you think that civil and political rights are fundamentally distinct from economic, social, and cultural rights? Are the legal duties involved in protecting economic, social, and cultural rights clear enough, or are the latter too vague and "aspirational"? Should states spend more of their resources on social safety nets and foreign aid, or would these policies be counterproductive and stifle economic growth?

of economic, social, and cultural rights being legally enforced has been a major reason why human rights NGOs have ignored these rights historically. One side in this debate argues not just that legal enforcement is possible for economic, social, and cultural rights, but also, and regardless, that legalization is not required anyway for these rights to be valid.[23]

More practically, does the attempt to ensure universal access to food, housing, and health care lead governments to become inefficient, corrupt, and dictatorial, or does it spur pro-poor growth and democratic participation? This was a central battleground of the Cold War, and the debate between neoliberalists and social democrats remains a key fissure in global economic policy. As the process of globalization has led societies throughout the world to open themselves to trade, privatize public assets, and reduce government intervention in the economy (as neoliberalists would recommend), protests have broken out like wildfire among those left unprotected by the new policies. This debate has also taken center stage in the struggle to enact health care reform in the United States beginning in 2009, as well as in the ongoing legislative fights over the US budget deficit.

While this debate about economic, social, and cultural rights remains unresolved, the majority of human rights NGOs and activists have taken sides. In the years since the Cold War ended, most human rights NGOs in the West have begun to accept the legitimacy of food, housing, and health care as important rights.[24] Groups like Amnesty International have incorporated economic, social, and cultural rights into their mission statements, and new NGOs have arisen that are specifically devoted to the rights to food, housing, and health care. Human rights NGOs in the West have finally heard the appeals from activists in the East and South to take these rights seriously. Today, the United States remains the only major actor that denies the equal legitimacy of economic, social, and cultural rights compared to civil and political rights.

This change, however, has not come without controversy. Some human rights activists worry that, even if economic, social, and cultural rights are valid human rights, they are not well suited to the kind of tactics that NGOs are adept at using. As Kenneth Roth, executive director of Human Rights Watch, explained, human rights NGOs have been successful because they employ naming and shaming strategies; that is, they identify specific violations by governments and compel them to stop.[25] According to Roth, many violations of economic, social, and cultural rights are complex and structural, so they do not easily fit into legal strategies and naming and shaming campaigns. As a result, NGOs should limit their efforts to focusing on "arbitrary and discriminatory" behavior by governments (e.g., burning down houses), which NGOs can have a greater impact in confronting, rather than issues of "distributive justice" (e.g., how a government should spend its budget). Other human rights NGOs, however, are moving headlong into distributive issues, analyzing government budgets and putting pressure on them to prioritize care of the poor and most vulnerable.[26] This has led to a dilemma for human rights activists. Should they focus their limited resources on using tactics that they know best, to the exclusion of important rights? Or should they devote their attention to the most pressing human rights, at the risk of spreading themselves too thin and having a limited impact on such a big and complex problem?[27]

> **Think Again**
>
> If you were the director of a human rights NGO, where would you spend your limited resources? For example, would you lobby to have individual political prisoners released (in which case you could see tangible results if successful), or would you lobby to change trade and foreign aid policies that affect the poor?

This is another debate that remains unresolved. One thing, however, is clear. Food, housing, and health care, which were long considered the "poor stepsisters" in the field of human rights, are now gaining much more attention from human rights NGOs, states, and international organizations in their efforts to make a real difference in the lives of the billion people who still suffer the horrible deprivation of extreme poverty.

Notes

1. Daniel Whelan, *Indivisible Human Rights: A History* (Philadelphia: University of Pennsylvania Press, 2010).

2. The Universal Declaration of Human Rights is available at http://www.un.org/en/documents/udhr.

3. Henry Shue, *Basic Rights* (Princeton: Princeton University Press, 1996), p. 19.

4. Paul Collier, *The Bottom Billion: Why the Poorest Countries Are Failing and What Can Be Done About It* (Oxford: Oxford University Press, 2007).

5. Lucie E. White and Jeremy Perelman, eds., *Stones of Hope: How African Activists Reclaim Human Rights to Challenge Global Poverty* (Palo Alto: Stanford University Press, 2011), jacket cover.

6. Joanne Bauer, "The Challenge to International Human Rights," in *Constructing Human Rights in the Age of Globalization,* edited by Mahmood Monshipouri et al. (Armonk, NY: Sharpe, 2003).

7. Isaiah Berlin, *Four Essays on Liberty* (Oxford: Oxford University Press, 1970).

8. For example, Nobel Prize–winning economist Amartya Sen showed that widespread famine has never occurred in modern democracies, because democratic governments must ultimately respond when people's suffering is so severe. See Amartya Sen, *Development as Freedom* (New York: Knopf, 1999), pp. 160–188.

9. Paul Hunt, *Reclaiming Social Rights: International and Comparative Perspectives* (Sudbury, MA: Dartmouth Publishing, 1996).

10. Shue, *Basic Rights,* p. 52.

11. Daniel Chong, *Freedom from Poverty: NGOs and Human Rights Praxis* (Philadelphia: University of Pennsylvania Press, 2010), pp. 44–47.

12. Asbjørn Eide, "Human Rights Requirements for Social and Economic Development," *Food Policy* 21, no. 1 (1996): 23–39.

13. For a range of specific examples, see Paul J. Nelson and Ellen Dorsey, *New Rights Advocacy: Changing Strategies of Development and Human Rights NGOs* (Washington, DC: Georgetown University Press, 2008); White and Perelman, *Stones of Hope*; Chong, *Freedom from Poverty.*

14. Eide, "Human Rights Requirements."

15. Patrus Anunias, "Implementing the Human Right to Food in Brazil," *World Hunger Notes,* February 8, 2009, http://www.worldhunger.org/articles/08/hrf/ananias.htm.

16. Jeffrey Sachs, *The End of Poverty: Economic Possibilities for Our Time* (New York: Penguin, 2005), pp. 288–308.

17. Shue, *Basic Rights,* p. 221, n. 5; emphasis added.

18. Berlin, *Four Essays on Liberty,* p. 122.

19. Aryeh Neier, "Perspectives on Economic, Social, and Cultural Rights," lecture at the Washington College of Law, American University, Washington, DC, January 19, 2006, http://www.wcl.american.edu/podcast/audio/20060119_WCL_Neier.mp3?rd=1.

20. Chong, *Freedom from Poverty,* pp. 56–58.

21. Philip Alston, "U.S. Ratification of the Covenant on Economic, Social, and Cultural Rights: The Need for an Entirely New Strategy," *American Journal of International Law* 84, no. 2 (1990): 383.

22. Thomas Sowell, "Poverty and Inequality: A Question of Injustice?" *The Economist*, March 11, 2004, http://www.economist.com/opinion/displayStory.cfm ?story_id=2499118.

23. See Saladin Meckled-García and Başak Çali, eds., *The Legalization of Human Rights* (London: Routledge, 2006), pp. 11–26.

24. See, for example, Nelson and Dorsey, *New Rights Advocacy*; and Chong, *Freedom from Poverty*.

25. Kenneth Roth, "Defending Economic, Social, and Cultural Rights: Practical Issues Faced by an International Human Rights Organization," *Human Rights Quarterly* 26, no. 1 (2004): 63–73.

26. A working group of NGOs has been created through the International Network for Economic, Social, and Cultural Rights for precisely this purpose. See "Budget Analysis and ESCR," http://www.escr-net.org/workinggroups/working groups_show.htm?doc_id=430934, accessed August 4, 2011.

27. For a description of how this dilemma has caused tensions within Amnesty International, see Stephen Hopgood, *Keepers of the Flame: Understanding Amnesty International* (Ithaca: Cornell University Press, 2006).

13

Do Transnational Corporations Violate Human Rights?

Walking through a Walmart store for the first time can be an overwhelming experience for any consumer. The company's slogan, "Save Money, Live Better," greets you on a sign over the front door. As you enter the giant warehouse-sized store, you might first approach the grocery section, where food items from every corner of the world line the shelves. You might pass by bananas from Honduras, soy sauce from Japan, cleaning products from France, or frozen fish transported thousands of miles from Namibia to your hometown. A few aisles away from the grocery section, you can find all varieties of clothing for men, women, and children, produced in China, Bangladesh, Lesotho, Mexico, and elsewhere. Next you might visit the electronics, toys, hardware, home furnishings, jewelry, pharmacy, or lawn and garden sections of the store. After shopping for all of your consumer needs, you then proceed to the cashier, where you are shocked to discover that you just paid a fraction of the cost that your ten different neighborhood stores would have charged you for purchasing the same items.

How can Walmart provide such a wide variety of consumer products at such low prices? It is because Walmart has perfected a business model that takes full advantage of the globalized economy, by relying on low margins and high volumes of sales. In other words, Walmart makes a tiny profit on each item that it sells, but it sells so many items that its total profits are enormous. In fact, Walmart has used this model to become one of the three largest **transnational corporations (TNCs)** in the world, with over $400 billion in annual revenues.[1] In order be profitable with this kind of business model, Walmart must run its operations very efficiently, buying products from its suppliers around the world at the lowest possible cost and cutting its overhead expenses. Walmart can use its size and buying power to negotiate lower prices from its suppliers, and lower taxes from the countries in which it operates. By selling such a high volume of consumer goods, it can take advantage of the efficiencies inherent in an economy of scale.

For example, much of the food that Walmart sells is produced within the **industrial food system**, which relies on factory farms using modern technology (for example, tractors, chemical pesticides, and fertilizers) to produce and transport large quantities of food around the globe. Many of the manufactured products that Walmart sells are made in export processing zones in developing countries, which are areas that have lower taxes and deregulated factories in order to attract foreign investment. Walmart is the prototypical example of a TNC that has succeeded in the current era of globalization, in which goods and services are being produced and transported across the world at an unprecedented scale and speed. In today's global economy, most of the products that we buy have raw materials that originate in one set of countries, are manufactured or processed in another set of countries, and then are sold in an entirely different set of countries.

Walmart's success is therefore inextricably linked to the integration of the global economy. Globalization, in turn, has been facilitated by the expansion of neoliberal economic policies in most of the world's states. In the past few decades, many states have adopted policies that reduce the government's role in their own economy, and increase the role of private actors such as investors, entrepreneurs, and TNCs. Neoliberal policies include measures such as the following:

- Increasing foreign exports and imports, by reducing trade barriers such as tariffs and quotas.
- Encouraging foreign investment, by lowering corporate taxes and other restrictions on the foreign ownership of businesses.
- Privatization, or selling government-owned industries to private investors.
- Deregulation, or eliminating labor rights and environmental laws that regulate how businesses can function.
- Reducing government spending, to open up space for private markets to fill.

Many of these neoliberal policies were imposed on developing countries in the 1980s by the **International Monetary Fund (IMF)** and **World Bank**, as a condition for receiving badly needed loans from these international institutions. The IMF and World Bank believed that these policies would stimulate private markets in poor countries and result in economic growth that would benefit everyone. Neoliberal policies were therefore explicitly designed to increase the power and global reach of TNCs like Walmart. In this task they succeeded, as many TNCs grew in size in the latter part of the twentieth century to rival some of the world's largest states.

Walmart has certainly succeeded in earning profits and expanding its operations, but has its growth come at the expense of human rights? Walmart has come under heavy criticism from human rights activists who allege that it cuts costs by trampling over the rights of factory workers, farmers, poor communities, retail-store employees, and its own customers. In response, Walmart's supporters claim that its role in the global economy actually improves human rights, and that any individual violations that may occur are not the responsibility of the company as a whole.

Argument 1
Transnational corporations such as Walmart systematically violate human rights.

According to this argument, Walmart has become one of the world's largest corporations by systematically violating human rights around the world. These violations are not unique to Walmart; in fact, they are symptomatic of some of the fundamental problems in the global economy, and of the inherent weaknesses of neoliberal economics. Walmart, because of its low-cost business model, is a particularly egregious violator.

First, let us examine Walmart's grocery section, and how the industrial food system violates human rights. When food is produced on such a massive scale, it often displaces small family farmers in poor countries, who depend on farming for their survival. Walmart purchases huge quantities of agricultural products from other TNCs such as Cargill and Chiquita, which own large tracts of land in developing countries. When TNCs dominate the most fertile land in developing countries, poor farmers are pushed to the margins. The only option for many small farmers is to grow cash crops for export, rather than undertake subsistence farming for their families and local communities, or to go to work for the corporations for low wages. Moreover, the large corporations are able to take advantage of economies of scale, invest in pesticides and fertilizers, and often receive subsidies from governments in wealthy countries. This allows the TNCs to produce the bananas, fish, soy sauce, and other food products at a very low cost. While this might be good for Walmart's customers, who see the benefit at the cash register, it is bad for small farmers in poor countries, who cannot compete with the TNCs and cannot earn enough money for their cash crops. Peasant farmers are therefore run out of business, denied the right to own land and earn a decent livelihood. This process has been repeated over and over again in developing countries over the past few decades, resulting in millions of rural families moving to the cities in a desperate search for employment. Because not enough jobs or infrastructure exists in the cities for the massive influx of people, urban areas have become centers of slums, unemployment, crime, and the spread of disease.

Moreover, the primary reason why factory farms operated by Walmart's suppliers are so efficient in producing cheap food is because they rely so heavily on artificial inputs that harm the environment and cause health problems to everyone involved in the process. The cows, pigs, chickens, and fish that make their way onto Walmart's shelves are raised in horrifying conditions. They are packed together in small spaces, sitting in their own feces, injected with hormones to grow quickly, then shot full of antibiotics to prevent the diseases that these living conditions create. While animal rights are technically not human rights, these animals should at least have the right not to be brutally exploited just to save Walmart's customers a few dollars. Additionally, the animals are not the only ones harmed by factory farms. Because the farms rely on chemical pesticides, fertilizers, and gasoline-powered machines, the waste runoff from these farms pollutes the surrounding communities. Land that is located close to industrial farms is rendered less productive, and local communities see an increase in waterborne and other illnesses. This pollution violates the right to livelihood and the right to health, particularly in less developed countries where citizens are already vulnerable to the problems caused by poverty.

In addition, the industrial food system threatens the health of Walmart's own customers. While the price of the food is undeniably cheap, the industrial chemicals inevitably find their way into the food, making it less healthy than organic or naturally produced food. The industrial food system operated by TNCs has resulted in an increase in health problems in wealthy countries, such as cancer, heart disease, diabetes, resistance to antibiotics, and food allergies.[2]

One example of Walmart's role in the industrial food system and the negative effects produced by it is the story of Atlantic salmon.[3] Walmart purchases the majority of its Atlantic salmon from the nation of Chile, which does not even border the Atlantic Ocean. The salmon are produced on aquaculture farms, and raised from birth to death in overcrowded tanks. The salmon are injected with seventy-five times the level of antibiotics injected into salmon produced in other countries. The industrial waste from these farms is largely unregulated by the Chilean government, which adopted neoliberal policies in the 1980s under pressure from the IMF during the reign of its authoritarian leader Augusto Pinochet. The waste from these farms has entered the ocean and threatens the livelihoods of local fishermen and the health of coastal communities. Many local fishermen and farmers have therefore been pushed into working on the factory farms for minimum wages in poor conditions.[4] Labor conditions on these farms have also been deregulated by the Chilean government. Because these conditions have allowed Walmart's suppliers to produce fish so cheaply, Walmart is able to sell Atlantic salmon for $5 per pound.

Next, let us continue our human rights tour through the sections of Walmart where clothes, toys, electronics, and household products are sold. As in the case of food, many of these products are manufactured in countries that have deregulated their environmental and labor laws, reduced corporate taxes, and opened themselves to foreign investment in order to attract TNCs. Because Walmart's business model relies on the purchase of these products at the lowest possible price, there are tremendous pressures for its suppliers to cut costs. Many of these suppliers operate sweatshops, which pay unlivably low wages to their workers, force them to work overtime without pay, provide unsafe working conditions, and prevent employees from forming unions. The factories often hire children, foreign immigrants, and uneducated women, because these groups are perceived to be more dexterous and obedient, thus making them more efficient workers.

For example, in 1996 an investigation by the National Labor Committee found that Walmart's clothing suppliers in Bangladesh and Honduras hired children as young as twelve, who were routinely beaten, forced to work up to fourteen hours a day for seven days a week, and paid as low as 7 cents per hour.[5] Another investigation, in 2011, found that Walmart's clothing suppliers in Jordan engaged in beatings of workers, forced overtime, payment lower than the national minimum wage, and even the rape of female employees.[6] Workers at the factories in Jordan were primarily migrants from Sri Lanka, who slept in dormitories provided by the factories, which lacked decent living conditions.

Indeed, because workers in sweatshops often migrate to the export processing zones from rural areas or foreign countries, they are often held in debt bondage. This is a form of modern-day slavery and human trafficking, in which an impoverished worker takes a loan in order to migrate to the factory, but the loan takes them months or years to pay off. Thus, because of the low wages earned by the worker and the exorbitant interest rates of the loan, the worker is essentially forced to work in the factory for free. In 2012, some of these indebted migrant workers revolted at a factory in Thailand that supplies Walmart, a revolt that the supplier subsequently suppressed.[7]

Similar kinds of working conditions exist in factories all over the world. While neoliberal economic policies purport to help grow economies by creating jobs and increasing investment, in reality they have resulted in a **race to the bottom**, in which governments lower their labor and environmental standards in order to attract foreign investment. Governments in less developed countries often do not even enforce their minimal regulations, out of fear that large corporations will move their operations elsewhere.[8] Large TNCs like Walmart are able to negotiate with, pressure, or bribe government officials into permitting these sweatshops to exist. For example, in 2012 Walmart was found to have given the Mexican government millions of dollars in bribes to obtain construction permits throughout the country.[9] Neoliberal policies have increased the size of corporations like Walmart, and corporations have translated that economic power into political power.

The globalized, neoliberal economic system in which TNCs like Walmart operate and the human rights violations that it produces illustrate what is known as **dependency theory**. Dependency theory explains why some states have not succeeded in developing while other states are wealthy and prosperous. In contrast to neoliberalists, dependency theorists argue that the current global economic system is inherently exploitative, allowing the rich and powerful to manipulate the poor and developing states in order to benefit themselves.[10] As a result, TNCs like Walmart are able to take advantage of the cheap resources and labor in developing countries; however, instead of these countries and people prospering from their involvement with Walmart, their economies remain stagnant and in many cases their people are worse off.

The last stop in our tour of Walmart's human rights abuses takes place at the cash register, where we discover that even workers in wealthy countries are exploited for the cheap prices that Walmart's customers pay at the register. Cashiers and other employees at Walmart's retail stores are offered low pay and inadequate health care benefits.[11] These employees are unable to organize and bargain collectively for better wages and working conditions, because Walmart has systematically harassed and opposed union activists in its stores.[12] For example, Walmart has included anti-union propaganda in its training materials for new employees, and it has fired and discriminated against union activists.

All of these activities are clearly human rights violations. The Universal Declaration of Human Rights provides for the freedom from slavery in Article 4; the right to earn fair wages, have decent working conditions, and form unions in Article 23; and the right to health and an adequate livelihood in Article 25. Countries that have ratified the International Covenant on Economic, Social, and Cultural Rights have legally committed themselves to protecting these rights, as have countries that are members of the **International Labour Organization (ILO)**. Although Walmart and other TNCs are not held directly accountable under these international treaties, they are responsible for upholding the national standards that should be based upon these international treaties.[13]

In sum, according to this argument Walmart and other TNCs like it systematically violate human rights as a result of failed neoliberal economic policies. Neoliberalism has opened up less developed countries to the influence of large corporations, while lowering labor and environmental standards in those countries. Poor farmers are unable to compete with large agribusiness in wealthy countries; poor laborers are unable to organize and collectively bargain for better working conditions; and poor communities are unable to prevent environmental degradation of their own land. TNCs like Walmart are able to exploit these gaps in the global economy to produce consumer goods cheaply, making huge profits for their wealthy shareholders. Walmart's customers might be saving money, but the world is not living better.

Argument 2
Transnational corporations such as Walmart improve human rights.

According to this argument, Walmart improves the lives of millions of people around the world. By distributing consumer goods with unprecedented efficiency, Walmart helps ensure that basic needs are accessible to low-income customers. Its economic activities also have spillover effects that benefit workers, their families, and their surrounding communities. Neoliberal policies have facilitated this process by making it easier and cheaper to transport goods across national borders. Globalization and industrialization have resulted in economic growth and a massive increase in poor people's standard of living across the globe.

Walmart does indeed source its grocery products from all corners of the globe, participating in the industrial food system. But this system should be viewed as an enormous human rights success, rather than a violation of rights. Large factory farms are able to produce huge quantities of food at a fraction of the cost of traditional farming methods. This was proven by the **green revolution**, in which industrial agricultural technologies were transferred to developing countries in the 1960s and beyond. These technologies included mechanized farming equipment, irrigation infrastructure, climate-controlled storage facilities, high-yielding seeds, and chemical pesticides and fertilizers. The green revolution resulted in the skyrocketing of agricultural production in the countries where these technologies were adopted.[14] This is critical to human rights because many of these countries, such as China, India, and the Philippines, suffered from chronic hunger and were at risk of widespread famine. Industrial agricultural technology and a globally integrated food system have helped feed billions of people across the world. Thanks to the industrial food system, world grain production increased by 260 percent from the 1960s to the 1980s,[15] and the average person in the developing world is now able to consume 25 percent more calories than before the green revolution.[16] Cheap and widely available food benefits poor consumers as much as wealthy ones. With global population expected to rise to over 10 billion people in the next few decades, it is more important than ever to produce and distribute high quantities of affordable food.[17]

According to this argument, the belief that the globalized, neoliberal economy is exploitative and has led to the underdevelopment of the poorest countries is incorrect. Rather, as according to modernization theory, all countries and economies must undergo a similar, albeit sometimes painful, process of development.[18] For example, although it is true that some peasant farmers cannot compete with the efficiency of larger factory farms, and so must move out of farming and into a new profession, this is not the fault of industrial agriculture, or of Walmart's purchasing of industrial food. Subsistence farming is simply an outdated technique, and the process of development inevitably requires a shift in the way that economies are structured. All developed countries have gone through a similar transition, as the United States did in the nineteenth and early twentieth centuries, when family farms were sold to large corporations and farmers went to the cities to find employment. The result of this industrial transition was a massive increase in wealth and living standards in these countries. While economic shifts always displace some people, the overall effect for human rights in developing countries has been and should continue to be overwhelmingly positive.

Therefore, the answer to this problem is not to restrict the activities of TNCs like Walmart, but rather to increase their activities, especially in poor, developing countries.

Regarding the case of Atlantic salmon farming in Chile, while it is true that aquaculture facilities are not pristine, and create some environmental challenges, again this is no different than the case of most US factories of the past century. Chile has experienced dynamic economic growth in the years since it adopted the neoliberal economic policies that attracted foreign investment. Chile's gross domestic product grew from roughly $20 billion in 1983 to $250 billion in 2011, thanks to a 150-fold increase in foreign investment over the same period. The average Chilean family tripled their annual income over that period.[19] Once a country like Chile grows economically, it gains the capacity to clean up its waste and improve its environmental regulations. Globalization and economic development in Chile also helped to spur a democratic transition in the 1990s, as a growing middle class demanded greater accountability from its government. Walmart's purchase of Atlantic salmon in Chile has contributed to the process of encouraging economic growth, distributing healthy food, and expanding democratic freedoms.

What about the other consumer products that Walmart sells, which are made in factories around the world, factories that critics label as "sweatshops"? These manufacturing facilities, on the whole, provide far better working conditions in developing countries than subsistence farming could ever offer. Subsistence farmers are vulnerable to the weather and natural disasters, and often face economic insecurity in the seasons when their crops are not in harvest. In contrast, factories provide a stable form of income and working conditions that are an improvement over work on a subsistence farm. This is why millions of people line up to get the jobs offered in the factories of Walmart's suppliers. These people are not forced into these working conditions; they desperately want these jobs because they represent economic progress. It is true that workers in these factories earn low wages, work long hours, and do not receive the same kinds of health and safety benefits as workers in wealthy countries. However, these are the exact same conditions that existed in US and European factories in the past century. The working conditions that exist in these factories may not be attractive to an American worker today, but they represent a step forward for poor workers, toward greater economic empowerment.

The presence of these factories also has spillover effects that benefit local communities in developing countries. The suppliers that make Walmart's products not only create jobs in these communities, but also build infrastructure such as roads and public utilities, pay taxes to support local governments, train people to use new technologies, and transfer Western values that are consistent with human rights. This is why countries that have become more integrated into the global economy have on average achieved greater economic growth and an increase in living standards for their poorest citizens.[20] Chile's economic success story has been shared by countries such as China, Thailand, South Korea, India, Turkey, and Mexico. The successes of globalization have reduced the percentage of the world's people living in extreme poverty by over half in the past few decades. This means that almost a billion people today are able to meet their basic needs, and achieve their right to an adequate livelihood, who were not able to do this before the recent spread of globalization.

Some legitimate human rights violations do exist in some of these factories. When women are raped, immigrants are held as slaves, or child labor laws are violated, then someone should be held accountable. But this is not the responsibility of TNCs like Walmart, because Walmart has very little control over the actual working conditions that prevail at these factories. The suppliers of Walmart's products are subcontractors, meaning that they are independent companies that are not legal subsidiaries of Walmart. Walmart simply purchases the products at a contracted price; the factories themselves are owned by a different corporation in the country where it operates. Walmart has neither the resources nor the authority to monitor and regulate all of the labor and environmental practices that occur at every link of its supply chain. It is the responsibility of the corporations that actually own the factories to regulate their manufacturing processes.

> **Think Again**
>
> Why do you think people would line up to work in such poor conditions? Do you think they perceive these factory jobs as an opportunity for empowerment? Or do they seek these jobs out of desperation and a lack of other options?

Walmart's legal obligation is to comply with all of the national laws that apply in the countries where it operates. In general, Walmart does comply with these laws. If these laws insufficiently protect labor and environmental rights in developing countries, or they are unenforced, then this is the responsibility of the governments of the countries involved. For example, Walmart cannot be held accountable for a low minimum wage in China; the Chinese government is responsible. Although Walmart's activities have positive benefits for human rights around the world, TNCs are obligated primarily to their shareholders to make a profit. If they do not make a profit, they cease to exist, and the jobs and economic benefits that the TNCs provide would disappear alongside them.

In sum, according to this argument Walmart's low-cost, high-volume business model has been a boon to poor workers in developing countries, as well as to customers in wealthy countries. Neoliberalism has resulted overall in economic growth that has raised the living standards of the world's poorest people. People are not only saving money, but also living better. Although some people inevitably get displaced or exploited in this process, it is the responsibility of their own national governments to provide the appropriate remedies or hold the actual violators accountable.

* * *

Conclusion

The arguments elaborated here illustrate the fact that the debate about the effect of transnational corporations is not just about Walmart's specific practices, but also about the broader impact that global economic integration has had on human rights. As states have increasingly adopted neoliberal policies, opening their economies to global trade and investment, TNCs have become ever more important actors in the protection or violation of human rights. Because TNCs operate across multiple states, it is often difficult to hold them accountable to any single set of national or international laws. As a result, human rights organizations have charged many corporations, including Walmart, of systematically circumventing national laws in order to exploit people for higher profits.

Human rights experts are somewhat divided about the overall impact of neoliberalism and economic globalization on the protection of human rights. Those who are optimistic about the effects of globalization believe that increased trade and foreign investment lead to the spread of information and cultural exchange, putting pressure on authoritarian regimes to implement democratic reforms.[21] Indeed, there is some statistical evidence showing that states with higher levels of foreign investment engage in greater protection of civil and political rights. Optimists also believe that neoliberalism produces economic growth, which helps poor people achieve their economic and social rights.[22]

On the other hand, critics of neoliberalism argue that, even when free trade succeeds in producing economic growth, most of this growth bypasses or actively displaces the poor.[23] Governments become aligned with foreign investors and corporations, and abdicate their responsibility to care for their own citizens. Developing states fail to protect their own struggling industries, which remain unable to compete with the large TNCs. States reduce their rates of corporate taxation and reduce their spending on social security, making their poorest citizens more vulnerable to poverty and disease. States eliminate labor and environmental regulations, making it easier for corporations to exploit workers and the land. Even as corporations outsource their jobs to developing nations, blue-collar workers in wealthy states also suffer from unemployment or depressed wages.

Whichever side is correct in this debate, both sides do agree that corporations can commit some serious human rights violations in the global economy (see Figure 13.1). However, the global reach of TNCs makes it difficult to devise effective remedies for these violations when they occur. Many people would argue that governments should be responsible for regulating the economic activities that occur on their own territory. The problem is that some of these governments are authoritarian and corrupt, and are more interested in profiting from the special deals that they strike with TNCs than in protecting their own citizens. Even if a state is genuinely interested in labor and environmental regulations, less developed states have little leverage over foreign investors and corporations. If these states raise the cost of doing business too much, then TNCs like Walmart will simply shift their purchasing contracts to a state where production is cheaper. So there is tremendous competitive pressure for poorer states to eliminate these regulations. These competitive pressures also exist for the corporations themselves, particularly the ones that own the factories or farms directly. Many of these corporations, including those that supply Walmart's products, operate on razor-thin profit margins, and so if their labor costs rise, then they will not be able to compete successfully.

In order to overcome this "race to the bottom," some experts have recommended that states work together to implement a set of common global regulations, which would prevent corporations from shifting production to the state with the lowest standards. However, for the same reason that states failed to integrate rules on workers' rights and labor standards into the World Trade Organization and global trade regime, the problem with this approach is the level of international coordination that would be required for such global standards. Some states, such as China and India, have a strong self-interest in maintaining the status quo, because their large pool of cheap labor has given them a competitive advantage in the global economy and sparked economic growth. Even if states could come together and agree on stronger labor and environmental rules, the system of global monitoring and enforcement would have to be powerful

---

Figure 13.1 Unocal's Complicity with Human Rights Abuses

Unocal was a major oil and natural gas company based in California (it later merged with Chevron, one of the world's largest TNCs). In the 1990s, Unocal managed the construction of the Yadana gas pipeline in the nation of Burma, which was run by one of the world's most repressive dictatorships. Human rights groups such as EarthRights International documented serious human rights abuses that were committed during Unocal's construction of the pipeline, such as forced labor, forced relocation, land confiscation, and the torture, rape, and murder of the pipeline's opponents.[24] Human rights activists called on Unocal to end these violations, but the corporation denied responsibility, claiming that it had no control over abuses committed by the authoritarian government.

EarthRights International, with legal assistance from the Center for Constitutional Rights, responded by suing Unocal in a US court in California. The lawsuit, *Doe v. Unocal*, was filed on behalf of thirteen Burmese peasants who had suffered abuses.[25] Under the **Alien Tort Claims Act** of 1789, US courts were given the authority to award damages to foreign nationals who suffered personal injury outside the United States. Human rights activists argued that Unocal hired Burmese military units to secure construction of the pipeline, knowing that these units were responsible for human rights violations. When the courts decided in 2002 that the lawsuit could proceed, Unocal settled the case out of court, compensating the Burmese villagers an unspecified sum of money. This marked the first time in history that the Alien Tort Claims Act was successfully used in the United States to enforce human rights standards against a corporation.

Unfortunately, the successful lawsuit has not ended the violations taking place along the Yadana gas pipeline. Construction on the pipeline was completed in 1998, and it is now managed by a consortium of corporations from France, Thailand, Burma, and the United States. The pipeline runs through a region where an ethnic minority group, the Karen, are involved in a civil war with the Burmese military. The military has continued to protect the pipeline, to benefit from foreign investment, and to commit human rights violations in its war against the Karen people.

---

and intrusive in order to ensure that some states do not cheat the system. Though people might debate the merits of having such a strong international enforcement body, the existence of so broad a body is currently not feasible. As a result, other experts have recommended less overarching measures at the global level, such as the **Tobin tax**, proposed by Nobel Prize–winning economist James Tobin. Tobin suggested that all financial transactions that cross national borders could be taxed a small amount, perhaps 0.5 percent of their value, in order to raise billions of dollars each year. The funds collected could then be put into a global fund to assist populations who are displaced by economic globalization.[26] Although ideas like this have been embraced by many human rights advocates, they have never taken hold at the international level.

Because states have not proven to be effective regulators of the global economic system, many human rights organizations have turned their attention on the largest TNCs themselves. Human rights activists have targeted most of the major global brands in the past two decades, such as Nike, Gap, Starbucks, McDonald's, ExxonMobil, and many others. Realizing that the major corporations must maintain a decent reputation in order to continue making profits, activists shine the spotlight on human rights violations in order to exercise some leverage over the corporation responsible. Large TNCs like Walmart, Nike, or Starbucks do not want their brand names associated with slavery, child labor, and environmental destruction. Protesters have demonstrated outside retail stores, written letters, worked through the media, and even attended shareholder meetings to pressure corporations to adopt voluntary codes of conduct to govern their operations around the world.

Human rights organizations have been largely successful in this effort. Most of the world's major corporations have promised to monitor the labor and environmental practices that occur throughout their supply chain, and even occasionally submit to independent outside monitoring. This movement has come to be known as **corporate social responsibility**—the idea that corporations can still make their customers happy, and continue to make profits, by paying more attention to the impact of their operations on human rights and the environment. Even Walmart, which human rights organizations condemned for many years, finally committed itself to corporate social responsibility in 2005. Walmart now produces an annual "global responsibility" report detailing the results of internal audits that the corporation conducts on its suppliers throughout the world.[27] Factories that supply Walmart's products are encouraged to improve their energy efficiency and their labor standards, and factories that fail Walmart's audits are dropped by the corporation. In 2008 Walmart led a group of clothing retailers in pressuring the authoritarian government of Uzbekistan to crack down on child labor in the cotton industry, and forced its suppliers to trace their sources of cotton.[28] Walmart has also expanded its offerings of local and organic produce in its retail stores. In addition, Walmart has earned industry awards for its commitment to diversity in the workplace, and for its support for humanitarian relief in natural disasters such as Hurricane Katrina.[29]

Thus, for Walmart and many other large TNCs, the move toward corporate social responsibility has seemed to make a difference in their labor and environmental practices. While human rights organizations have not been able to reform states' economic policies, they have successfully affected the TNCs directly. However, some human rights activists remain unconvinced. They argue that corporations' commitments to social responsibility amount to little more than public relations campaigns, and have resulted in few improvements for farmers, the working poor, or their communities. They accuse Walmart of whitewashing (or in the case of environmental practices, **greenwashing**) its destructive economic activities, simply to present a good face to its customers.[30] For example, a 2010 investigation into Walmart's sourcing of supposedly socially responsible jewelry in Bolivia found that its mining of gold and silver was just as environmentally and socially destructive as the mining practices of socially irresponsible companies.[31] And in 2012, the biggest pension fund in the Netherlands made an unprecedented move to divest itself from Walmart, after Walmart failed to reform its anti-union practices.[32] In fact, cases of corporations sidestepping their own social responsibility promises have become so common that they have given rise to the "business and human rights" movement. This movement seeks to reduce the negative impact of TNCs like Walmart by holding them accountable to international human rights law, rather than relying on voluntary codes of conduct.[33]

One alternative solution to the problems of the neoliberal global economy is to support **fair trade**. Fair trade companies question the assumption that the only purpose of a corporation is to make a profit. Instead, these companies make it their primary mission to maximize the benefit that poor workers, poor communities, and other stakeholders receive. Companies like Equal Exchange and Ten Thousand Villages use global economic linkages to ensure that workers are paid a living wage, provided safe and healthy working conditions, and have a positive environmental impact while remaining financially sustainable. Of course, the ultimate power to decide whether fair trade will succeed rests with consumers, who can vote with their wallets whether to support companies that place human rights at the forefront of their mission.

In sum, as neoliberal policies have integrated the world's economies and increased the power of transnational corporations, globalization has produced both positive and negative effects. Although the global activities of TNCs have come under unprecedented scrutiny by human rights activists, it remains to be seen whether corporate social responsibility represents a substantial movement of the larger TNCs toward truly fair trade, or is mere window-dressing to conceal ongoing human rights abuses.

Notes

1. Walmart Annual Report, 2012, p. 19, http://www.walmartstores.com/sites/annual-report/2012/default.aspx.

2. Leo Horrigan, Robert S. Lawrence, and Polly Walker, "How Sustainable Agriculture Can Address the Environmental and Human Health Harms of Industrial Agriculture," *Environmental Health Perspectives* 110, no. 5 (May 2002): 445–456.

3. Charles Fishman, "The Story of Wal-Mart and Chilean Salmon," *Salon,* January 23, 2006, http://reclaimdemocracy.org/walmart/2006/fishman_chile_salmon_farm.php.

4. Jimmy Langman, "Atlantic Salmon a Fishy Tale: Chilean Industry Criticized for Pollution, Sneaky Labeling," *San Francisco Chronicle,* April 1, 2002, http://www.sfgate.com/green/article/Atlantic-Salmon-a-fishy-tale-Chilean-industry-2858353.php.

5. Labor and Worklife Program, "Children Found Sewing Clothing for Wal-Mart, Hanes, and Other U.S. and European Companies," Harvard Law School, October 2006, http://www.law.harvard.edu/programs/lwp/NLC_childlabor.html.

6. Charles Kernigan, "Sexual Predators and Serial Rapists Run Wild at Wal-Mart Supplier in Jordan" (Pittsburgh: Institute for Global Labour and Human Rights, June 2011).

7. UNI Global Union, "UNI Calls on Walmart to End Debt Bondage in Thailand," May 15, 2012, http://www.uniglobalunion.org/Apps/UNINews.nsf/vwLkpById/E04FE63DF1BC8639C12579FF00429D1D.

8. John Ruggie, "Protect, Respect, and Remedy: A Framework for Business and Human Rights," UN Human Rights Council, April 7, 2008, http://www2.ohchr.org/english/bodies/hrcouncil/docs/8session/A-HRC-8-5.doc.

9. David Barstow, "Vast Mexico Bribery Case Hushed Up by Wal-Mart After Top-Level Struggle," *New York Times,* April 22, 2012.

10. J. Samuel Valenzuela and Arturo Valenzuela, "Modernization and Dependency: Alternative Perspectives in the Study of Latin American Underdevelopment," *Comparative Politics* 10, no. 4 (July 1978): 535–557.

11. Susanna Kim, "Walmart Cuts Employee Health Benefits," *ABC News,* October 21, 2011, http://abcnews.go.com/blogs/business/2011/10/walmart-cuts-employee-health-care-benefits.

12. Carol Pier, "Discounting Rights: Wal-Mart's Violation of US Workers' Right to Freedom of Association," Human Rights Watch, May 1, 2007, http://www.hrw.org/reports/2007/04/30/discounting-rights-0.

13. Ruggie, "Protect, Respect, and Remedy."

14. Gordon Conway, *The Doubly Green Revolution: Food for All in the Twenty-First Century* (New York: Comstock, 1999), chap. 4.

15. Henery W. Kindall and David Pementel, "Constraints on the Expansion of the Global Food Supply," *Ambio* 23, no. 3 (May 1994): 198–205.

16. Conway, *The Doubly Green Revolution.*

17. Robert S. Chen, "Global Agriculture, Environment, and Hunger: Past, Present, and Future Links," *Environmental Impact Assessment Review* 10, no. 4 (1990): 335–358.

18. Valenzuela and Valenzuela, "Modernization and Dependency."

19. Google Public Data, http://www.google.com/publicdata, accessed July 20, 2012. All figures reported in constant US dollars.

20. David Dollar, "Globalization, Inequality, and Poverty Since 1980," World Bank Development Research Group, November 2001, ftp://www.econ.bgu.ac.il /courses/Globalization_and_Development/Notes/Globalization-inequality-and -poverty.pdf.

21. Julie Harrelson-Stephens, "Achieving Human Rights: The Globalization Debate," in *Exploring International Human Rights,* edited by Rhonda L. Callaway and Julie Harrelson-Stephens (Boulder: Lynne Rienner, 2007).

22. Paul Krugman, "In Praise of Cheap Labor: Bad Jobs at Bad Wages Are Better Than No Jobs at All," *Slate,* March 27, 1997, http://www.slate.com /articles/business/the_dismal_science/1997/03/in_praise_of_cheap_labor.html.

23. Robert McCorquodale and Richard Fairbrother, "Globalization and Human Rights," in *Exploring International Human Rights,* edited by Rhonda L. Callaway and Julie Harrelson-Stephens (Boulder: Lynne Rienner Publishers, 2007).

24. EarthRights International, "The Yadana Pipeline," http://www.earthrights .org/campaigns/yadana-pipeline, accessed July 22, 2012.

25. *Doe v. Unocal,* 248 F.3d 915, US Court of Appeals, Ninth Circuit (2001).

26. James Tobin, "A Proposal for International Monetary Reform," *Eastern Economic Journal* 4, nos. 3–4 (July–October 1978): 153–159.

27. Walmart's reports on global responsibility are available through the Social Funds website, at http://www.socialfunds.com/csr/profile.cgi/1908.html, accessed July 22, 2012.

28. Marc Gunther, "Wal-Mart: A Bully Benefactor," *CNNMoney,* December 5, 2008, http://money.cnn.com/2008/12/02/news/companies/walmart_gunther.fortune /index.htm.

29. See, for example, the "2010 Awards and Recognition" section of Wal-mart's 2011 report on global responsibility, at http://www.walmartstores.com/sites /ResponsibilityReport/2011/awards.aspx, accessed July 22, 2012.

30. Stacy Mitchell, "Walmart's Greenwash," Institute for Local Self-Reliance, March 2012, http://www.ilsr.org/wp-content/uploads/2012/03/walmart-greenwash -report.pdf.

31. Rachel Cernansky, "Walmart's Human Rights– and Eco-Friendly Jewelry Line Is Neither," *AlterNet,* January 7, 2011, http://www.alternet.org/environment /149453/walmart's_human_rights-_and_eco-friendly_jewelry_line_is_neither ?page=1.

32. Lila Shapiro, "Walmart Blacklisted by Major Pension Fund over Poor Labor Practices," *Huffington Post,* January 5, 2012, http://www.huffingtonpost.com /2012/01/05/walmart-blacklist-abp-pension-fund_n_1186384.html.

33. Joanne Bauer, "Business and Human Rights: An Interview with Joanne Bauer," University of Navarre, IESE Business School, September 2011, http:// www.iese.edu/es/files/%20La%20vision%20de...%20(inglés)_tcm5–71120.pdf.

14

Does the Right to Health Justify a Violation of Property Rights?

AIDS has become one of the most deadly diseases of the twenty-first century. AIDS likely began in West Africa in the early twentieth century, but it exploded into a global pandemic in the 1990s. HIV was first identified in the United States in 1981, as a virus that primarily affected homosexual males, intravenous drug users, and recipients of blood transfusions. However, HIV quickly spread to new populations and new regions. By 2010, there were 34 million people living with HIV/AIDS, the majority being located in sub-Saharan Africa or Asia.[1] Although there are still high-risk groups who are more vulnerable to contracting HIV, the virus has spread to men, women, and children, and AIDS kills approximately 2 million people each year. Poverty has become the single greatest risk factor for contracting HIV.

Beginning in the early 1990s, medical researchers began to develop a range of antiretroviral drugs that would make it possible for people living with HIV/AIDS to stay alive longer. Although several medications are used in combination in antiretroviral treatments, the most common drug is azidothymidine (AZT), which was first created under a grant from the US National Institutes of Health.[2] The US pharmaceutical company GlaxoSmithKline developed AZT for clinical use, and acquired a patent to sell the medication to the public. Several other drug companies, such as Bristol-Myers Squibb, Merck, and Pfizer, also developed and patented components of antiretroviral drugs. Today, antiretrovirals are used not only to keep HIV from spreading in the body, but also to prevent the transmission of HIV from pregnant mothers to their children. These medicines are now keeping millions of people alive who would otherwise be dead.

And yet, over a decade after antiretroviral drugs became widely available in the United States, only a tiny fraction of AIDS patients in low- and middle-income countries were receiving the medicine. As of 2003, fewer than 10 percent of people suffering from AIDS could gain access to treatment, which meant that AIDS was a death sentence for the overwhelming majority of people who contracted it.[3] In part, this was because the countries of sub-Saharan Africa, where HIV spread most quickly, lacked adequate health infrastructure, such as clinics, doctors, nurses, and health educators. As a result, many AIDS patients did not get tested for HIV early enough, or did not know about ways to prevent and treat the disease. However, a major reason why the rate of treatment was so low in poor countries was because they could not afford the cost of the antiretroviral drugs. GlaxoSmithKline and other pharmaceutical companies charged over $12,000 per year for the drug regimen, while the average annual income in many developing countries was less than $1,000. There was no way for the governments of these countries or their citizens to afford the medicine that was widely available in wealthy countries.

The prices of antiretroviral drugs throughout the world remained high because most states are members of the World Trade Organization, an international body designed to facilitate more open trade. One treaty that governs membership in the WTO is the **TRIPS (Trade Related Aspects of Intellectual Property Rights) Agreement**, in which states promise to respect the patents, or intellectual property rights, held by corporations in other countries.[4] In other words, states promised not to infringe on the patents for antiretroviral drugs held by the major US pharmaceutical companies. As such, they could not produce less expensive generic versions of antiretrovirals.

In the late 1990s, several developing countries decided to violate these intellectual property rights in order to expand AIDS treatment for their citizens. They used a loophole in the TRIPS Agreement to produce generic versions of antiretroviral drugs, or import them from other countries. For example, an Indian pharmaceutical company created Nevirapine, a generic version of AZT, which it sold to developing countries for only $350 per yearly treatment regimen.[5] It represented a discount of over 95 percent compared with the patented antiretroviral drugs. Similar generic drugs were produced in Brazil and Thailand under these WTO exceptions. Countries like South Africa, home to nearly a third of all pregnant women infected with HIV, began importing antiretrovirals from India and elsewhere.

A group of Western pharmaceutical companies that held the patents for antiretroviral drugs responded by suing the South African government in 1998 for violating their intellectual property rights. The drug companies were trying to prevent the less expensive generic drugs from entering the South African market. This enraged South African AIDS activists, and sparked a series of protests throughout the country. Similarly, the US government threatened to impose economic sanctions against South Africa, and filed a claim against Brazil in the WTO for violating the TRIPS Agreement. This also incited a round of protests from human rights activists in the United States, who argued that corporations and their allies in government were prioritizing profits over people's basic needs.

Although the United States does not explicitly recognize any human right to health, most other countries do. Article 12 of the International Covenant on Economic, Social, and Cultural Rights recognizes the right to "enjoyment of the highest attainable standard of physical and mental health." Many of the countries involved in the dispute over antiretroviral drugs have also incorporated the right to health into their national constitutions. For example, Article 27 of the South African constitution declares that "everyone has the right to have access to health care services" and that "no one may be refused emergency medical treatment." However, all of these countries have also recognized the right to own private property. For example, Article 17 of the Universal Declaration of Human Rights, and Article 25 of the South African constitution, protect the right to own property, including intellectual property.

Thus, when human rights conflict with each other, as in the case of access to medicine, which right should take precedence? Does the right to health, if it truly exists, allow countries to violate intellectual property rights? Would violating pharmaceutical patents even be effective in improving treatment for poor people infected with HIV, or might it prove to be counterproductive? Are there better ways to think about health care than through the lens of human rights? This debate will provide different perspectives on these questions.

Argument 1
Poor countries should violate patent laws if necessary to protect the right to health.

According to this argument, pharmaceutical corporations such as Glaxo-SmithKline and Merck put profits ahead of people's lives when they try to enforce their patents against developing countries. Because health is necessary for the realization of other rights such as property rights, one can say that the right to health is more basic than the right to intellectual property and should take precedence. Therefore, poor countries that cannot afford the price of patented drugs have a legitimate reason to violate patent law in order to save lives. Indeed, the actions of countries like Brazil and South Africa were not even violations of the TRIPS rules, and do not threaten the drug companies' main sources of profit. Focusing attention on the human right to health can motivate nations to improve all aspects of their health care systems, resulting in millions of lives being saved.

First, it must be recognized that the production of inexpensive generic drugs is entirely consistent with WTO rules and international law. The TRIPS Agreement allows for countries to manufacture their own generic drugs if these drugs are "essential medicines" that are necessary to stem a "national health emergency."[6] In 2002 the WHO added antiretroviral drugs to its approved list of essential medicines.[7] There is simply no question that the AIDS pandemic has become a national health emergency in many countries throughout sub-Saharan Africa, the Caribbean, and Asia. Likewise, there is no question that the cost of patented drugs has prevented developing countries from providing them to people who need them.

According to this argument, violating intellectual property rights to save lives is also legitimate under international human rights law. The right to health is a basic human right. It is central to human dignity, and foundational to the protection of many other human rights. At the same time, the right to own property is a secondary right that can be limited in a variety of circumstances. Private property is often expropriated, even by the most democratic and capitalist countries, when it is necessary to serve the public interest. For centuries, the United States and most other democratic countries have seized private property in order to build highways, railroads, and public utilities under the principle of eminent domain. Saving lives and averting national health emergencies are far more justifiable reasons to expropriate property than these more common applications of eminent domain.

> **Think Again**
>
> The WHO keeps a list of "essential medicines," to which all countries should have affordable access, for the purpose of public health. What medicines do you think should be on the list? What if only 100 people died from a disease because they couldn't afford the medication? Should that be considered an essential medicine? Would you think differently if the dying person were a member of your family?

In addition, US opposition to the move by Brazil and South Africa to use the loopholes in the TRIPS Agreement to produce generic drugs was transparently hypocritical. While the United States was arguing that the threat of HIV/AIDS did not truly constitute a national emergency, it was simultaneously claiming its own "national emergency" exception to the TRIPS Agreement in order to generically produce a treatment for anthrax in 2001.[8] The anthrax attacks in the United States killed a total of five people; AIDS has killed 30 million.

Furthermore, allowing poor countries to infringe on drug patents to treat major pandemics will not destroy the Western pharmaceutical companies' profits. Drug companies like Merck and Pfizer spend less than 1 percent of their research and development budgets on the diseases that primarily affect poor countries.[9] The major drug companies spend the overwhelming majority of their research funds on chronic diseases and other health conditions experienced in wealthy countries, because these diseases are the main sources of their profit. Pharmaceutical companies are making billions of dollars on medicines for conditions such as hypertension, depression, high cholesterol, weight loss, and erectile dysfunction, not on antiretroviral drugs. Moreover, there is very little chance that cheap antiretroviral drugs sold in developing countries will leak back into wealthy countries and distort their markets. Wealthy patients tend to distrust medicines originating in developing countries, and have private insurance that would pay for more expensive drugs. The market in the United States for inexpensive drugs manufactured elsewhere, such as India, is in reality quite small.

In the unlikely event that the violation of patents were to threaten the profitability of Western drug companies, it would still represent a better outcome for health and human rights than the current system. Why must private companies and their wealthy investors benefit from the treatment of deadly diseases? Why do health care and the provision of medicine need to produce such exorbitant profits? Although opponents of this argument claim that the profit motive is necessary to incentivize innovation and the development of new drugs, and that strict patent enforcement is the only way to protect profits, there are better ways to provide affordable medicines to people in an economically sustainable manner. Most of the initial research on the medicines that treat diseases that disproportionately affect poor people is already funded by governments and philanthropists, not corporations. This was the case with the development of AZT and other antiretroviral drugs, and continues to be the case with the development of an HIV vaccine. Approximately 90 percent of the funding to develop an HIV vaccine comes from governments, via international agencies such as the **Global Fund to Fight AIDS, Tuberculosis, and Malaria**, or from private charities, such as the Bill and Melinda Gates Foundation.[10] Once new drugs are developed, the patents could be turned over to NGOs like One-

World Health to conduct clinical trials and develop commercial applications, rather than allowing the large pharmaceutical corporations to retain the patents for these medications.[11]

In addition, these organizations could still make a return on their financial investment, while keeping the price of medicines affordable, by negotiating advance purchase agreements with the governments of developing countries.[12] These agreements would ensure that once a new drug or vaccine is developed, it would be bought in high volume. Alternatively, Thomas Pogge has suggested creating an institution, funded by governments, that would reward manufacturers proportionally to the impact that their drug has on the global disease burden.[13] Clearly, strictly enforceable patents and high prices are not necessary as an incentive to develop new medicines.

Although the cost of medicine is not the only barrier to accessing health care in developing countries, and although the health infrastructure is weak in many poor countries, which makes it difficult to provide high-quality health care even when medicine is affordable, these cultural and economic barriers are not insurmountable, and reducing the cost of medicine is an important part of the solution. When drugs and other life-saving technologies are expensive and therefore inaccessible in poor countries, frustrated doctors and other health professionals become more likely to seek employment in wealthy countries. This contributes to the so-called brain drain and weakens the health infrastructure even further. On the other hand, when a nation is truly committed to improving the health of its citizens, then it can make dramatic improvements in its health infrastructure, expand access to medicine, and achieve tangible results. For example, the international NGO Doctors Without Borders conducted clinical trials of AZT in South Africa and proved to the world that poor, rural, and illiterate patients could comply with a strict regimen of daily medication. Indeed, NGOs have achieved better rates of compliance with antiretroviral treatment programs in Africa than the rates found in the United States.[14] When antiretroviral drugs ultimately became more affordable in developing countries, treatment rates for AIDS skyrocketed. While highly trained doctors and modern hospitals are still rare in many poor countries, these countries have achieved tremendous gains in health by focusing their attention on the use of smaller health clinics and **community health workers** to reach the most vulnerable populations. Community health workers receive just enough training to diagnose the most common illnesses, and then they use that training to ensure that people in the community are getting tested for diseases, complying with treatment regimens, and meeting their basic needs.[15] In sum, with the support of international NGOs and foreign aid from wealthy governments, developing nations have found cost-effective ways to improve their health infrastructure and expand access to life-saving treatments.

The opponents of this argument claim that thinking about health as a human right is a waste of resources, because treating AIDS is more expensive than preventing HIV or treating malaria. In a world of scarce resources, they say, not everyone can be treated, as the process of triage dictates. Yet this choice, between treatment and prevention, is a false one. Treating people suffering from AIDS does not conflict with HIV prevention, because it has been demonstrated that once people know they can afford treatment and improve their health, they are more likely to get tested and educated about how to prevent the spread of HIV.[16] Indeed, the relevant trade-off is not between treatment of different diseases at the expense of others, but between a nation's commitment to health care and its other priorities. When a developing country spends a third of its budget on its military, surely it can find new resources for health care if it reprioritizes its government spending. When the United States spends $700 billion on its military budget, surely it can find an extra $10 billion to eliminate the world's most deadly diseases. Human rights standards require us to try to save every human life, using the maximum resources available, starting with the most vulnerable people. The human right to health requires all nations of the world to make the commitment to save the most lives possible. While not every person can be treated immediately, there is simply no excuse for letting a person die when a treatment can be made available and affordable.

Argument 2
Poor countries should not violate patent laws in their efforts to provide inexpensive medicine.

According to this argument, human rights standards do not give countries any justification to violate patent laws in the name of expanding health care. Although health care is of course an important service that meets a basic human need, it is best provided through an efficient market system. Millions of people suffer from AIDS and other deadly diseases, not because of the cost of patented drugs, but because of other reasons related to poverty. When developing countries threaten the ability of pharmaceutical companies to make a fair return on their investment, this results in less access to high-quality medical care in the long run. Thus, thinking about health care as a human right is ultimately counterproductive.

The global AIDS pandemic is truly a human tragedy, but it is not the fault of the Western drug companies. The main causes of the spread of AIDS in poor countries are the lack of health infrastructure, low levels of education, and the lack of government support. Throughout sub-Saharan Africa, there are only about 15 physicians and 70 nurses per 100,000 people, which is ten to twenty times smaller than the ratio in wealthy countries.[17] This means that there are not enough doctors and nurses to test everyone and prescribe treatment. Moreover, even when medicine is prescribed to AIDS patients in poor countries, they often do not have the level of education needed to comply with the treatment regimen. The antiretroviral regimen is complicated, and requires multiple doses of several different pills at specific times, every day for the rest of the patient's life. Andrew Natsios, the director of the US Agency for International Development, argued in 2001 that funds spent on antiretroviral treatments in Africa are a waste of money because African AIDS patients "don't know what Western time is. . . . You have to take these drugs a certain number of hours each day, or they won't work."[18] This is especially relevant in rural areas, where residents have little access to medical clinics and their treatment cannot be adequately supervised and adjusted.

AIDS is also proliferating because of the lack of sex education and preventive health. In many poor countries, where the average level of education stops at primary school, many unscientific and inaccurate myths are perpetuated about the causes of AIDS. For example, in some countries, large portions of the population believe that mosquitoes can transfer HIV, that HIV was invented by the West to kill Africans and homosexuals, or even that having sex with a virgin can cure AIDS.[19] Indeed, former South African president Thabo Mbeki questioned the fact that the HIV virus was the cause of AIDS, and believed that vitamin supplements could prevent HIV transmission.

Additionally, even when the poorest people do receive antiretroviral treatments, they often suffer from so many other health problems that the antiretrovirals are not fully effective. It provides little benefit to treat someone for AIDS while they remain untreated for malnutrition, diarrhea, malaria, or tuberculosis. All of these diseases are less expensive and less complicated to treat than AIDS, and yet millions of people in poor countries die from these diseases every year. This is proof that the intellectual property rights that result in a higher cost of medicine are not the main impediment to better health care in developing countries. The main impediments are the health, education, and governance systems in those countries. Countries like South Africa, India, and Brazil would be better off investing public money into training doctors and nurses, and building medical clinics, rather than violating international law and fighting with pharmaceutical companies.

Intellectual property rights do not place "profits over people," as critics charge. Patents are necessary in order to stimulate innovation and ensure that new medicines are developed. Pharmaceutical companies spend millions and sometimes billions of dollars researching and developing clinical uses for new drugs. If they cannot protect their investments by patenting their inventions, then these new drugs would never become available to anyone. Indeed, while antiretroviral drugs are helpful in extending life and improving the health of AIDS patients, the only way that the world will truly conquer AIDS is by developing a vaccine for HIV. Patents therefore give drug companies the incentive to invest money into research for a desperately needed HIV vaccine.

Critics of intellectual property rights argue that drug companies' profits will not be harmed by the production of generic antiretroviral drugs in poor countries. They say that, since poor people and their governments cannot afford the prices offered by Merck and GlaxoSmith-Kline, these corporations will not lose much revenue in these countries anyway. However, the violation of intellectual property rights will indeed ruin the global pharmaceutical market, and threaten the safety of existing medicines. The generic drugs sold in poor countries can leak into the markets of wealthy countries, undercutting the drug companies' main source of income. A generic antiretroviral drug bought for $350 per yearly treatment regimen in South Africa can easily be resold over the Internet in the United States or Europe. As well, while poor countries today are claiming the right to infringe only on patents for antiretroviral drugs for AIDS, why would they stop at these drugs? In the future, they may claim the right to violate patents on medicines for cancer, high blood pressure, diabetes, or other diseases whose treatment constitutes a multibillion-dollar industry in the developed world. Indeed, the Indian manufacturer Cipla is currently producing low-cost generic drugs to treat cancer, and is planning to expand into a wide range of diseases that affect both the developing world and the developed world. According to one analyst, "the battle ten years ago over AIDS medicines was a small skirmish compared with the one likely to erupt over cancer, diabetes and heart medicines."[20] If developing countries are allowed to continue violating drug patents, then Western drug companies will not be able to compete. Not only would these generic drugs undercut the market in developed countries, but because they are produced in developing countries they would be subject to lower safety standards and therefore pose a potentially harmful threat to consumers.

Intellectual property rights therefore do not put "profits over people"; rather, they ensure that profits can be earned by making people healthier. Using the incentive system of the private market is the most efficient way to provide high-quality medicines to the most people. When drug patents are violated, even if it might result in a short-term expansion of treatment, it comes at a cost to rich and poor countries alike, in that better medicines will not be developed in the future.

Universal, high-quality health care is obviously an important goal to strive toward. But thinking about health care as a fundamental human right is unhelpful and potentially counterproductive. In a world of scarce resources, critical decisions must be made about who can receive care, and what kinds of health problems should receive the most attention. In health care, this is known as triage. Because it is impossible to save everyone, limited resources must be directed toward remedies that can save the most people in the most cost-effective way. Providing antiretro-viral treatments for people who are already infected with HIV is one of the least cost-effective health interventions available in developing countries. In the best of cases, antiretroviral treatments extend life for only a few years, at a high cost. Meanwhile, when billions of health care dollars are shifted toward AIDS treatment, they are shifted away from HIV prevention, malaria, respiratory infections, maternal mortality, and many of the other deadly health conditions that plague poor countries. Although AIDS is one of the leading causes of death in developing countries, millions of people also die each year from diarrhea, malaria, tuberculosis, pneumonia, and complications from childbirth.[21] Some economists estimate that if the resources spent on AIDS treatment were simply shifted toward preventing HIV infection, then between three and seventy-five new infections could be prevented for every additional year of life given to an AIDS patient.[22]

Many AIDS activists call for universal access to antiretroviral drugs, regardless of cost, because they argue that human rights require everyone to receive equal treatment. Although their passion is understandable, their argument is incorrect. Indeed, international human rights law explicitly states that the right to health is limited by the availability of resources. Article 2 of the International Covenant on Economic, Social, and Cultural Rights calls on states to "take steps . . . to the maximum of its available resources, with a view toward achieving progressively" the right to health. Developing countries therefore have no right to violate international patent law in the name of providing a right to health. More people would be saved if developing countries directed their limited resources toward improving the overall health infrastructure, or providing better health education so that infections can be prevented. Intellectual property rights are not a barrier to saving lives; they are necessary in order to save lives, because they provide an incentive to develop more potent and cost-effective drugs.

* * *

Conclusion

The battle that developing countries like Brazil and South Africa fought against the United States and its pharmaceutical companies over the patents for antiretroviral drugs took place over a decade ago, and has largely been won by the developing countries, at least in regard to antiretrovirals. After the United States filed a claim in the WTO that Brazil had violated the TRIPS Agreement, protests from US and Brazilian human rights activists grew so loud that the George W. Bush administration dropped its WTO dispute in 2001.[23] Brazil has since taken advantage of its ability to manufacture inexpensive generic antiretroviral drugs by providing them free of charge to its citizens.[24] By 2010, virtually all Brazilian AIDS patients who needed antiretroviral drugs were receiving them. While this has not reduced the overall number of HIV infections in Brazil, it has cut the mortality rate from AIDS almost in half.[25]

In South Africa, the road to expanded AIDS treatment was somewhat more complicated. In 2001 the Western drug companies, which had sued the government of South Africa for violating their patents, dropped their lawsuit in response to widespread protests in the country. This allowed South Africa to continue to import generic antiretroviral drugs, but because the administration of President Thabo Mbeki held false beliefs about HIV infection, these drugs were not distributed to AIDS patients. It was not until a South African human rights group sued the government and started a nationwide campaign for universal distribution of antiretroviral drugs that the South African government finally expanded treatment.[26] In the landmark 2002 case of *Minister of Health v. Treatment Action Campaign,* the South African high court found that the country's constitution required the government to provide antiretroviral drugs to HIV-infected pregnant women.[27] In the ensuing years, as a result of further advocacy by the Treatment Action Campaign and other human rights groups, South Africa has dramatically increased antiretroviral treatment, which is now supplied to nearly 80 percent of AIDS patients who need the medication.[28]

Similar stories are being played out throughout the developing world. Several developing countries, such as Botswana, Cambodia, Cuba, and Rwanda, have achieved near-universal health insurance coverage for AIDS patients (see Figure 14.1).[29] New HIV infections and AIDS-related deaths are declining around the world.[30] Over 2 million people in poor countries are alive today because they have gained access to less expensive antiretroviral drugs.[31] Although the world is a long way from conquering the pandemic, for the first time human rights activists can see the possibility of an end to AIDS. These successes are attributable not only to the reduced cost of antiretroviral drugs, but also to a range of holistic approaches to HIV and other diseases. Nations like Uganda and Thailand have worked to destigmatize AIDS and educate their populations about ways to prevent the spread of HIV. Other nations have adopted the community health model, and strengthened their health infrastructures to combat their most deadly diseases. And while medical researchers have not yet developed a proven HIV vaccine, clinical trials are proceeding on several possible drugs, and a successful vaccine is expected within the next decade.[32]

While human rights activists have largely won the global debate over AIDS and antiretroviral drugs, the broader debate over health care, human rights, and intellectual property remains. If developing countries can infringe on patents for AIDS drugs with impunity, why not drugs for malaria, tuberculosis, pneumonia, and other diseases that afflict the poor? For that matter, since heart disease, cancer, and diabetes are on the rise in developing countries, why not violate the patents on drugs for the diseases that are widespread in wealthy countries? Determining when a disease constitutes a "national health emergency" is a sensitive topic, and the broader the definition becomes, the more that the violation of intellectual property will cut into the profits of the major pharmaceutical corporations. Although governments and philanthropists can reasonably be relied on to fund the development of some new medicines, many people doubt their ability to pursue technological innovation at the same pace as private corporations.

Thus we return to the question of whether the free market is the most efficient and equitable way to deliver high-quality health care. Virtually all of the developed countries in the world, from Canada to Japan to the European Union, have answered no. Their governments have imposed higher tax rates on their citizens in order to provide them with universal health care for all essential treatments. These governments also control the prices that physicians, hospitals, and pharmaceutical companies can charge for their services, ensuring that the health system remains somewhat affordable. The United States is an exception in this regard, as it relies on lower taxes, private insurers, and fewer government regulations over health care providers. The US system, however, cannot be viewed as any more efficient or equitable. While the free market system has resulted in the highest-quality health

Figure 14.1 The Rwandan Health Care System

When the central African country of Rwanda was decimated by genocide in 1994, it was already one of the poorest places on Earth, with an annual per capita income of under $300. In a nation of 7 million people, Rwanda had only a handful of physicians and hospitals. It was ravaged by deadly illnesses including diarrhea, pneumonia, malnutrition, and increasingly AIDS. As part of a plan to rebuild the country in the aftermath of war, President Paul Kagame embarked on a bold endeavor to reform the Rwandan health care system.[33]

Kagame's plan centered on providing national health insurance coverage to all Rwandans. Insurance premiums cost only $2 per year, and they cover preventive care and treatments for the most common deadly diseases. If a citizen needs advanced treatment for more complicated conditions such as cancer, heart attack, or stroke, they must purchase supplemental private insurance. Yet over 90 percent of Rwandans have the basic insurance coverage, a higher rate than the United States has achieved.

Rwanda has been able to provide near-universal coverage at such a low cost because it has implemented a community-based model of health care made famous by Paul Farmer's work with the NGO Partners in Health. Community health workers are trained and paid a monthly stipend to make daily house calls in their villages and ensure that people's basic needs are met. The total cost of the Rwandan health care system is roughly $30 per person, so the government receives international aid from organizations such as the Clinton Foundation and the Global Fund to Fight AIDS, Tuberculosis, and Malaria. The government is slowly increasing its own health care budget each year, and hopes to become self-reliant within the next decade.

The results of Rwanda's health care reforms have been dramatic. Nearly everyone infected with HIV has access to treatment, at a cost of only $150 per year.[34] Life expectancy is on the rise, and deaths from childbirth and malaria are down sharply. A Rwandan journalist once remarked after meeting an American exchange student that it was "absurd, ridiculous, that I had health insurance and she didn't . . . and if she got sick, her parents might go bankrupt. The saddest thing was the way she shrugged her shoulders and just hoped not to fall sick."[35]

care in the world for the wealthiest citizens of the United States, it has produced great inequality in terms of life expectancy, child mortality, and other health outcomes.[36] Over 40 million people in the United States have no health insurance, and often their only recourse when becoming sick is to go to a hospital's emergency room, which is far more expensive than preventive care. This system has resulted in US citizens spending twice as much of their annual incomes on health care as do the citizens of other industrialized countries, while achieving poorer health outcomes.[37] According to a study by Harvard University, medical expenses play a significant role in 62 percent of all personal bankruptcies in the United States.[38]

These problems with the US health care system led to the passage of the **Affordable Care Act** in 2010,[39] which subsidizes health care for low-income citizens, mandates that everyone purchases health insurance, and increases the regulation of health care providers. The new law helped to fulfill President Barack Obama's campaign promise to treat health care as a fundamental right, rather than as a commodity or privilege that only the wealthy could afford.[40] However, this law sparked a major controversy in the United States, as protesters argued that "Obamacare" violated individual freedom by increasing taxes, forcing people to buy health insurance, and imposing governmental restrictions over private corporations. Thus, the debate about the right to health, intellectual property rights, and the free market seems far from resolved.

Notes

1. Joint United Nations Programme on HIV/AIDS (UNAIDS), *World AIDS Day Report 2011* (Geneva), p. 10, http://www.unaids.org/en/media/unaids/content assets/documents/unaidspublication/2011/jc2216_worldaidsday_report_2011 _en.pdf.

2. Samuel Broder, "The Development of Antiretroviral Therapy and Its Impact on the HIV-1/AIDS Pandemic," *Antiviral Research* 85, no. 1 (2009): 1–2.

3. Avert, "Universal Access to AIDS Treatment: Targets and Challenges," http://www.avert.org/universal-access.htm#contentTable0, accessed July 24, 2012.

4. See the World Trade Organization, "Pharmaceutical Patents and the TRIPS Agreement," September 21, 2006, https://www.wto.org/english/tratop_e/trips_e /pharma_ato186_e.htm.

5. Amy Nunn, *The Politics and History of AIDS Treatment in Brazil* (New York: Springer, 2009), p. 121.

6. World Trade Organization, "Pharmaceutical Patents and the TRIPS Agreement."

7. World Health Organization, "WHO Takes Major Steps to Make HIV Treatment Accessible," April 22, 2002, http://www.who.int/mediacentre/news/releases /release28/en/index.html.

8. Martiga Lohn, "A Bitter Pill for the WTO," *Mother Jones,* November 9, 2001, http://www.motherjones.com/politics/2001/11/bitter-pill-wto.

9. Families USA Global Health Initiative, "Fighting the World's Most Devastating Diseases: A Plan for Closing the Research Gap," February 2008, http:// www.familiesusa.org/assets/pdfs/closing-research-gap.pdf.

10. UNAIDS, HIV Vaccines, and Microbicides Resource Tracking Working Group, "Tracking Funding for Preventive HIV Vaccine Research & Development," June 2005, http://data.unaids.org/una-docs/vaccinestrackingfundingjune 2005_report_en.pdf.

11. For more information on OneWorld Health, see the organization's website, at http://www.oneworldhealth.org/about-us, accessed July 25, 2012.

12. Ernst R. Berndt and John A. Hurvitz, "Vaccine Advance Purchase Agreements for Low-Income Countries: Practical Issues," *Health Affairs* 24, no. 3 (May 2005): 653–665.

13. Thomas Pogge, "Human Rights and Global Health: A Research Program," *Metaphilosophy* 36, no. 2 (January 2005): 182–209.

14. Jonathan Wolff, *The Human Right to Health* (New York: Norton, 2012), p. 71. See also "Africa: House Calls and Health Care," *PBS Now,* September 11, 2009, http://www.pbs.org/now/shows/537/transcript.html.

15. See the work of Paul Farmer and Partners in Health, described in Tracy Kidder, *Mountains Beyond Mountains* (New York: Random, 2003).

16. Paul Farmer, "Global AIDS: New Challenges for Health and Human Rights," *Perspectives in Biology and Medicine* 48, no. 1 (Winter 2005): 10–16.

17. Bernhard Liese and Gilles Dussault, "The State of the Health Workforce in Sub-Saharan Africa," Africa Region Human Development Working Paper (Washington, DC: World Bank, September 2004), p. 4.

18. John Donnelly, "Prevention Urged in AIDS Fight: Natsios Says Fund Should Spend Less on HIV Treatment," *Boston Globe,* June 7, 2001.

19. Keyan G. Tomaselli, "(Re)Mediatizing HIV/AIDS in South Africa," *Cultural Studies, Critical Methodologies* 9, no. 4 (June 2009): 570–587.

20. Gardiner Harris, "China and India Making Inroads in Biotech Drugs," *New York Times,* September 19, 2011.

21. World Health Organization, "The Top Ten Causes of Death," Fact Sheet no. 310, February 2007, http://www.who.int/mediacentre/factsheets/fs310/en/.

22. William Easterly, *The White Man's Burden* (New York: Penguin, 2006), p. 255.

23. Sarah Joseph, "Pharmaceutical Corporations and Access to Drugs: The 'Fourth Wave' of Corporate Human Rights Scrutiny," *Human Rights Quarterly* 25, no. 2 (May 2003): 425–452.

24. Nunn, *The Politics and History of AIDS Treatment in Brazil.*

25. Avert, "HIV and AIDS in Brazil," http://www.avert.org/aids-brazil.htm #contentTable1, accessed July 25, 2012.

26. William Forbarth, "Cultural Transformation, Deep Institutional Reform, and ESR Practice: South Africa's Treatment Action Campaign," in *Stones of Hope: How African Activists Reclaim Human Rights to Challenge Global Poverty,* edited by Lucie E. White and Jeremy Perelman (Palo Alto: Stanford University Press, 2010).

27. *Minister of Health v. Treatment Action Campaign,* 5 S.A. 721 (2002).

28. Avert, "HIV and AIDS in South Africa," http://www.avert.org/aidssouth africa.htm#contentTable5, accessed July 25, 2012.

29. UNAIDS, *World AIDS Day Report 2011,* p. 20.

30. Ibid., p. 9.

31. Ibid., p. 6.

32. Alyssa A. Botelho, "Scientists Hunting for an AIDS Vaccine May Be Getting Close," *Washington Post,* July 23, 2012.

33. Donald G. McNeil Jr., "A Poor Nation, with a Health Plan," *New York Times,* June 15, 2010.

34. "Africa: House Calls and Health Care."

35. McNeil, "A Poor Nation."

36. Karen Davis, Cathy Schoen, and Kristof Stremikis, "Mirror, Mirror on the Wall: How the Performance of the U.S. Health Care System Compares Internationally, 2010 Update" (New York: Commonwealth Fund, June 23, 2010).

37. Ibid.

38. David U. Himmelstein, Deborah Thorne, Elizabeth Warren, and Steffie Woolhandler, "Medical Bankruptcy in the United States, 2007: Results of a National Study," *American Journal of Medicine* 122, no. 8 (August 2009): 741–746.

39. The full title of the health care reform is the Patient Protection and Affordable Care Act (PL 111–148, 124 Stat. 119).

40. In the October 7, 2008, presidential debate, moderator Tom Brokaw asked the question, "Is health care in America a privilege, a right, or a responsibility?" Obama replied, "I believe it should be a right for every American."

15

Do Wealthy States Have an Obligation to Give Foreign Aid?

Sein is a ten-year-old girl who lives in the small town of Mae Sot in western Thailand.[1] Her home, an unstable structure of bamboo stalks and corrugated tin, sits on the Mae Sot garbage dump. The dump is a square mile of trash piled twenty feet high, where her parents work to recycle scraps of plastic for about a dollar a day. Each time a garbage truck comes to deliver its payload, the 200 residents of the dump gather around the fresh pile of trash to pick through its contents. Sein and her baby sister spend most of their days walking barefooted around the dump, trying to avoid broken glass, rotten food, and the occasional dog's skull. Her friends play games like sliding down the side of the garbage mountain in a sled fashioned from an old car fender. Sein and her sister wash themselves in the small reservoir a few feet from the garbage pile, which is colored turquoise with chemical runoff from the dump. Sein's family lives here because it is their only option for survival, having fled civil war and political oppression in their home country of Burma. Because they cannot earn enough money to meet their basic needs, they receive some food, clean drinking water, health care, and schooling from international aid agencies.

Sein is one of the 1.3 billion people on the planet who live in extreme poverty, defined by the World Bank as earning less than $1.25 per day.[2] About 2.5 billion people live on less than $2 per day. Every day, roughly 30,000 people die from causes related to extreme poverty, such as chronic malnutrition, dirty water, and preventable diseases. While every country has some **relative poverty** in comparison with its average income level, people like Sein live in **absolute poverty** (also called extreme poverty), which prevents them from meeting their basic physical needs. The largest number of poor people overall live in South Asia, but sub-Saharan Africa has the highest percentage of people living in poverty. About 70 percent of people in absolute poverty live in rural areas, unable to secure an adequate livelihood through their agricultural work.[3]

Extreme poverty is directly related to a wide range of human rights violations. Obviously, extreme poverty threatens the ability of people to achieve an adequate livelihood, which affects their housing, nutrition, and health. Poverty also prevents children from receiving a decent education, as many are unable to pay school fees or are forced to work in order to supplement their families' meager incomes. Furthermore, poverty makes it more difficult to hold public officials accountable, and poor countries are more likely to have authoritarian governments. Poor countries are more susceptible to government corruption, because public officials are often paid poorly and economic resources are centralized and more easily lootable.[4] Racial discrimination and gender inequality are also common in the poorest societies, which produce human rights abuses such as sexual violence against women.[5] The extreme poor are also more vulnerable to violations in the workplace, as their desperation often forces them into substandard working conditions.

These conditions should not come as a surprise, as the world has been aware of the scale and depth of extreme poverty for many decades. Because people in poverty are dependent on outside assistance to meet some of their basic needs, and because poor people seem caught in a trap that they cannot escape, wealthy nations have long provided foreign aid in order to ameliorate these conditions. Foreign aid comes from many different sources. Aid can come from private individuals and charitable foundations, usually channeled through humanitarian NGOs such as CARE or Oxfam. More commonly, foreign aid comes from wealthy governments, and is given directly to a developing country (**bilateral aid**), or channeled through an international organization such as the World Bank or the World Health Organization (**multilateral aid**). In total, wealthy people and states give approximately $30 billion each year in private aid, $100 billion in bilateral aid, and $40 billion in multilateral aid.[6]

Foreign aid can be packaged in different forms, and serve many different purposes. Some aid is given in response to emergencies and natural disasters, while the goals of other kinds of aid are to stimulate economic growth, support political reforms, and provide economic stability during financial crises.[7] Some aid comes in the form of cash transfers that are deposited directly into a developing country's treasury, in order to bolster the government's budget, while other aid is designated for specific projects, such as the construction of a school or highway. In some cases, aid comes in the form of loans that must be repaid to the donor over time, at a below-market interest rate, while other aid is given freely as a grant. Some aid is conditional, requiring for example that the recipient country enact certain political or economic reforms that the donor demands, while other aid is unconditional. Finally, some aid comes in the form of in-kind assistance, such as bags of grain or a technical expert's advice, rather than cash. Thus, a small proportion of all foreign aid is targeted directly toward people living in conditions like those that Sein experiences, or in forms that they can personally use.

The world's wealthiest countries have come together numerous times to express their commitment to help end extreme poverty. Beginning in 1970, the member states of the **Organization for Economic Cooperation and Development (OECD)** set a goal to each contribute 0.7 percent of their total income (gross domestic product) to ending extreme poverty.[8] Although this promise of 0.7 percent has been repeated many times, it is not a legally binding commitment. The United States has never fully endorsed a specific target amount for development aid, and most OECD countries have failed to reach the 0.7 percent goal so far, more than forty years after it was initially proposed.

In 2000, all the nations of the world came together again to reaffirm their expressed commitment to ending extreme poverty by signing the **Millennium Development Goals (MDGs)**. The MDGs are a series of eight benchmarks that all countries hope to achieve by 2015. They include, for example, halving the percentage of people living on less than a dollar a day, halving the proportion of malnourished people, cutting the child mortality rate by two-thirds, providing universal HIV/AIDS treatment, and providing universal primary education.[9] The eighth goal calls on wealthy states to assist this process in the least-developed countries, not just by providing them with foreign aid, but also by instituting a range of policies that would benefit the poor. Such favorable policies toward developing countries could include lowering tariffs on their exports, forgiving the debt that they have accrued, encouraging private investment, and transferring to them technologies that they need. Overall, while there has been important progress made on some of the MDGs, it appears that several of the goals will not be reached by 2015.

Thus, while the world recognizes the urgency of extreme poverty, the consistency of its actions has not yet matched the loftiness of its commitments. For example, of the OECD states that have pledged to give 0.7 percent of their GDP, only five have succeeded in doing so and the average percentage given by OECD states is around 0.4 percent of GDP.[10] At question here is whether wealthy countries have a moral obligation, and perhaps also a legal obligation, to help end extreme poverty in developing countries, and whether human rights provide a sufficient basis to demand such aid.

These questions in turn are related to a number of controversies about human rights and poverty. For example, does the existence of poverty itself constitute a human rights violation, or is poverty simply an unfortunate part of the human condition? How can individuals, private enterprises, national governments, and international donors simultaneously be held responsible for ending poverty? Is poverty best ended through governmental action, or through the invisible hand of the marketplace? Is foreign aid even effective in giving people like Sein a chance at a better livelihood over the long term? This is the debate to which we now turn.

Argument 1
Wealthy states do have an obligation to give foreign aid.

According to this argument, human rights do require wealthy states to give foreign aid to the least-developed states. This is because freedom from poverty is a fundamental right that explicitly creates both national and international obligations. When national governments are unable to free their own people from poverty, and outside donors are able to make a tangible impact, then they must provide assistance. Although some foreign aid is wasted and counterproductive, this is not an inherent characteristic of foreign aid. When targeted and packaged correctly, foreign aid can save lives and plant the seeds for long-term economic growth.

First, it must be recognized that the existence of extreme poverty is itself a violation of human rights. Centuries ago, the world simply did not have the capability to provide for everyone's needs, and so at that time the existence of poverty was not a human rights violation. But today, in a world of plenty, over a billion people suffer while others live in luxury. Because the world is capable of providing for everyone's needs, the continuance of poverty is an injustice, not a misfortune. By giving foreign aid, wealthy states trade a less basic right (the right to dispose of one's income as one pleases) in exchange for a more basic right (the right to an adequate livelihood).[11] Not only that, but as dependency theory suggests,

> **Think Again**
>
> People in wealthy states commonly say, "We cannot help people in distant countries until we solve our problems here at home." How would you respond to this statement? What do you think human rights experts would say about this?

wealthy states are also intricately involved in the causes of poverty in developing states. Many wealthy states took part in colonialism, slavery, and the exploitation of natural resources throughout Africa, Asia, and Latin America, which left these regions underdeveloped. Wealthy states continue to take advantage of the global economy, gaining access to cheap resources and making deals with dictators for their own benefit, which leads to the underdevelopment of the poorest, most vulnerable states. Thus, because wealthy states participate in an integrated world system that enriches their own citizens, they have a responsibility to help fulfill the basic rights of the people who are left behind by that system.[12] Foreign aid is a matter of justice, based on a moral and historical debt that wealthy states owe to poor states, and not simply a matter of charity.

Virtually all states have acknowledged the universal right to an adequate standard of living, which includes at least a minimum level of housing, food, clean water, sanitation, health care, and other material needs.[13] The former UN High Commissioner for Human Rights has stated, "No social phenomenon is as comprehensive in its assault on human rights as poverty."[14] And as other human rights experts have noted, "Anyone anywhere who suffers from severe poverty not of their own choosing is having their economic rights violated. If we were to actually enforce economic rights, there would be no involuntary poverty anywhere in the world."[15] Although international law places primary duty on the developing state itself to take all possible steps to eliminate poverty, international law also recognizes that the least-developed states do not have sufficient resources to fully address poverty within their own countries. This is why states are obligated to take steps to end poverty "individually and through international assistance and cooperation, especially economic and technical."[16] The duty to provide foreign aid is clear in international human rights law.

It is true that human rights law does not single out any particular wealthy state, or stipulate any funding target that they must reach. It simply states that everyone must help address extreme poverty, using their maximum available resources. The vagueness of the obligation does make it difficult to enforce on any single state. However, international coordination can help to fill this gap, by using diplomacy to ensure that all wealthy states are doing their part. No single state should have to shoulder the burden itself.

According to this argument, wealthy states have a duty to assist the poor. But why should this assistance come in the form of foreign aid? Why not, as opponents of this argument suggest, simply focus on opening these countries to foreign trade and investment, and let them develop on their own? The reason against this suggestion is that trade and investment are not enough to pull the least-developed countries out of poverty. Many of these nations are crippled by financial debt, cut off from major trade routes, mired in civil war, burdened with deadly diseases, and vulnerable to natural disasters. The least-developed countries are locked in a downward economic spiral, described by some economists as a poverty trap.[17] The prevalence of extreme poverty makes it more difficult for these countries to achieve sustainable economic growth, and thus makes it difficult for them to attract private investment or sell their products to the world.

Of course, foreign aid would be morally required only if it were actually proven to be effective. But although a great deal of foreign aid, as it is currently constituted, does not create long-term solutions for people in poverty, this is not because foreign aid is inherently ineffective, or because the governments of developing countries are hopelessly corrupt. It is because most of the official aid flowing from wealthy states is self-interested and politically driven, rather than targeted toward truly addressing the needs of the poor. For example, the top recipients of US foreign aid are Israel, Egypt, Afghanistan, Pakistan, Jordan, Colombia, and Mexico.[18] It is clear from this list that the main purpose of US foreign aid is to support the war on terrorism, the war on drugs, and other political interests. Most of these countries are not even poor, by global standards, and aid to these countries, especially Israel and Egypt, is not directed toward helping those in need or stimulating the economy, but rather to ensure military cooperation. Thus, while critics of foreign aid like to explain that wealthy states have given over \$2 trillion since the end of World War II, in fact very little of this aid has gone to the least-developed countries. According to one estimate, the average person in sub-Saharan Africa receives a meager \$12 in aid per year from the entire world.[19]

Even the aid that is directed toward the least-developed countries is not necessarily packaged in a way that serves the interests of the poor. Many wealthy states give **tied aid**, meaning that poor countries are legally required to spend up to 70 percent of the aid amount on products and services originating in the wealthy states themselves. While this benefits the consultants and corporations of the wealthy states, it makes foreign aid less efficient, and results in less aid actually reaching its intended beneficiaries. For example, the United States has tied its food aid to corporate interests for several decades. Instead of supporting the poorest farmers in developing countries with agricultural tools, the United States buys grain from its own agricultural corporations, transports it thousands of miles using US shipping companies, and distributes it using US nongovernmental organizations. This system not only is less efficient, but also often hurts farmers in poor countries who cannot sell their food in local markets when they must compete with free food from the United States.

Although the aid system has sometimes encouraged corruption in developing states, this is not because aid inherently fuels corruption, but because wealthy states have knowingly given aid to corrupt governments when it serves their political interests. For example, the World Bank has given loans to dictators in countries like Chad, China, and the Philippines to build large infrastructure projects such as oil pipelines, hydroelectric dams, and nuclear power plants. Corrupt government officials then skim a percentage of these loans to line their own pockets. The World Bank has also conditioned its loans to compel governments to implement neoliberal reforms that shrink the social safety net and hurt the poor. Infrastructure projects sometimes displace whole communities of poor people, or perhaps never get completed. And even if such projects are completed, they sometimes benefit only the elite neighborhoods in the major cities at the expense of the poor communities. As a result, the developing nation becomes saddled with a debt that it was unable to repay. This is the kind of foreign aid that hurts rather than helps the poor.

However, foreign aid does not have to be this way. Aid that is targeted to the poorest communities, and packaged in a form that increases local self-reliance, can hugely reduce extreme poverty. This is called the **rights-based approach to development**: using aid to empower the most destitute people from the bottom up, rather than focusing exclusively on economic growth and hoping that the benefits trickle down. Increasingly, both states and NGOs are fashioning their aid policies with the human rights of the poorest people in mind.[20] Nobel Prize–winning economist Amartya Sen has called this "support-led" development, in contrast to export-oriented growth.[21] In other words, aid can be used to build the capabilities and productivity of the poorest people, which stimulates economic growth as they participate in their local market rather than relying on selling cheap products to the rest of the world.

Rights-based approaches to development include programs like paying rural families to enroll their children in school, so that they do not have to work in the fields. Such a compensation program could be focused on enrolling girls, who are often underrepresented in education, and could include a daily meal in school to supplement children's nutrition. Programs like these have helped to increase school enrollments throughout the developing world, so that for the first time in history, roughly the same numbers of girls are attending primary school as are boys.[22] Other effective bottom-up solutions to poverty include support for microenterprises, which are small, informal businesses operated by the poor themselves to supplement their incomes. For example, the Grameen Bank, an NGO in Bangladesh, has helped millions of poor women increase their incomes by providing them with small loans, business training, health education, and a community support structure.[23] Grameen's clients might own a sewing machine, or a grocery cart, or a cell phone that members of the community can use. These are just a couple of the many examples of successful programs funded by foreign aid.

According to economist Jeffrey Sachs, if investments are truly targeted toward five areas that directly affect the most vulnerable people, then foreign aid can make a big difference in ending extreme poverty.[24] These areas are (1) agriculture, to ensure that farmers have the tools they need to increase their productivity; (2) health care, to cure treatable diseases; (3) sanitation, to prevent diseases from spreading in the first place; (4) education, to build a work force for the next generation; and (5) energy, to provide clean electricity and fuel. Sachs believes that if wealthy states approach their goal of providing 0.7 percent of their GDP in foreign aid, and if the aid is targeted toward proven solutions in these areas, then extreme poverty can be dramatically reduced within two decades.

But won't corrupt governments simply steal and misappropriate the aid that is intended for these communities? Not necessarily, because there are effective ways to use foreign aid to circumvent or reform corrupt governments, if wealthy states are well coordinated and not beholden to their own interests. For example, international donors could channel their aid through NGOs and community-based organizations, rather than directly subsidizing governments themselves. Or, in cases where direct government support is necessary, donors could insist that the recipient prove that they have addressed corruption, and that they are truly committed to ending extreme poverty in their country, before they receive any funding. This is what the United States does with its Millennium Challenge Corporation, which directs a portion of US foreign aid toward extreme poverty. Governments that receive US aid through the Millennium Challenge Corporation must demonstrate that they are eliminating corruption and expanding the protection of rights for their citizens.[25] Thus, while corruption and economic mismanagement are still problems throughout the world, smartly designed aid can be used to promote reforms that benefit everyone.

In sum, according to this argument human rights do obligate wealthy states to give foreign aid to the least-developed states. Wealthy states have benefited from economic globalization, and they have the capability to make a difference in poor people's basic rights. While not all aid is effective, foreign aid that is properly designed and targeted can help a billion people achieve a decent livelihood. Failure to make every possible effort in this regard is an injustice.

Argument 2
Wealthy states do not have an obligation to give foreign aid.

Clearly extreme poverty is a human tragedy, and people should be encouraged to give to charitable causes. According to this argument, however, wealthy states cannot be held accountable for the poverty that occurs in the least-developed countries, and wealthy states cannot create truly effective solutions to poverty across distant borders. As a result, human rights are simply not useful instruments for dealing with the problems of poverty, and they are not applicable to the economic policies that extend across international borders.

As argued in Chapter 12, poverty by itself is not a human rights violation. Indeed there are some circumstances in which people are made poor by human rights violations, for example, by discrimination or ethnic cleansing. However, the majority of the poor did not have their rights directly violated by anyone; they became poor through an extremely complex system that could include unfortunate weather, political conflict, economic cycles, and bad luck. Who should be held responsible for "violating" the rights of the poor when such circumstances conspire against them? It is one thing to set goals to reduce poverty, but it is quite another to claim that people's fundamental rights are being violated by poverty, and to lay blame at the feet of industrialized nations.

Human rights law recognizes that the primary authority responsible for protecting people's rights is their own state. If the governments of poor countries are not using their own resources to the maximum possible extent to put an end to poverty, then they are the ones who should be held accountable.[26] Indeed, according to some economists, the corruption, economic mismanagement, and outright theft that occur in poor countries represent the single greatest barrier to development.[27] Many of the nations of sub-Saharan Africa and elsewhere are richly endowed with natural resources, such as oil, gold, and diamonds. Yet these resources are exploited in order to benefit the elite few, while millions go hungry. Profits from the sale of these resources are often used to bolster the security apparatus of the state, rather than being used for poverty reduction. During the 1990s, which some economists considered the "lost decade" of economic stagnation, governments in sub-Saharan Africa spent 2.3 percent of GDP on their own militaries, which is larger than the world average. Some nations, such as Eritrea, spent over 20 percent of GDP on their militaries.[28] Other governments decided to embrace ruinous economic policies in the name of socialism or anticolonialism. For example, Zimbabwe's authoritarian government confiscated farmland from white farmers, which destroyed agricultural production, drove up inflation, and devastated the economy. In short, the problem of extreme poverty is not due to a gap in commitment from international donors, but to a gap in democracy and good governance within Africa, Asia, and other less developed regions of the world.

If human rights did confer a duty on wealthy states to help the poor, then who exactly would be responsible to provide this assistance, and to whom? Even the United States, as the world's wealthiest country, does not have the resources to provide foreign aid to all of the hundred-plus developing countries, or even to the forty-eight least-developed countries that need it.[29] Do OECD countries have an obligation to send aid to Zimbabwe, even though President Robert Mugabe is known to be one of the most corrupt leaders on the planet? Does the Chinese government have an obligation to send foreign aid, even though its average citizen is not nearly as wealthy as an OECD citizen? Human rights work best when a clear violator can be identified and held accountable for a specific action. In the case of global poverty, humanitarians typically make appeals that "everyone" must do their part to contribute. The problem is, when "everyone" is responsible, then no one truly is, because it is impossible to hold states individually accountable for their overlapping global obligations. This is why the system of foreign aid so easily degenerates into a game in which wealthy states make lofty promises that they have no real intention of fulfilling. Because states cannot be held responsible for a duty to aid a distant country, it is far better to conceive of development aid as either an act of charity that individuals can make out of goodwill, or an act of political discretion that states can make to achieve their national interests and values. Describing foreign aid as a transnational duty grounded in human rights only confuses the issue and brings us no closer to reaching an end to poverty.

Another significant problem with thinking about foreign aid as a human right is the fact that international aid is largely ineffective in reducing poverty. According to economist William Easterly, wealthy countries have given over $2.3 trillion in foreign aid over the past six decades.[30] Why are so many countries still poor after having so much money injected into them? They remain poor because foreign aid is simply not a good way to stimulate economic growth in poor countries. Some economists have found, after examining dozens of countries over a period of several decades, that countries receiving large amounts of aid did not grow any faster than countries receiving little or no aid.[31] One reason for this might be that, because people are so poor, the aid is spent on consuming immediate needs, rather than investing in the future.[32] Another reason is that an influx of aid can cause a society to suffer from high inflation, which makes it difficult to sell products abroad and inhibits economic growth.[33] Yet another possible reason is that the high rate of population growth could overwhelm any positive economic growth that the country experienced.[34]

While there is no shortage of reasons why foreign aid has been ineffective in developing countries, perhaps the biggest cause is corruption. Much of the aid that has been given to poor countries has been used to swell the size of government budgets, which gives government officials an incentive to protect their own turf and expand their own bureaucratic empires. By increasing the power of government bureaucrats instead of poor citizens, foreign aid entrenches the very problems it attempts to solve. It makes developing governments dependent on wealthy states, and exacerbates the problem of corruption.

It is true that foreign aid can save some lives in the short run, simply by injecting resources into a place of scarcity. However, real poverty reduction can only happen with long-term economic growth, and growth can only happen when a developing country commits itself to policies that attract international trade and investment. Because foreign aid causes countries to focus more on donors than potential customers, it actually hinders countries from moving toward the path of development. It would be more helpful for developing countries to raise the capital that they need through the open marketplace, by selling bonds to private investors.[35] Raising money from private investors would impose discipline on the governments of poor countries, and would help end their corruption and mismanagement, because these governments would know that they could not seek forgiveness of their debts if their development programs do not work. Poor nations such as China, South Korea, and Botswana have been able to overcome poverty, but not because they have received an influx of foreign aid. As modernization theory would suggest, these countries have succeeded because they have been able to integrate themselves into the global economy, attract foreign investment, and sell their products to the world. It is not foreign aid that has led to their growth, but rather the modernization of their societies, cultures, and economic policies.

In sum, according to this argument human rights do not obligate wealthy states to provide foreign aid to the least-developed states. Although it is a good and humane act to give charity in response to a natural disaster or other humanitarian crisis, such acts of charity are at the discretion of a wealthy government, not a moral or legal obligation. To the extent that people may have a human right to be free from poverty, hunger, or disease, they should exercise this right against the government of their own state, which is the main barrier to economic growth in the developing world. Foreign aid is not helpful in eliminating extreme poverty because aid comes with too many unintended consequences that result in corruption and economic stagnation.

* * *

Conclusion

We should remember that both sides in this debate believe that extreme poverty is a tragedy; they simply propose different approaches to solving it. We should also keep in mind that the world has achieved enormous gains in the fight against poverty over the past generation. While over a billion people still remain in destitute conditions, another billion have gained the capacity to meet their daily needs. Whereas in 1981, 52 percent of the developing world lived in absolute poverty, by 2008 only 22 percent did.[36] This has been due to the policies advocated by both sides of the debate. On the one hand, economic growth fueled by the private market and international trade has led to hundreds of millions of poor people increasing their incomes, especially in East Asia. Foreign aid had very little to do with the resounding success of the so-called Asian Tigers and other emerging economies of the developing world. On the other hand, foreign aid has also resulted in measurable successes in poor countries, in areas such as expanding access to education, increasing productivity in agriculture, and improving public health. As such, progress is being made to meet about half of the Millennium Development Goals in about half of the regions of the world by 2015, which will make a tangible difference in the lives of millions of people.[37] Of course, over a billion people are still left behind, so much work remains to be done.

As of 2013, only five countries have fulfilled their promise of giving 0.7 percent of their GDP in aid: Sweden, Norway, Luxembourg, Denmark, and the Netherlands.[38] The United States, because of the overwhelming size of its economy, gives the largest amount of foreign aid in absolute terms ($30 billion per year), but this is only 0.2 percent of its GDP, which ranks it fifth lowest among wealthy states.[39] In recent years, many wealthy states have committed themselves to increasing their foreign aid in pursuit of the MDGs, but the economic recession that has gripped the world since 2008 seems to have cut into the aid budgets of wealthy countries. European states in the midst of a severe debt crisis, such as Spain and Greece, cut their foreign aid by over 30 percent in 2011.[40] And while the foreign aid budget of the United States remains relatively stable, there is significant public pressure to cut foreign aid in order to reduce the US budget deficit. In one poll, 71 percent of Americans recommended a cutback in foreign aid, despite the fact that the aid budget contributed only a miniscule amount to the deficit.[41] No other US government program received anywhere near this level of support for budget cutting. Thus, the commitment by wealthy states to provide aid remains fragile, even as the successes of aid are being more widely shared.

Notes

1. I visited the Mae Sot garbage dump in 2011 and 2012, and thank Ashin Sopaka, King Zero, and the Best Friend Library for introducing me to children like Sein.

2. World Bank, "New Estimates Reveal Drop in Extreme Poverty, 2005–2010," February 29, 2012, http://go.worldbank.org/4K0EJIDFA0.

3. United Nations, "Despite Gains, Bulk of World's Poor Live in Rural Areas, UN Report Finds," December 6, 2010, http://www.un.org/apps/news/story.asp?NewsID=36967&Cr=rural&Cr1.

4. Eric Chetwynd, Frances Chetwynd, and Bertram Spector, "Corruption and Poverty: A Review of Recent Literature" (Washington, DC: Management Systems International, January 2003).

5. Gita Sen, "Poverty as a Gendered Experience: The Policy Implications," *Poverty in Focus* 13 (January 2008): 6–7.

6. Organization for Economic Cooperation and Development (OECD), "DAC1 Official and Private Flows," OECD Stat Extracts, http://stats.oecd.org/Index.aspx?DatasetCode=TABLE1, accessed July 27, 2012.

7. Steven Radelet, "A Primer on Foreign Aid," Working Paper no. 92 (Washington, DC: Center for Global Development, July 2006).

8. OECD, "History of the 0.7% ODA Target," June 2010, http://www.oecd.org/dac/stats/45539274.pdf.

9. For the complete list of UN Millennium Development Goals, see http://www.un.org/millenniumgoals, accessed July 30, 2012.

10. OECD, "History of the 0.7% ODA Target."

11. See, for example, Peter Singer, "The Singer Solution to World Poverty," *New York Times,* September 5, 1999. See also Henry Shue, *Basic Rights* (Princeton: Princeton University Press, 1996).

12. Thomas Pogge, *World Poverty and Human Rights: Cosmopolitan Responsibilities and Reforms* (Cambridge: Polity, 2002).

13. See the Universal Declaration of Human Rights, Article 25; and the International Covenant on Economic, Social, and Cultural Rights (ICESCR), Article 11.

14. United Nations High Commissioner for Human Rights, "Human Rights Dimensions of Poverty," *UNHCHR Online,* http://www.ohchr.org/english/issues /poverty/index.htm; Internet, accessed December 1, 2005.

15. Shareen Hertel and Lanse Minkler, eds., *Economic Rights: Conceptual, Measurement, and Policy Issues* (Cambridge: Cambridge University Press, 2007), p. 2.

16. ICESCR, Article 2(1).

17. Jeffrey Sachs, *The End of Poverty: Economic Possibilities for Our Time* (New York: Penguin, 2005), p. 19.

18. Daniel Tovrov, "Top Ten Largest Recipients of U.S. Aid," *International Business Times,* February 6, 2012.

19. Sachs, *The End of Poverty,* p. 310.

20. Daniel Chong, *Freedom from Poverty: NGOs and Human Rights Praxis* (Philadelphia: University of Pennsylvania Press, 2010).

21. Amartya Sen, *Development as Freedom* (New York: Knopf, 1999), p. 46.

22. UK Department for International Development, "Girls' Education: Toward a Better Future for All" (London, January 2005).

23. See the Grameen Bank website, at http://www.grameen-info.org, accessed August 3, 2012.

24. Sachs, *The End of Poverty,* p. 232.

25. See the Millennium Challenge Corporation website, at http://www.mcc .gov/pages/selection, accessed August 3, 2012.

26. See ICESCR, Article 2(1).

27. See, for example, Dambisa Moyo, *Dead Aid: Why Aid Is Not Working and How There Is a Better Way for Africa* (New York: Farrar, Straus, and Giroux, 2009).

28. Kwabena Gyimah-Brempong, "Researching Military Expenditures in Africa: Findings and Lessons for Researchers" (Solna, Sweden: Stockholm International Peace Research Institute, May 6, 2002).

29. The United Nations (through its Statistics Division), as well as the World Bank and International Monetary Fund, use the informal categories of "developed" and "developing" to group countries. These are loosely based on levels of income, industrial standards, and ranking on the Human Development Index, but there is no universal standard for classifying countries. The "least-developed" countries are those at the bottom of these rankings.

30. William Easterly, *The White Man's Burden* (New York: Penguin, 2006), p. 11.

31. Ibid., p. 44.

32. Peter Boone, "Politics and the Effectiveness of Foreign Aid," Discussion Paper no. 272 (London: London School of Economics, Centre for Economic Performance, December 1995).

33. This is known as "Dutch disease," in reference to the failure of natural gas reserves in the Netherlands to stimulate economic growth following their discovery in 1959.

34. For an argument to this effect, see Garrett Hardin, "Lifeboat Ethics: The Case Against Helping the Poor," *Psychology Today,* September 1974.

35. Moyo, *Dead Aid.*

36. World Bank, "New Estimates Reveal Drop in Extreme Poverty."

37. United Nations, "Millennium Development Goals: 2012 Progress Chart," http://www.un.org/millenniumgoals/pdf/2012_Progress_E.pdf.

38. OECD, "Net Official Development Assistance from DAC and Other OECD Members in 2011," April 4, 2012, http://www.oecd.org/dac/aidstatistics/50060310 .pdf.

39. Ibid.

40. Ibid.

41. "This Week's Economist/YouGov Poll," *The Economist,* April 7, 2010, http://www.economist.com/blogs/democracyinamerica/2010/04/economistyougov _polling.

Part 4

Conclusion

16

Advancing Human Rights Through Debate

This series of debates has been designed to encourage critical and creative thought about international human rights. You may have learned about certain human rights violations for the first time. Perhaps you began reading this book with strong opinions about an issue like free speech or female circumcision, and those opinions were challenged by reading an opposing perspective. Perhaps your opinions were strengthened by reading the evidence in favor of your own perspective on a particular issue. Or perhaps you discovered a way to integrate aspects of both sides of a debate into an interesting new synthesis.[1] Whatever the outcome, these debates demonstrate that there is more than one reasonable perspective about how human rights are defined and implemented.

The conventional wisdom about the nature of human rights is that they act as a kind of legal and political trump card. In other words, in the midst of cultural differences, power politics, and economic trade-offs, human rights supposedly hold the promise of ending the messy process of deliberation by appealing to a universal, absolute threshold that can never be crossed. According to human rights activists, all government policies will naturally produce a certain amount of good or harm, but there is nothing that can justify violating basic human dignity: some actions are absolutely and always wrong. Thus, for example, most human rights NGOs have denounced any use of torture to interrogate terror suspects, because even if these methods were to be proven effective in stopping future attacks, the Geneva Conventions unequivocally prohibit torture in all circumstances. For groups like Amnesty International, torture crosses the universal threshold that human rights are supposed to provide. Similarly, when President

241

Obama drew a "red line" in 2012 over the use of chemical weapons in Syria's civil war, he was attempting to play the human rights trump card.[2] Although combatants inevitably die in the midst of war, Obama claimed that because chemical weapons indiscriminately kill and injure innocent people, their use can never be justified.

Contrary to the conventional wisdom, this book has shown that an appeal to human rights does not necessarily end political debate or trump other policy considerations. As the examples of torture and chemical weapons demonstrate, when human rights violations are alleged, the actual response to these violations must take into account considerations of national interests, cultural differences, interpretations of international law, the reliability of international institutions, and competing rights claims. Even in supposedly unambiguous cases like the use of torture and chemical weapons, there are no easy solutions that states and international institutions are currently able to impose. Instead of trumping other political concerns, human rights provide a particular kind of argument that can extend or reframe a political controversy. By making a human rights claim, activists are attempting to place basic human dignity at the center of these policy debates. This does not end debate, but it does provide an important tool for political activists trying to influence the policymaking process.

The debates throughout this book have been waged on a variety of different battlegrounds. Some debates include a significant philosophical and cultural element, exposing disagreements about what human rights really are, who should have them, and how they should be delineated. For example, Chapter 1 outlined different approaches to justifying why humans should have universal rights. Chapter 10 asked whether human rights should apply to fetuses, and Chapter 11 examined whether female circumcision is a human rights violation or simply a cultural practice that offends Westerners. The debates on economic and social rights explored how these rights might be balanced against competing rights claims. These debates point to the fact that the boundaries of what we call "human rights" are still shifting and open to interpretation.

Other debates are primarily legal and political, as various interpretations of international law or competing political interests vie to determine how human rights are actually enforced. For example, in what circumstances does national censorship of free speech constitute a violation of international law? Even if Western states agree that China is abusing its citizens' rights, should they respond with coercive measures that pressure it to stop? Are international institutions effective in enforcing human rights law? Should the United States potentially threaten its national interests by joining the International Criminal Court or ceasing torture of terror suspects? Even in cases where we might gain consensus on the philosophical questions (for example, if we agree that torture is always a human rights violation), there are still no easy answers about how to enforce these norms.

At this point, you may be tempted to respond to these controversies with a sense of cynical resignation. If human rights fail to provide a trump card in policy deliberations, and each side has compelling arguments in the debates that ensue, why enter the debates in the first place? If ongoing debate is inevitable, and political interests are always part of the calculus, is true progress on human rights even possible? Perhaps the best outcome we can expect is for human rights to occasionally coincide with the self-interests of the most powerful states, as the realists argue. For example, the international slave trade ended only when Britain, the most powerful state in the eighteenth century, determined that it had a domestic interest in compelling other states to end the practice.[3] Similarly, one might hope that the United States continues on the path of global hegemony, since the United States has both the power, and occasionally the motivation, to intervene on behalf of human rights around the world. In this scenario, arguing on behalf of human rights would have little benefit, other than to serve as a pretext for powerful states to pursue their self-interests.

However, the history of human rights does not lend itself to such a cynical interpretation. Despite the fact that Western powers have implemented human rights inconsistently and hypocritically, human rights have made unmistakable progress over the past century. International pressure to end the racist system of apartheid in South Africa was led by transnational organizations and small states, and only later joined by the United States.[4] Key reforms such as the abolition of the death penalty, criminal accountability for human rights violators, and the protection of LGBT rights are expanding despite, and not because of, the support of the current global hegemon. Advances in the legal and practical protection of economic and social rights have been led by countries of the global South, despite the US government's active opposition to these rights. In the twenty-first century, human rights are a central part of the most important political debates around the world, and power politics cannot explain this phenomenon by itself.

Constructivists offer an alternative explanation for the historical progress that human rights have achieved, and the debates contained in this book play a central role in their account. For constructivists, politics is inherently a battle of ideas, rather than simply a competition over interests and resources. This battle of ideas takes place through political dialogue and debate, and over time some ideas simply win out. According to Thomas Risse, argumentation is key to the spread of human rights, because international politics is characterized by "truth-seeking" behavior as much as it is by power and self-interests.[5] When social activists and policymakers are able to engage in open debate, this allows for the better argument to win in the long run. Although powerful states are sometimes able to ignore compelling arguments in favor of their self-interests, power politics plays a lesser role in human rights because states have tied themselves to a wide array of human rights treaties. By publicly committing themselves to protect human rights, states have forced themselves to justify their behavior in these terms, opening themselves up to debate and argumentation.

Thus, in the constructivist view of the world, engaging in these debates is crucial to the advancement of human rights. This is especially true in democracies, which have institutionalized the right to free speech, open access to information, and the right to protest, which are prerequisites to a fair debate. Recall that Britain ultimately committed itself to ending the slave trade in the eighteenth century not because of its economic or geopolitical interests, but because activists such as William Wilberforce successfully engaged in parliamentary debate about the moral evil of slavery. Wilberforce's arguments were reinforced by a growing antislavery movement among the British population, which ensured that this debate could receive a fair hearing and not be ignored by powerful interests. The combination of grassroots protests and open debate has led to similar advances throughout recent history, in women's rights, labor rights, disability rights, LGBT rights, civil rights, and much more.

Arguing and organizing on behalf of human rights is important not only in democracies, but also across the planet. As the world has become more globally integrated over the past few decades, it has created new opportunities for debate to cross national borders.[6] Increasingly, people across all societies are able to exchange ideas and social values, which has facilitated global debates about human rights. The spread of transnational advocacy networks—groups of activists united across national borders for a single cause—has forced states and powerful interests across the world to justify their actions in terms of human rights.[7] Human rights have become the universal moral language that activists use to evaluate the actions of governments.

This does not mean that power is rendered irrelevant, or that progress for human rights (however defined) is inevitable. Many roadblocks still stand in the way of progress. It simply means that any future advancement in human rights depends critically on people engaging in the kind of debates examined here, and creating space for the better argument to win.

Notes

1. The process of using debate to reach an integrative new idea is often referred to as "Hegelian dialectics." See Gustav E. Mueller, "The Hegel Legend of Thesis-Antithesis-Synthesis," *Journal of the History of Ideas* 19, no. 3 (1958): 411–414.

2. See White House, "Remarks by the President to the White House Press Corps," August 20, 2012, http://www.whitehouse.gov/the-press-office/2012/08/20/remarks-president-white-house-press-corps.

3. Stephen Krasner, *Sovereignty: Organized Hypocrisy* (Princeton: Princeton University Press, 1999), pp. 106–109.

4. Audie Klotz, "Norms Reconstituting Interests: Global Racial Equality and U.S. Sanctions Against South Africa," *International Organization* 49, no. 3 (1995): 451–478.

5. Thomas Risse, "'Let's Argue': Communicative Action in World Politics," *International Organization* 54, no. 1 (2000): 1–39.

6. Ibid., p. 20.

7. Margaret E. Keck and Kathryn Sikkink, *Activists Beyond Borders: Advocacy Networks in International Politics* (Ithaca: Cornell University Press, 1998).

Glossary

absolute poverty. The level of poverty at which people struggle to meet their basic survival needs.

Abu Ghraib. Prison in Iraq that became notorious worldwide when it was discovered in 2004 that US personnel had committed abuses against the prisoners held there.

Affordable Care Act. Legislation passed by the US Congress in 2010 that expands government-subsidized health care for low-income populations.

Alien Tort Claims Act. Part of the US Judiciary Act of 1789 that allows US courts to hear human rights–based cases that occur outside the United States.

American Civil Liberties Union (ACLU). Nongovernmental organization founded in 1920 that seeks to protect and promote the individual liberties guaranteed under the US Constitution.

American exceptionalism. The idea that, because the United States is a world superpower with an exemplary national legal system, it is inherently different from other states and cannot be held to the same rules and procedures of international law.

Amnesty International. Independent, international nongovernmental organization created in 1961 that campaigns for the worldwide protection of human rights as enumerated in the Universal Declaration of Human Rights.

Asian values. Set of cultural standards put forth by Asian leaders asserting that people living in Asian cultures follow a unique set of values different from those in the West.

asylum. Protection or refuge given by a foreign nation to a person or group of people fleeing their home country because of a well-founded fear of persecution.

Bangkok Declaration. Declaration put forth by Asian governments in 1993 asserting the importance of Asian values and national sovereignty.

basic rights. According to Henry Shue, basic rights are those rights that are foundational to the exercise of other rights. Basic rights include subsistence rights and personal security rights.

bilateral aid. Foreign aid given by a government directly to a recipient country.

Bush Doctrine. US policy approach followed by the post–September 11, 2001, administration of George W. Bush that pushed for the aggressive pursuit of terrorists and state sponsors of terrorism, sometimes at the expense of violating human rights.

247

CIA black sites. Top-secret Central Intelligence Agency facilities used to detain terror suspects outside the United States; accused of engaging in torture and other rights abuses.

civil and political rights. Class of rights guaranteeing an individual the freedom to participate in civil and political life, such as freedom of speech and universal suffrage.

Code of Hammurabi. Legal code put forward by the Babylonian king Hammurabi in 1772 B.C.E. Considered one of the first written constitutions, it granted some of his subjects a handful of rights.

collective enforcement. Method used to hold states accountable to treaties that they are party to, by which the other state parties collectively impose diplomatic, economic, and military sanctions for noncompliance.

collectivism. The notion that a person's duty to family and society takes precedence over a person's individual autonomy.

command liability. The idea that leaders who order human rights abuses are just as criminally responsible as the soldiers who carry out those orders.

community-based organizations. Grassroots organizations of individuals that provide local services and advocacy.

community health workers. Members of poor communities, usually in developing countries, who are trained to provide basic health care.

complementarity. A principle by which the International Criminal Court claims jurisdiction over a case only when it is determined that national courts are unable or unwilling to provide a fair trial.

confrontation. An approach to human rights enforcement that relies on coercive measures, such as diplomatic threats, economic sanctions, and military force.

constructivism. International relations theory claiming that people and states are motivated by their ideas, which give actors their interests in a given situation.

Convention Against Torture. Treaty signed in 1984 that established freedom from torture as a nonderogable right. Ratified by 154 states as of 2013.

Convention on the Elimination of All Forms of Discrimination Against Women (CEDAW). Treaty signed in 1979 that grants women specific protections under international law on the assumption that women are vulnerable to specific kinds of abuses. Ratified by 187 states as of 2013.

Convention on the Rights of the Child. Treaty signed in 1989 that outlines the rights of all people younger than age eighteen. Ratified by 193 states as of 2013.

corporate social responsibility. Voluntary commitments made by private corporations to respect human rights and the environment in their business practices.

crimes against humanity. Grave affronts to human dignity that are committed as part of a widespread attack or systematic policy.

cultural relativism. The notion that human rights cannot be universally applied to all people because different cultures have different values and beliefs.

Defamation of Religion. Controversial resolution passed annually by various United Nations committees until 2011, decrying the stereotyping, intolerance, and discrimination against religions, specifically Islam.

dependency theory. Theory claiming that the rules that govern economic globalization are unfair, allowing the rich and powerful countries to exploit the weak and poor.

economic, social, and cultural rights. Class of rights guaranteeing an individual access to the socioeconomic means necessary to a dignified life, such as food, housing, and health care.

engagement. Method of human rights implementation that increases involvement with a human rights violator with the intention of encouraging reform through the exchange of ideas and norms.

enhanced interrogation. Interrogation techniques authorized by the post–September 11, 2001, administration of George W. Bush that went beyond those outlined in the US Army Field Manual to include waterboarding, sleep and sensory deprivation, exposure to hypothermia, and stress positions.

essentialism. Philosophical justification for human rights claiming that all humans share innate characteristics that provide them with dignity and rights.

extraordinary rendition. The act of transferring detainees across national borders without judicial oversight.

fair trade. Policies that support businesses whose primary purpose is to improve the livelihoods of their workers, producers, and the environment.

female circumcision. A cultural practice common in sub-Saharan Africa and the Middle East that involves the removal, in part or in whole, of the external female genitalia. Also known as female genital mutilation or female genital cutting.

freedom of speech. The right of people to publicly express their opinions without fear of government censorship.

Geneva Conventions. Series of treaties, agreed on by virtually all states, governing the treatment of prisoners of war, noncombatants, and sick and wounded soldiers during war.

genocide. The deliberate and systematic attempt to destroy, in whole or in part, a racial, political, or cultural group.

Global Fund to Fight AIDS, Tuberculosis, and Malaria. International organization founded in 2002 that provides funding for programs that combat the spread of AIDS, tuberculosis, and malaria.

green revolution. The spread of industrial agricultural technologies, including high-yielding seeds, pesticides, and fertilizers, to developing countries beginning in the 1960s.

greenwashing. Marketing strategy by which companies portray questionable activities as environmentally friendly in order to increase their profits.

Guantanamo Bay. US naval base located in Guantanamo Bay, Cuba, that has been used since September 11, 2001, to detain and interrogate suspects in the war on terrorism.

habeas corpus. Legal principle that guarantees a prisoner the right to be brought before a judge and confront the evidence against them.

hate crime. A crime motivated by prejudice or bias against a group of people.

hate speech. Any speech that attacks a person or group of people based on their membership in a particular racial, sexual, ethnic, religious, or political group.

Human Rights Watch. Independent, international nongovernmental organization founded in 1978 that investigates and advocates for human rights worldwide.

human trafficking. The illegal transfer of humans usually for commercial purposes such as sexual slavery, forced labor, or the harvesting of organs.

humanitarian intervention. The use of military force against a state with the ostensible goal of advancing human rights and protecting civilians in that state.

hybrid courts. Court system composed of a mixture of national and international elements.

inalienable. The principle that human rights are inherent to being human, and can never be lost for any reason.

individual accountability. The norm that individual human rights violators should be held criminally accountable for their actions, rather than the states that they represent.

individualism. The notion that a person's individual autonomy takes precedence over a person's duty to family and society.

indivisible. The principle that all human rights are equally important to the achievement of human dignity and thus that no one right should be given priority over others.

industrial food system. Global agricultural system based on large corporations using industrial technologies to produce large quantities of single crops of food.

intergovernmental organizations (IGOs). Organizations whose membership is composed of states, based on treaties or agreements.

International Court of Justice (ICJ). Judicial body of the United Nations that arbitrates disputes that are voluntarily submitted by the states involved, and provides legal advice and opinions to the UN General Assembly and other agencies.

International Covenant on Civil and Political Rights (ICCPR). Treaty signed in 1966 that establishes the civil and political rights of all individuals, such as freedom of speech, the right to life, due process, and political participation. Ratified by 167 states as of 2013.

International Covenant on Economic, Social, and Cultural Rights (ICESCR). Treaty signed in 1966 that outlines the economic, social, and cultural rights of all people, such as food, housing, education, and health care. Ratified by 161 states as of 2013.

International Criminal Court (ICC). Created by the Rome Statute in 2002, the ICC is the first permanent international court designed to prosecute individuals for human rights violations, specifically genocide, war crimes, and crimes against humanity.

International Criminal Tribunal for Rwanda (ICTR). Ad hoc tribunal established by the United Nations to prosecute crimes committed during the 1994 genocide in Rwanda.

International Criminal Tribunal for the former Yugoslavia (ICTY). Ad hoc tribunal established by the United Nations to prosecute crimes committed during the wars in the former Yugoslavia in the 1990s.

international humanitarian law. Body of international law, governing armed conflict, that seeks to minimize the destructive effects of war.

International Labour Organization (ILO). Founded in 1919 to protect and promote workers' rights and encourage fair working conditions. Became the first United Nations specialized agency in 1946.

International Monetary Fund (IMF). International organization founded in 1945 that provides loans to governments to promote financial stability and economic growth. Membership comprises 188 countries as of 2013.

jus cogens. Legal principle that certain values in international law cannot, under any circumstances, be disregarded by any state.

Just War doctrine. Set of military ethics that outline the criteria to determine when the use of force is justified. The international community has largely agreed that these criteria must be met in order to invoke the Responsibility to Protect doctrine.

League of Democracies. An alternate mechanism of human rights enforcement proposed by John McCain. This league would be composed of self-selected, "like-minded" democracies that would theoretically be more fit to judge human rights abuses than is the United Nations Human Rights Council.

legal positivism. Philosophical position claiming that rights are not inherent and are only real when they are granted by law and enacted and enforced by a government.

lese majeste laws. Laws restricting speech that defames or criticizes a ruling sovereign or state leader.

liberalism. International relations theory based on the primacy of individual freedom and the ability of states to cooperate peacefully through trade, democracy, and international institutions.

Magna Carta. The charter forced on King John of England in 1215 delineating the civil and political rights of the English nobility and wealthy landowners.

Military Commissions Act. US law passed in 2006 that tried to suspend certain legal rights of enemy combatants such as the right to habeas corpus.

Millennium Development Goals (MDGs). Set of eight development goals that 189 countries pledged in 2000 to achieve by 2015, such as reducing poverty by half, halting the spread of HIV/AIDS, and decreasing maternal mortality rates.

modernization theory. Theory claiming that societies evolve internally as they develop, such that industrialization, urbanization, economic liberalization, and civil and political rights tend to advance alongside one another.

multilateral aid. Aid provided by a group of countries, or by an organization representing a group of countries.

naming and shaming. Confrontational tactic used to raise awareness and opposition against human rights abusers in order to pressure them to reform, most commonly used by nongovernmental organizations and intergovernmental organizations.

natural law. Philosophical position claiming that human rights are inherent because humans are the only creatures who have the ability to reason and free choice.

negative rights. According to Isaiah Berlin, negative rights are those rights that are fulfilled by governments and individuals refraining from taking any action, such as freedom of speech and freedom from torture.

neoliberalism. Set of economic policies that focus on increasing the role of free markets, deregulation, and privatization, and decreasing the authority of government over economic policy.

nonderogable. The principle that certain rights cannot be violated under any circumstances whatsoever, even in times of emergency.

non-essentialism. Philosophical position claiming that rights are not an essential or inherent characteristic of being human, but rather are created by humans based on a social process.

nongovernmental organizations (NGOs). Private independent organizations created by individuals that provide services or conduct legal and political advocacy.

North Atlantic Treaty Organization (NATO). Alliance of twenty-eight states from North America and Europe, founded in 1949, to provide its members with a system of collective security following World War II.

Organization for Economic Cooperation and Development (OECD). International organization composed of thirty-four states, founded in 1961, to promote economic progress and international trade.

Organization of the Islamic Conference. Organization of fifty-six Islamic states, founded in 1969, that work together to foster Muslim solidarity and protect their interests.

Ottawa Treaty. Treaty drafted in 1997 that attempts to eliminate the use of landmines. Ratified by 161 states as of 2013.

Patriot Act. Post–September 11, 2001, legislation granting the US government greater power to gather intelligence, regulate financial transactions, and secure the country's borders.

personhood amendments. Amendments of US state constitutions that define legal personhood as beginning at the moment of conception, in an attempt to make abortion illegal.

positive rights. According to Isaiah Berlin, positive rights are those rights that require action on the part of the government or other actors in order to be fulfilled, such as the rights to food, housing, and health care.

proportionality. One of the six criteria for military intervention outlined in the Responsibility to Protect doctrine, requiring that the scale and intensity of military force should be the minimum necessary to accomplish humanitarian goals.

race to the bottom. According to dependency theory, the process by which economic globalization has forced developing countries to continuously lower their labor and environmental standards in order to compete with one another.

ratification. The final stage in a state's acceptance of a treaty, making the treaty legally binding upon that state.

realism. International relations theory claiming that individuals and states constantly struggle for power in order to achieve their self-interests.

relative poverty. The condition when a group's standard of living is lower than the average standard of living in their society.

Responsibility to Protect (R2P). Nonbinding doctrine, adopted by member states of the United Nations in 2005, that redefines state sovereignty by giving the international community the responsibility to intervene when a state is unwilling or unable to stop atrocities against its own citizens.

rights-based approach to development. Concept of development that focuses on using aid to empower the poorest people within a society, as opposed to focusing exclusively on economic growth.

Rome Statute. Treaty, effective in 2002, that established the International Criminal Court.

rule of law. The principle that all people and institutions are subject to the laws of the land, which are enforced through an independent judiciary.

social constructivism. Philosophical position claiming that rights are not inherent, but are based on norms to which people implicitly or explicitly consent.

social contract. The idea that, according to natural law, rational and free-thinking individuals will choose a social order that protects their rights.

sovereign immunity. The long-held norm that sovereigns and leaders should be immune from prosecution in order to maintain political stability.

Special Court for Sierra Leone. Hybrid court established to try offenses that occurred during the civil war in Sierra Leone after 1996.

Special Rapporteurs. Independent experts employed by the United Nations Human Rights Council to report on specific human rights abuses.

spiral model. Theory claiming that states entrap themselves by making public commitments to human rights, thereby leading to a spiral of increasing enforcement and socialization of human rights norms.

tied aid. Foreign aid that is provided under the condition that the recipient spends a proportion of the aid on goods and services produced in the donor's country.

time, place, and manner (TPM) restrictions. Legal restrictions on freedom of speech that limit the time, place, and manner of a protest in the interest of public order.

Tobin tax. Proposed tax on all international financial transactions with the aim of stabilizing currency values and raising revenue to meet development goals.

transitional justice. The process by which states attempt to redress human rights violations by providing mechanisms for accountability.

transnational advocacy networks. Decentralized groups of activists and nongovernmental organizations united across national borders to advocate for a single cause.

transnational corporations (TNCs). Large corporations, such as Walmart and Chevron, that operate in multiple countries. Also known as multinational corporations (MNCs).

TRIPS (Trade Related Aspects of Intellectual Property Rights) Agreement. Agreement administered by the World Trade Organization, effective as of 1996, according to which states promise to respect the patents held by individuals and corporations in other states. Ratified by 158 states as of 2013.

truth commissions. Mechanism of transitional justice according to which human rights violations are publicly acknowledged by the state, but violators are typically not criminally prosecuted.

Truth and Reconciliation Commission (TRC). Truth commission established in post-apartheid South Africa to allow perpetrators the option to publicly confess their crimes in exchange for amnesty.

United Nations Commission on Human Rights. Intergovernmental body that monitored and reported on human rights abuses from 1946 until 2006, when it was replaced by the UN Human Rights Council.

United Nations High Commissioner for Human Rights. Agency responsible for coordinating human rights policy among the many agencies and committees in the UN system.

United Nations Human Rights Council (UNHRC). Intergovernmental body within the United Nations whose purpose is to monitor and report on human rights violations around the world, and make recommendations for their improvement. Replaced the UN Commission on Human Rights in 2006.

United Nations Security Council. Charged with the maintenance of international peace and security, this is the only mechanism in the UN system that has military enforcement capability.

universal. The notion that, by virtue of our common humanity, all humans share the same rights regardless of cultural background.

Universal Declaration of Human Rights (UDHR). Nonbinding resolution adopted by the United Nations in 1948 as the first internationally agreed set of human rights, serving as the basis for international human rights law.

universal jurisdiction. Legal principle asserting that a state or international organization can claim jurisdiction over certain heinous crimes regardless of where the crime was committed or the nationalities of the parties involved.

Universal Periodic Review. Mechanism of the United Nations Human Rights Council that requires every state to report annually on its human rights performance.

viability. The point at which a fetus is able to sustain itself outside the mother's body.

victor's justice. The situation whereby the victor of a conflict doles out justice by prosecuting the crimes committed by enemies and not by allies.

Vienna Convention on Consular Relations. Treaty signed in 1963 that established a framework for consular relations between countries, providing certain rights for suspects accused of committing crimes abroad.

war crimes. Acts carried out as part of a military campaign that violates international humanitarian law.

waterboarding. Method of torture used post–September 11, 2001, as part of the George W. Bush administration's "enhanced interrogation" program, that involved pouring water over a prisoner's face to simulate drowning.

World Bank. International financial institution established in 1944 that provides long-term loans to developing countries to finance specific development projects. Membership comprises 188 countries as of 2013.

World Health Organization (WHO). International organization established in 1948 under the auspices of the United Nations to monitor and improve international public health.

World Trade Organization (WTO). International organization established in 1995 to increase free trade among countries by institutionalizing a set of global rules for trade. Membership comprises 159 states as of 2013.

Bibliography

Abrams, Floyd. "Citizens United and Its Critics." *Yale Law Journal Online,* September 29, 2010. http://yalelawjournal.org/the-yale-law-journal-pocket-part/constitutional -law/citizens-united-and-its-critics.

Achbar, Mark, and Peter Wintonick. *Manufacturing Consent: Noam Chomsky and the Media.* Zeitgeist Films, 2002.

"Africa: House Calls and Health Care." *PBS Now,* September 11, 2009. http://www .pbs.org/now/shows/537/transcript.html.

Ailslieger, Kristafer. "Why the United States Should Be Wary of the International Criminal Court: Concerns over Sovereignty and Constitutional Guarantees." *Washburn Law Journal* 39, no. 1 (1999): 80–105.

Alanis, Mark C., and Richard S. Lucidi. "Neonatal Circumcision: A Review of the World's Oldest and Most Controversial Operation." *Obstetrical and Gynecological Survey* 59, no. 5 (May 2004): 379–395.

Albon, Chris R. "The Libyan No-Fly Zone Debate: A Cheat Sheet." *UN Dispatch,* March 7, 2011. http://www.undispatch.com/the-libyan-no-fly-zone-debate-a-cheat-sheet.

Alston, Philip. "Reconceiving the UN Human Rights Regime: Challenges Confronting the New UN Human Rights Council." *Melbourne Journal of International Law* 7, no. 1 (2006): 185–224.

———. "U.S. Ratification of the Covenant on Economic, Social, and Cultural Rights: The Need for an Entirely New Strategy." *American Journal of International Law* 84, no. 2 (1990): 383.

Althaus, Frances A. "Female Circumcision: Rite of Passage or Violation of Rights?" *International Family Planning Perspectives* 23, no. 3 (September 1997): 130–133.

American Civil Liberties Union. "Secret Service Ordered Local Police to Restrict Anti-Bush Protestors at Rallies, ACLU Charges in Unprecedented Nationwide Lawsuit." September 23, 2003. http://www.aclu.org/free-speech/secret-service-ordered-local -police-restrict-anti-bush-protesters-rallies-aclu-charges-u.

Amnesty International. "Death Sentences and Executions in 2011." March 2012. http://www.amnesty.org/en/library/info/ACT50/001/2012/en.

———. "Economic, Social, and Cultural Rights: Questions and Answers." 1998. http:// www.amnestyusa.org/pdfs/escr_qa.pdf.

———. "Libya Human Rights." http://www.amnestyusa.org/our-work/countries/middle
-east-and-north-africa/libya, accessed June 26, 2012.

———. "What Is Female Genital Mutilation?" September 30, 1997. http://www.amnesty
.org/en/library/info/ACT77/006/1997.

Anderson, Kenneth. "The Case for Drones." *Commentary,* June 2013.

"Anti-Gay Preachers Banned from UK." *BBC News,* February 19, 2009. http://news.bbc
.co.uk/2/hi/uk_news/england/hampshire/7898972.stm.

Anunias, Patrus. "Implementing the Human Right to Food in Brazil." *World Hunger Notes,* February 8, 2009. http://www.worldhunger.org/articles/08/hrf/ananias.htm.

"Arson and Death Threats as Muhammad Caricature Controversy Escalates." *Spiegel Online,* February 4, 2006. http://www.spiegel.de/international/cartoon-violence
-spreads-arson-and-death-threats-as-muhammad-caricature-controversy-escalates
-a-399177.html.

Avert. "HIV and AIDS in Brazil." http://www.avert.org/aids-brazil.htm#contentTable1, accessed July 25, 2012.

———. "HIV and AIDS in South Africa." http://www.avert.org/aidssouthafrica.htm
#contentTable5, accessed July 25, 2012.

———. "Universal Access to AIDS Treatment: Targets and Challenges." http://www.avert.org/universal-access.htm#contentTable0, accessed July 24, 2012.

Ba, Alice, and Matthew J. Hoffman. "Making and Remaking the World for IR 101: A Resource for Teaching Social Constructivism in Introductory Classes." *International Studies Perspectives* 4, no. 1 (March 2003): 15–33.

Baker, Bruce. "Twilight of Impunity for Africa's Presidential Criminals." *Third World Quarterly* 25, no. 8 (2004): 1487–1499.

Bauer, Joanne. "Business and Human Rights: An Interview with Joanne Bauer." University of Navarre, IESE Business School, September 2011. http://www.iese.edu
/es/files/%20La%20vision%20de...%20(inglés)_tcm5-71120.pdf

———. "The Challenge to International Human Rights." In *Constructing Human Rights in the Age of Globalization,* edited by Mahmood Monshipouri et al. Armonk, NY: Sharpe, 2003.

Bauman, Richard A. *Human Rights in Ancient Rome.* London: Routledge, 1999.

Baxi, Upendra. "Human Rights Education: The Promise of the Third Millennium?" December 19, 1995. http://www.pdhre.org/dialogue/third_millenium.html.

Bell, Christine. *Peace Agreements and Human Rights.* Oxford: Oxford University Press, 2003.

Bellamy, Alex J. "Massacres and Morality: Mass Killing in an Age of Civilian Immunity." *Human Rights Quarterly* 34, no. 4 (2012): 927–958.

Bellamy, Alex J., and Paul D. Williams. "The New Politics of Protection? Côte d'Ivoire, Libya, and the Responsibility to Protect." *International Affairs* 87, no. 4 (2011): 825–850.

Bennett, Isabella. "Media Censorship in China." Council on Foreign Relations, March 7, 2011. http://www.cfr.org/china/media-censorship-china/p11515.

Benson, Pam, and Elaine Quijano. "Cheney Says Documents Show Interrogations Prevented Attacks." *CNN,* August 25, 2009. http://edition.cnn.com/2009/POLITICS
/08/25/terror.interrogations.

Berlin, Isaiah. *Four Essays on Liberty.* Oxford: Oxford University Press, 1970.

Berndt, Ernst R., and John A. Hurvitz. "Vaccine Advance Purchase Agreements for Low-Income Countries: Practical Issues." *Health Affairs* 24, no. 3 (May 2005): 653–665.

Bhattacharji, Preeti, and Carin Zissis. "Olympic Pressure on China." Council on Foreign Relations, June 17, 2008. http://www.cfr.org/china/olympic-pressure-china/p13270
#p7.

Boone, Peter. "Politics and the Effectiveness of Foreign Aid." Discussion Paper no. 272. London: London School of Economics, Centre for Economic Performance, December 1995.

Brancati, Dawn, and Jack Snyder. "The Libyan Rebels and Electoral Democracy." *Foreign Affairs,* September 2, 2011. http://www.foreignaffairs.com/articles/68241/dawn-brancati-and-jack-l-snyder/the-libyan-rebels-and-electoral-democracy.

Broder, Samuel. "The Development of Antiretroviral Therapy and Its Impact on the HIV-1/AIDS Pandemic." *Antiviral Research* 85, no. 1 (2009): 1–2.

Burke, Roisin. "Status of Forces Deployed on UN Peacekeeping Missions: Jurisdictional Immunity." *Journal of Conflict and Security Law* 16, no. 1 (2011): 63–104.

Carnegie Endowment for International Peace. "Reframing China Policy: U.S. Engagement and Human Rights in China." Public debate, Washington, DC, March 5, 2007. http://www.carnegieendowment.org/files/cds4_transcript.pdf.

Casey, Lee, and David Rivkin. "The International Criminal Court vs. the American People." Backgrounder no. 1249. Washington, DC: Heritage Foundation, February 5, 1999.

Center for Gender and Refugee Studies. "Fauziya Kassindja and the Struggle for Gender Asylum." http://cgrs.uchastings.edu/about/kasinga.php.

Center for Reproductive Rights. "Female Genital Mutilation (FGM): Legal Prohibitions Worldwide." New York, December 11, 2008.

Central Intelligence Agency. "GDP (Official Exchange Rate)." In *The World Factbook, 2012.* https://www.cia.gov/library/publications/the-world-factbook/fields/2195.html.

Cernansky, Rachel. "Walmart's Human Rights– and Eco-Friendly Jewelry Line Is Neither." *AlterNet,* January 7, 2011. http://www.alternet.org/environment/149453/walmart's_human_rights-_and_eco-friendly_jewelry_line_is_neither?page=1.

Chen, Robert S. "Global Agriculture, Environment, and Hunger: Past, Present, and Future Links." *Environmental Impact Assessment Review* 10, no. 4 (1990): 335–358.

Chen, Shaohua, and Martin Ravallion. "The Developing World Is Poorer Than We Thought, but No Less Successful in the Fight Against Poverty." Washington, DC: World Bank, August 2008.

Chesler, Phyllis. "Ban the Burqa? The Argument in Favor." *Middle East Quarterly* 17, no. 4 (2010): 33–45.

Chetwynd, Eric, Frances Chetwynd, and Bertram Spector. "Corruption and Poverty: A Review of Recent Literature." Washington, DC: Management Systems International, January 2003.

Chong, Daniel. *Freedom from Poverty: NGOs and Human Rights Praxis.* Philadelphia: University of Pennsylvania Press, 2010.

Cohen, Adam. "Why Spewing Hate at Funerals Is Still Free Speech." *Time,* September 29, 2010. http://www.time.com/time/nation/article/0,8599,2022220,00.html.

Cohn, Marjorie. "Under U.S. Law Torture Is Always Illegal." *CounterPunch,* May 8, 2008. http://www.counterpunch.org/2008/05/06/under-u-s-law-torture-is-always-illegal.

Cole, Alison. "A Landmark Decision for International Justice." March 14, 2012. http://www.lubangatrial.org/2012/03/14/a-landmark-decision-for-international-justice/.

Collier, Paul. *The Bottom Billion: Why the Poorest Countries Are Failing and What Can Be Done About It.* Oxford: Oxford University Press, 2007.

Commission for Historical Clarification. *Guatemala: Memory of Silence.* Guatemala City, 1999.

Conway, Gordon. *The Doubly Green Revolution: Food for All in the Twenty-First Century.* New York: Comstock, 1999.

Cook, Rebecca J., and Bernard M. Dickens. "Human Rights Dynamics of Abortion Law Reform." *Human Rights Quarterly* 25, no. 1 (2003): 1–59.

Cortright, David, and George A. Lopez, eds. *Smart Sanctions: Targeting Economic State-craft*. Boulder: Rowman and Littlefield, 2002.

Crook, John R. "State Department Hails U.S. Accomplishments in UN Human Rights Council; United States to Seek Election to Another Term." *American Journal of International Law* 105, no. 3 (2011): 592–594.

Cushman, Tom. *A Matter of Principle: Humanitarian Arguments for the War in Iraq.* Berkeley: University of California Press, 2005.

Davis, Karen, Cathy Schoen, and Kristof Stremikis. "Mirror, Mirror on the Wall: How the Performance of the U.S. Health Care System Compares Internationally, 2010 Update." New York: Commonwealth Fund, June 23, 2010.

Dickinson, Laura A. "The Promise of Hybrid Courts." *American Journal of International Law* 97, no. 2 (April 2003): 295–310.

Dollar, David. "Globalization, Inequality, and Poverty Since 1980." World Bank Development Research Group, November 2001. ftp://www.econ.bgu.ac.il/courses/Globalization_and_Development/Notes/Globalization-inequality-and-poverty.pdf.

Doyle, Michael. "Liberalism and World Politics." *American Political Science Review* 80, no. 4 (1986): 1151–1169.

Dreyfuss, Robert. "Obama's NATO War for Oil in Libya." *The Nation,* August 23, 2011. http://www.thenation.com/blog/162908/obamas-nato-war-oil-libya#.

Dukalskis, Alexander, and Robert C. Johansen. "Measuring Acceptance of International Enforcement of Human Rights: The United States, Asia, and the International Criminal Court." *Human Rights Quarterly* 35, no. 3 (2013): 569–597.

EarthRights International. "The Yadana Pipeline." http://www.earthrights.org/campaigns/yadana-pipeline, accessed July 22, 2012.

Easterly, William. *The White Man's Burden.* New York: Penguin, 2006.

Eide, Asbjørn. "Human Rights Requirements for Social and Economic Development." *Food Policy* 21, no. 1 (1996): 23–39.

Erdman, Joanna N., Teresa DePineres, and Eszter Kismodi. "Updated WHO Guidance on Safe Abortion: Health and Human Rights." *International Journal of Gynecology and Obstetrics* 120 (2003): 200–203.

European Dignity Watch. "No Right to Abortion Under International Law." October 6, 2011. http://www.europeandignitywatch.org/de/day-to-day/detail/article/no-right-to-abortion-under-international-law.html.

Evans, Rebecca. "Pinochet in London, Pinochet in Chile: International and Domestic Politics in Human Rights Policy." *Human Rights Quarterly* 28, no. 1 (2006): 207–244.

Eye on the UN. "Human Rights Actions by the Human Rights Council." http://www.eyeontheun.org/browse-un.asp?ya=1&sa=1&u=344&un_s=0&ul=1&tp=1&tpn=Resolution, accessed June 22, 2012.

Families USA Global Health Initiative. "Fighting the World's Most Devastating Diseases: A Plan for Closing the Research Gap." February 2008. http://www.familiesusa.org/assets/pdfs/closing-research-gap.pdf.

Farmer, Paul. "Global AIDS: New Challenges for Health and Human Rights." *Perspectives in Biology and Medicine* 48, no. 1 (Winter 2005): 10–16.

Fishman, Charles. "The Story of Wal-Mart and Chilean Salmon." *Salon,* January 23, 2006. http://reclaimdemocracy.org/walmart/2006/fishman_chile_salmon_farm.php.

FitzGerald, Garrett. "The Truth Commissions of Guatemala: Pluralism and Particularity Within the Human Rights Paradigm." *Cult/ure* 5 (2010).

Foot, Rosemary. "Exceptionalism Again: The Bush Administration, the 'Global War on Terror,' and Human Rights." *Law and History Review* 26, no. 3 (2008): 707–725.

Forbarth, William. "Cultural Transformation, Deep Institutional Reform, and ESR Practice: South Africa's Treatment Action Campaign." In *Stones of Hope: How African*

Activists Reclaim Human Rights to Challenge Global Poverty, edited by Lucie E. White and Jeremy Perelman. Palo Alto: Stanford University Press, 2010.

Forsythe, David. *Human Rights in International Relations.* Cambridge: Cambridge University Press, 2012.

Fox, John, and François Godement. *A Power Audit of EU-China Relations.* London: European Council on Foreign Relations, 2009.

Fukuyama, Francis. *The End of History and the Last Man.* New York: Free Press, 1992.

Ghosh, Bobby. "A Top Interrogator Who's Against Torture." *Time,* April 24, 2009. http://www.time.com/time/nation/article/0,8599,1893679,00.html.

Gibney, Mark. *Five Uneasy Pieces: American Ethics in a Globalized World.* Boulder: Rowman and Littlefield, 2004.

Glendening, Marc. "Why Is Botswana Behaving As a European Puppet?" London: ICCwatch, March 19, 2010.

Guns, Wendy. "The Influence of the Feminist Anti-Abortion NGOs as Norm Setters at the Level of the UN." *Human Rights Quarterly* 35, no. 3 (2013): 673–700.

Gunther, Marc. "Wal-Mart: A Bully Benefactor." *CNNMoney,* December 5, 2008. http://money.cnn.com/2008/12/02/news/companies/walmart_gunther.fortune/index .htm.

Guo, Sanzhuan. "Implementation of Human Rights Treaties by Chinese Courts: Problems and Prospects." *Chinese Journal of International Law* 8, no. 1 (2009): 161–179.

Guttmacher Institute. "State Policies in Brief: An Overview of Abortion Laws." July 1, 2002. http://www.guttmacher.org/statecenter/spibs/spib_OAL.pdf.

Gyimah-Brempong, Kwabena. "Researching Military Expenditures in Africa: Findings and Lessons for Researchers." Solna, Sweden: Stockholm International Peace Research Institute, May 6, 2002.

Haas, Michael. *International Human Rights: A Comprehensive Introduction.* London: Routledge, 2008.

Hagan, John. "Voices of the Darfur Genocide." *Contexts* 10, no. 3 (Summer 2011): 22–28.

Hardin, Garrett. "Lifeboat Ethics: The Case Against Helping the Poor." *Psychology Today,* September 1974.

Harrelson-Stephens, Julie. "Achieving Human Rights: The Globalization Debate." In *Exploring International Human Rights,* edited by Rhonda L. Callaway and Julie Harrelson-Stephens. Boulder: Lynne Rienner, 2007.

Hawkins, Darren. "Universal Jurisdiction for Human Rights: From Legal Principle to Limited Reality." *Global Governance* 9, no. 3 (2003): 347–365.

Hayner, Priscilla B. *Unspeakable Truths: Transitional Justice and the Challenge of Truth Commissions.* New York: Routledge, 2001.

Heffner, Linda J. "Advanced Maternal Age: How Old Is Too Old?" *New England Journal of Medicine* 351 (November 2004): 1927–1929.

Hehir, Aidan, and Robert Murray, eds. *Libya, the Responsibility to Protect, and the Future of Humanitarian Intervention.* New York: Palgrave Macmillan, 2013.

Henshaw, Stanley K., Susheela Singh, and Taylor Haas. "The Incidence of Abortion Worldwide." *Family Planning Perspectives* 25, supplement (1999): S30–38.

Hentoff, Nat. "President Reagan's Torture Advice to President Obama." Cato Institute, May 20, 2009. http://www.cato.org/publications/commentary/president-reagans -torture-advice-president-obama.

Hertel, Shareen, and Lanse Minkler, eds. *Economic Rights: Conceptual, Measurement, and Policy Issues.* Cambridge: Cambridge University Press, 2007.

Himmelstein, David U., Deborah Thorne, Elizabeth Warren, and Steffie Woolhandler. "Medical Bankruptcy in the United States, 2007: Results of a National Study." *American Journal of Medicine* 122, no. 8 (August 2009): 741–746.

Hopgood, Stephen. *Keepers of the Flame: Understanding Amnesty International.* Ithaca: Cornell University Press, 2006.

Horrigan, Leo, Robert S. Lawrence, and Polly Walker. "How Sustainable Agriculture Can Address the Environmental and Human Health Harms of Industrial Agriculture." *Environmental Health Perspectives* 110, no. 5 (May 2002): 445–456.

Human Rights Office, Archdiocese of Guatemala. *Guatemala, Never Again!* Maryknoll, NY: Orbis, 1999.

Human Rights Watch. "DR Congo: ICC Arrest First Step to Justice." March 18, 2006. http://www.hrw.org/fr/news/2006/03/17/dr-congo-icc-arrest-first-step-justice.

———. *Getting Away with Torture: The Bush Administration and Treatment of Detainees.* New York, July 2011.

———. "Libya: New Era Needs Focus on Rights." October 20, 2011. http://www.hrw.org/news/2011/10/20/libya-new-era-needs-focus-rights.

———. "Libya: Revoke Draconian New Law." May 5, 2012. http://www.hrw.org/news/2012/05/05/libya-revoke-draconian-new-law.

———. "Myths and Facts About the International Criminal Court." http://www.hrw.org/legacy/campaigns/icc/facts.htm, accessed June 20, 2012.

———. "Sri Lanka: Report Fails to Advance Accountability." December 16, 2011. http://www.hrw.org/news/2011/12/16/sri-lanka-report-fails-advance-accountability.

Hunt, Paul. *Reclaiming Social Rights: International and Comparative Perspectives.* Sudbury, MA: Dartmouth Publishing, 1996.

"ICC Acquits Congolese Armed Group Leader." *African Press Organization,* December 18, 2012.

Ignatieff, Michael. *Human Rights as Politics and Idolatry.* Princeton: Princeton University Press, 2001.

"Interior Minister Resigns Rather Than Carry Out Gadhafi Orders." *CNN,* February 22, 2011. http://www.cnn.com/2011/WORLD/africa/02/22/libya.protests/.

International Commission on Intervention and State Sovereignty. *The Responsibility to Protect.* December 2001. http://responsibilitytoprotect.org/ICISS%20Report.pdf.

International Federation for Human Rights. "Bashar al-Assad: Criminal Against Humanity." Report no. 570a. Paris, July 2011.

Ishay, Micheline. *The History of Human Rights: From Ancient Times to the Globalization Era.* Berkeley: University of California Press, 2004.

Joint United Nations Programme on HIV/AIDS (UNAIDS). *World AIDS Day Report 2011.* Geneva.

Jones, Rachel K., and Kathryn Kooistra. "Abortion Incidence and Access to Services in the United States, 2008." *Perspectives on Sexual and Reproductive Health* 43, no. 1 (March 2011): 41–50.

Joseph, Rita. *Human Rights and the Unborn Child.* Leiden: Nijhoff, 2009.

Joseph, Sarah. "Pharmaceutical Corporations and Access to Drugs: The 'Fourth Wave' of Corporate Human Rights Scrutiny." *Human Rights Quarterly* 25, no. 2 (May 2003): 425–452.

Kallen, Evelyn. "Hate on the Net: A Question of Rights/A Question of Power." *Electronic Journal of Sociology* (1998). http://www.sociology.org/content/vol003.002/kallen.html.

Keck, Margaret E., and Kathryn Sikkink. *Activists Beyond Borders: Advocacy Networks in International Politics.* Ithaca: Cornell University Press, 1998.

Kelemen, Michele. "Activist's Escape Complicates Clinton's China Visit." *National Public Radio,* April 30, 2012. http://www.npr.org/2012/04/30/151707162/activists-escape-complicates-clintons-china-visit.

Kelly, Michael J. *Nowhere to Hide: Defeat of the Sovereign Immunity Defense for the Crimes of Genocide and the Trials of Slobodan Milosevic and Saddam Hussein.* New York: Peter Lang, 2005.

Kernigan, Charles. "Sexual Predators and Serial Rapists Run Wild at Wal-Mart Supplier in Jordan." Pittsburgh: Institute for Global Labour and Human Rights, June 2011.

Khan, Huma. "Catholic Church vs. Obama in Election Year Showdown." *ABC News,* January 30, 2012. http://abcnews.go.com/blogs/politics/2012/01/catholic-church -vs-obama-in-election-year-showdown.

Kidder, Tracy. *Mountains Beyond Mountains.* New York: Random, 2003.

Kim, Hunjoon, and Kathryn Sikkink. "Explaining the Deterrence Effect of Human Rights Prosecutions for Transitional Countries." *International Studies Quarterly* 54, no. 4 (2010): 939–963.

Kim, Susanna. "Walmart Cuts Employee Health Benefits." *ABC News,* October 21, 2011. http://abcnews.go.com/blogs/business/2011/10/walmart-cuts-employee-health -care-benefits.

Kindall, Henery W., and David Pementel. "Constraints on the Expansion of the Global Food Supply." *Ambio* 23, no. 3 (May 1994): 198–205.

Klotz, Audie. "Norms Reconstituting Interests: Global Racial Equality and U.S. Sanctions Against South Africa." *International Organization* 49, no. 3 (1995): 451–478.

Krasner, Stephen. *Sovereignty: Organized Hypocrisy.* Princeton: Princeton University Press, 1999.

Kritz, Neil J. "Coming to Terms with Atrocities: A Review of Accountability Mechanisms for Mass Violations of Human Rights." *Law and Contemporary Problems* 59, no. 4 (1997): 127–152.

Krugman, Paul. "In Praise of Cheap Labor: Bad Jobs at Bad Wages Are Better Than No Jobs at All." *Slate,* March 27, 1997. http://www.slate.com/articles/business/the _dismal_science/1997/03/in_praise_of_cheap_labor.html.

Labor and Worklife Program. "Children Found Sewing Clothing for Wal-Mart, Hanes, and Other U.S. and European Companies." Harvard Law School, October 2006. http://www.law.harvard.edu/programs/lwp/NLC_childlabor.html.

Leane, Geoffrey W. G. "Rights of Ethnic Minorities in Liberal Democracies: Has France Gone Too Far in Banning Muslim Women from Wearing the Burka?" *Human Rights Quarterly* 33, no. 4 (2011): 1032–1061.

Lee, Susan J., et al. "Fetal Pain: A Systematic Multidisciplinary Review of the Evidence." *Journal of the American Medical Association* 294, no. 8 (August 2005): 947–954.

Lemarchand, René. "Consociationalism and Power Sharing in Africa: Rwanda, Burundi, and the Democratic Republic of Congo." *African Affairs* 106, no. 422 (January 2007): 1–20.

Li, Yitan, and A. Cooper Drury. "Threatening Sanctions When Engagement Would Be More Effective: Attaining Better Human Rights in China." *International Studies Perspectives* 5, no. 4 (2004): 378–394.

Liese, Bernhard, and Gilles Dussault. "The State of the Health Workforce in Sub-Saharan Africa." Africa Region Human Development Working Paper. Washington, DC: World Bank, September 2004.

Lohn, Martiga. "A Bitter Pill for the WTO." *Mother Jones,* November 9, 2001. http:// www.motherjones.com/politics/2001/11/bitter-pill-wto.

Ludwig King, Elizabeth B. "Amnesties in a Time of Transition." *George Washington International Law Review* 41, no. 3 (2010): 577–618.

MacInnis, Laura. "UN Body Adopts Resolution on Religious Defamation." *Reuters,* March 26, 2009. http://www.reuters.com/article/2009/03/26/us-religion-defamation-idUSTRE52P60220090326.

MacLean, Emi. "Ríos Montt Genocide Trial Confronts Political Push-Back in Guatemala." Open Society Justice Initiative, April 18, 2013. http://www.opensociety foundations.org/voices/rios-montt-genocide-trial-confronts-political-push-back-guatemala.

Mancini, Marina. "A Brand New Definition for the Crime of Aggression: The Kampala Outcome." *Nordic Journal of International Law* 81, no. 2 (2012): 227–248.

Mayer, Jane. "Annals of Justice: Outsourcing Torture." *New Yorker,* February 14, 2005.

Mayerfeld, Jamie. "Who Shall Be Judge? The United States, the International Criminal Court, and the Global Enforcement of Human Rights." *Human Rights Quarterly* 25, no. 1 (February 2003): 93–129.

McCorquodale, Robert, and Richard Fairbrother. "Globalization and Human Rights." In *Exploring International Human Rights,* edited by Rhonda L. Callaway and Julie Harrelson-Stephens. Boulder: Lynne Rienner, 2007.

McCrudden, Christopher, and Brendan O'Leary. *Courts and Consociations: Human Rights Versus Power Sharing.* Oxford: Oxford University Press, 2013.

McMahon, Edward, and Marta Ascherio. "A Step Ahead in Promoting Human Rights? The Universal Periodic Review of the UN Human Rights Council." *Global Governance* 18, no. 2 (2012): 231–248.

Meckled-García, Saladin, and Başak Çali, eds. *The Legalization of Human Rights.* London: Routledge, 2006.

Mehler, Andreas. "Not Always in the People's Interest: Power-Sharing Agreements in African Peace Agreements." Working Paper no. 83. Hamburg: German Institute of Global and Area Studies, July 2008.

Mertus, Julie. "The New U.S. Human Rights Policy: A Radical Departure." *International Studies Quarterly* 4, no. 4 (November 2003): 371–384.

Miller, Lynn H. "The Contemporary Significance of the Doctrine of Just War." *World Politics* 16, no. 2 (January 1964): 254–286.

Mills, Kurt. "'Bashir Is Dividing Us': Africa and the International Criminal Court." *Human Rights Quarterly* 34, no. 2 (2012): 404–407.

Minkenberg, Michael. "Religion and Public Policy: Institutional, Cultural, and Political Impact on the Shaping of Abortion Policies in Western Democracies." *Comparative Political Studies* 35, no. 2 (2002): 221–247.

Mitchell, Stacy. "Walmart's Greenwash." Institute for Local Self-Reliance, March 2012. http://www.ilsr.org/wp-content/uploads/2012/03/walmart-greenwash-report.pdf.

Moffett, Sebastian. "NATO Underplayed Civilian Deaths in Libya: HRW." *Reuters,* May 14, 2012. http://news.yahoo.com/nato-underplayed-civilian-deaths-libya-hrw-0407 10456.html.

Momoh, Comfort, ed. *Female Genital Mutilation.* Abingdon: Radcliffe, 2005.

Morgenthau, Hans. *Politics Among Nations: The Struggle for Power and Peace.* New York: Knopf, 1948.

Morison, Linda, et al. "The Long Term Reproductive Health Consequences of Female Genital Cutting in Rural Gambia: A Community Based Survey." *Tropical Medicine and International Health* 6, no. 8 (August 2001): 643–653.

"Moroccan Jailed for King Insult." *BBC News,* October 27, 2008. http://news.bbc.co .uk/2/hi/africa/7693988.stm.

Morsink, Johannes. *The Universal Declaration of Human Rights: Origins, Drafting, and Intent.* Philadelphia: University of Pennsylvania Press, 1999.

Moyn, Samuel. *The Last Utopia: Human Rights in History.* Cambridge: Harvard University Press, 2010.

Moyo, Dambisa. *Dead Aid: Why Aid Is Not Working and How There Is a Better Way for Africa*. New York: Farrar, Straus, and Giroux, 2009.

Mueller, Gustav E. "The Hegel Legend of Thesis-Antithesis-Synthesis." *Journal of the History of Ideas* 19, no. 3 (1958): 411–414.

National Abortion Federation. "History of Abortion." http://www.prochoice.org/about _abortion/history_abortion.html, accessed July 16, 2012.

Neier, Aryeh. *The International Human Rights Movement: A History*. Princeton: Princeton University Press, 2013.

———. "Perspectives on Economic, Social, and Cultural Rights." Lecture at the Washington College of Law, American University, Washington, DC, January 19, 2006.

Nelson, Paul J., and Ellen Dorsey. *New Rights Advocacy: Changing Strategies of Development and Human Rights NGOs*. Washington, DC: Georgetown University Press, 2008.

Ngwena, Charles G. "Inscribing Abortion as a Human Right: Significance of the Protocol on the Rights of Women in Africa." *Human Rights Quarterly* 32, no. 4 (2010): 783–864.

Nichols Haddad, Heidi. "Mobilizing the Will to Prosecute: Crimes of Rape at the Yugoslav and Rwandan Tribunals." *Human Rights Review* 12 (2011): 109–132.

Noll, Christian. "The Betrayed: An Exploration of the Acholi Opinion of the International Criminal Court." *Journal of Third World Studies* 26, no. 1 (2009): 99–119.

Nunn, Amy. *The Politics and History of AIDS Treatment in Brazil*. New York: Springer, 2009.

Olarn, Kocha. "American Gets 2.5 Years for Insulting Thai Monarchy." *CNN*, December 8, 2011. http://www.cnn.com/2011/12/08/world/asia/thailand-american-insults/index.html.

Olsen, Tricia D., Leigh A. Payne, and Andrew G. Reiter. "The Justice Balance: When Transitional Justice Improves Human Rights and Democracy." *Human Rights Quarterly* 32, no. 4 (2010): 980–1007.

Orentlicher, Diane F. "Settling Accounts: The Duty to Prosecute Human Rights Violations of a Prior Regime." *Yale Law Journal* 100, no. 8 (1991): 2537–2615.

Organization for Economic Cooperation and Development. "DAC1 Official and Private Flows." http://stats.oecd.org/Index.aspx?DatasetCode=TABLE1, accessed July 27, 2012.

———. "History of the 0.7% ODA Target." June 2010. http://www.oecd.org/dac/stats /45539274.pdf.

———. "Net Official Development Assistance from DAC and Other OECD Members in 2011." April 4, 2012. http://www.oecd.org/dac/aidstatistics/50060310.pdf.

Pati, Roza. *Due Process and International Terrorism*. Leiden: Nijhoff, 2009.

Paul, Ron. "A Court of No Authority." April 8, 2002. http://www.rumormillnews .com/cgi-bin/archive.cgi?read=18922, accessed September 22, 2013.

Peterson, Jeremy. "Unpacking Show Trials: Situating the Trial of Saddam Hussein." *Harvard International Law Journal* 48, no. 1 (2007): 257–292.

Pier, Carol. "Discounting Rights: Wal-Mart's Violation of US Workers' Right to Freedom of Association." Human Rights Watch, May 1, 2007. http://www.hrw.org/reports /2007/04/30/discounting-rights-0.

Pigott, Robert. "Amnesty Ends Abortion Neutrality." *BBC News*, August 18, 2007. http://news.bbc.co.uk/2/hi/americas/6952558.stm.

Pogge, Thomas. "Human Rights and Global Health: A Research Program." *Metaphilosophy* 36, no. 2 (January 2005): 182–209.

———. *World Poverty and Human Rights: Cosmopolitan Responsibilities and Reforms*. Cambridge: Polity, 2002.

Potter, Deborah. "Indecent Oversight." *American Journalism Review* 26, no. 4 (September 2004): 80.

Power, Samantha. "Bystanders to Genocide." *The Atlantic,* September 2001.

Przeworski, Adam, and Fernando Limongi. "Modernization: Theories and Facts." *World Politics* 49, no. 2 (1997): 155–183.

Pugliese, Joseph. "Prosthetics of Law and the Anomic Violence of Drones." *Griffith Law Review* 20, no. 4 (2011): 931–961.

Radelet, Steven. "A Primer on Foreign Aid." Working Paper no. 92. Washington, DC: Center for Global Development, July 2006.

Rahman, Anika, and Nahid Toubia. *Female Genital Mutilation: A Guide to Laws and Policies Worldwide.* London: Zed, 2000.

Rayner, Moira. "History of Universal Human Rights—Up to WW2." December 3, 2005. http://www.universalrights.net/main/histof.htm.

Reagan, Ronald. "Farewell Address to the Nation." January 11, 1989. http://www.reagan foundation.org/pdf/Farewell_Address_011189.pdf.

Real Clear Politics. "Obama: Guantanamo Bay Is a Recruiting Tool for al Qaeda." September 10, 2010. http://www.realclearpolitics.com/video/2010/09/10/obama _guantanamo_bay_is_a_recruiting_tool_for_al-qaeda.html.

"Report: 108 Died in U.S. Custody." *CBS News,* February 11, 2009. http://www.cbs news.com/2100–224_162–680658.html.

Report of the Chilean National Commission on Truth and Reconciliation. Notre Dame, IN: University of Notre Dame Press, 1993.

Reporters Without Borders. "Press Freedom Index 2011/2012." January 25, 2012. http://en.rsf.org/press-freedom-index-2011-2012,1043.html.

Rhem, Kathleen T. "New Guantanamo Facility Safer for Guards, More Comfortable for Detainees." *American Forces Press Service,* January 11, 2007. http://www.defense .gov/news/newsarticle.aspx?id=2665.

Risse, Thomas. "'Let's Argue': Communicative Action in World Politics." *International Organization* 54, no. 1 (2000): 1–39.

Risse, Thomas, and Kathryn Sikkink. "The Socialization of International Human Rights Norms into Domestic Practice: Introduction." In *The Power of Human Rights: International Norms and Domestic Change,* edited by Thomas Risse, Stephen C. Ropp, and Kathryn Sikkink. Cambridge: Cambridge University Press, 1999.

Rosenfeld, Eli. "The Human Rights Council One Year On: Are We Any Better Off?" Report from a discussion hosted by the Century Foundation, Open Society Institute, and Friedrich Ebert Foundation, June 19, 2007. http://tcf.org/events/2007/ev188.

Roth, Kenneth. "Defending Economic, Social, and Cultural Rights: Practical Issues Faced by an International Human Rights Organization." *Human Rights Quarterly* 26, no. 1 (2004): 63–73.

———. "Was the War in Iraq a Humanitarian Intervention?" *Journal of Military Ethics* 5, no. 2 (2006): 84–92.

Ruggie, John. "Protect, Respect, and Remedy: A Framework for Business and Human Rights." UN Human Rights Council, April 7, 2008. http://www2.ohchr.org/english /bodies/hrcouncil/docs/8session/A-HRC-8-5.doc.

Sachs, Jeffrey. *The End of Poverty: Economic Possibilities for Our Time.* New York: Penguin, 2005.

Schofield, Philip. "Jeremy Bentham's 'Nonsense on Stilts.'" *Utilitas* 15 (2003): 1–26.

Sen, Amartya. *Development as Freedom.* New York: Knopf, 1999.

Sen, Gita. "Poverty as a Gendered Experience: The Policy Implications." *Poverty in Focus* 13 (January 2008): 6–7.

Serwer, Adam. "The Great Libya-Shariah Freakout of 2011." *Mother Jones,* October 26, 2011. http://www.motherjones.com/mojo/2011/10/great-libya-shariah-freakout -2011.

Shalev, Carmel. "Rights to Sexual and Reproductive Health: The ICPD and the Convention on the Elimination of All Forms of Discrimination Against Women." *Health and Human Rights* 4, no. 2 (2000): 38–66.

Shue, Henry. *Basic Rights*. Princeton: Princeton University Press, 1996.

Sikkink, Kathryn. *The Justice Cascade: How Human Rights Prosecutions Are Changing World Politics*. New York: Norton, 2011.

Silverman, Jon. "Ten Years, $900 Million, One Verdict: Does the ICC Cost Too Much?" *BBC News,* March 14, 2012. http://www.bbc.co.uk/news/magazine-17351946.

Singer, Peter. *Animal Liberation*. London: Pimlico, 1975.

Slack, Alison T. "Female Circumcision: A Critical Appraisal." *Human Rights Quarterly* 10, no. 4 (1988): 437–486.

Southern Poverty Law Center. "Westboro Baptist Church." http://www.splcenter.org/get -informed/intelligence-files/groups/westboro-baptist-church, accessed July 12, 2012.

Sowell, Thomas. "Poverty and Inequality: A Question of Injustice?" *The Economist,* March 11, 2004. http://www.economist.com/opinion/displayStory.cfm?story_id =2499118.

Sterio, Milena. "The United States' Use of Drones in the War on Terror: The (Il)Legality of Targeted Killings Under International Law." *Case Western Reserve Journal of International Law* 45, nos. 1–2 (Fall 2012): 197–214.

Sussman, Dalia. "Poll: Abortion Support Conditional." *ABC News,* January 22, 2003. http://abcnews.go.com/US/story?id=90413&page=1.

"This Week's Economist/YouGov Poll." *The Economist,* April 7, 2010. http://www .economist.com/blogs/democracyinamerica/2010/04/economistyougov_polling.

Tobin, James. "A Proposal for International Monetary Reform." *Eastern Economic Journal* 4, nos. 3–4 (July–October 1978): 153–159.

Tomaselli, Keyan G. "(Re)Mediatizing HIV/AIDS in South Africa." *Cultural Studies, Critical Methodologies* 9, no. 4 (June 2009): 570–587.

Toubia, Nahid. *Female Genital Mutilation: A Global Call to Action*. Berkeley: Women Ink, 1993.

Trotta, Daniel. "Iraq War Hits U.S. Economy: Nobel Winner." *Reuters,* March 2, 2008.

Truth and Reconciliation Commission. *Witness to Truth: Report of the Sierra Leone Truth and Reconciliation Commission*. Cape Town, 2004.

Turack, Daniel C. "Ending Impunity in Africa: The Charles Taylor Trial at the Special Court for Sierra Leone." *Journal of Third World Studies* 26, no. 2 (2009): 191–202.

UK Department for International Development. "Girls' Education: Toward a Better Future for All." London, January 2005.

Ulfstein, Geir, and Hege Fosund Christiansen. "The Legality of the NATO Bombing in Libya." *International and Comparative Law Quarterly* 62, no. 1 (2013): 159–171.

Umar, Muhammed Suyel. "Image of God: A Note on the Scriptural Anthropology." *Journal of Scriptural Reasoning* 4, no. 2 (October 2004).

UNAIDS, HIV Vaccines, and Microbicides Resource Tracking Working Group. "Tracking Funding for Preventive HIV Vaccine Research & Development." June 2005. http://data.unaids.org/una-docs/vaccinestrackingfundingjune2005_report_en .pdf

UNI Global Union. "UNI Calls on Walmart to End Debt Bondage in Thailand." May 15, 2012. http://www.uniglobalunion.org/Apps/UNINews.nsf/vwLkpById/E04FE 63DF1BC8639C12579FF00429D1D.

United Nations. "Convention on the Elimination of All Forms of Discrimination Against Women." *United Nations Treaty Collection.* http://treaties.un.org/Pages/View Details.aspx?src=TREATY&mtdsg_no=IV-8&chapter=4&lang=en, accessed July 17, 2012.

———. "Despite Gains, Bulk of World's Poor Live in Rural Areas, UN Report Finds." December 6, 2010. http://www.un.org/apps/news/story.asp?NewsID=36967&Cr =rural&Cr1.

———. "International Covenant on Civil and Political Rights." *United Nations Treaty Collection.* http://treaties.un.org/Pages/ViewDetails.aspx?src=TREATY&mtdsg_no =IV-4&chapter=4&lang=en, accessed July 13, 2012.

———. "Millennium Development Goals: 2012 Progress Chart." http://www.un.org /millenniumgoals/pdf/2012_Progress_E.pdf.

United Nations Department of Economic and Social Affairs. "World Abortion Policies 2007." New York, April 2007.

United Nations Fourth World Conference on Women. "Platform for Action." Beijing, September 1995.

United Nations High Commissioner for Human Rights. "Human Rights Dimensions of Poverty." *UNHCHR Online.* http://www.ohchr.org/english/issues/poverty/index .htm, accessed December 1, 2005.

United Nations International Conference on Population and Development. "Summary of the Programme of Action." Cairo, March 1995.

United Nations News Centre. "In Historic Vote, General Assembly Creates New Human Rights Council." March 15, 2006. http://www.un.org/apps/news/story.asp?News ID=17811&Cr=rights&Cr1=council.

United Nations Office of the High Commissioner for Human Rights. "Background Information on the Human Rights Council." http://www.ohchr.org/EN/HRBodies /HRC/Pages/AboutCouncil.aspx, accessed June 22, 2012.

———. "Human Rights Bodies." http://www.ohchr.org/EN/HRBodies/Pages/Human RightsBodies.aspx, accessed June 22, 2012.

"U.S. and Coalition Casualties." *CNN,* http://www.cnn.com/SPECIALS/war.casualties /table.iraq.html.

US-China Business Council. "U.S.-China Trade Statistics and China's World Trade Statistics." https://www.uschina.org/statistics/tradetable.html, accessed June 13, 2012.

US Department of State. *American Service-Members' Protection Act.* June 30, 2003. http://www.state.gov/t/pm/rls/othr/misc/23425.htm.

Valenzuela, J. Samuel, and Arturo Valenzuela. "Modernization and Dependency: Alternative Perspectives in the Study of Latin American Underdevelopment." *Comparative Politics* 10, no. 4 (July 1978): 535–557.

van der Schyff, Gerhard, and Adriaan Overbeeke. "Exercising Religious Freedom in the Public Space: A Comparative and European Convention Analysis of General Burqa Bans." *European Constitutional Law Review* 7, no. 3 (2011): 424–452.

"Vice President Tells West Point Cadets That 'Bush Doctrine' Is Serious." *American Forces Press Service,* June 2, 2003. http://www.defense.gov/news/newsarticle .aspx?id=28921.

Vriens, Lauren. "Troubles Plague UN Human Rights Council." Council on Foreign Relations, May 13, 2009. http://www.cfr.org/un/troubles-plague-un-human-rights -council/p9991.

Weber, Max. *Politics as a Vocation.* Minneapolis: Fortress, 2000.

Weiss, Thomas G. "RtoP Alive and Well After Libya." *Ethics and International Affairs* 25, no. 3 (2011): 287–292.

Wendt, Alexander. *Social Theory of International Politics.* Cambridge: Cambridge University Press, 1999.

West, Eleanor T. "World Voices: The Libya Debate." *World Policy* Blog, March 23, 2011. http://www.worldpolicy.org/blog/2011/03/23/worldvoices-libya-debate.

Whelan, Daniel. *Indivisible Human Rights: A History.* Philadelphia: University of Pennsylvania Press, 2010.

Whelan, Daniel, and Jack Donnelly. "The Reality of Western Support for Economic and Social Rights: A Reply to Susan L. Kang." *Human Rights Quarterly* 31, no. 4 (2009): 1030–1054.

White, Lucie E., and Jeremy Perelman, eds. *Stones of Hope: How African Activists Reclaim Human Rights to Challenge Global Poverty.* Palo Alto: Stanford University Press, 2011.

White House. "Remarks by the President to the White House Press Corps." August 20, 2012. http://www.whitehouse.gov/the-press-office/2012/08/20/remarks-president-white-house-press-corps.

Williams, Ian. "Applying 'Responsibility to Protect' to Syria No Cakewalk." *Washington Report on Middle East Affairs* 31, no. 4 (2012): 35–36.

Williams, Linda A. "Eradicating Female Circumcision: Human Rights and Cultural Values." *Health Care Analysis* 6 (1998): 33–35.

Wilson, Richard Ashby, ed. *Human Rights in the War on Terror.* Cambridge: Cambridge University Press, 2005.

Wolff, Jonathan. *The Human Right to Health.* New York: Norton, 2012.

World Bank. "New Estimates Reveal Drop in Extreme Poverty, 2005–2010." February 29, 2012. http://go.worldbank.org/4K0EJIDFA0.

World Health Organization. "Female Genital Mutilation." Fact Sheet no. 241. February 2012. http://female circumcision.who.int/mediacentre/factsheets/fs241/en/index.html.

———. "The Top Ten Causes of Death." Fact Sheet no. 310. February 2007. http://www.who.int/mediacentre/factsheets/fs310/en/.

———. "WHO Takes Major Steps to Make HIV Treatment Accessible." April 22, 2002. http://www.who.int/mediacentre/news/releases/release28/en/index.html.

World Trade Organization. "Pharmaceutical Patents and the TRIPS Agreement." September 21, 2006. https://www.wto.org/english/tratop_e/trips_e/pharma_ato186_e.htm.

Yip, Winnie Chi-Man, et al. "Early Appraisal of China's Huge and Complex Health Care Reforms." *The Lancet* 379, no. 9818 (March 2012): 833–842.

Yoo, John. *The Powers of War and Peace: The Constitution and Foreign Affairs After 9/11.* Chicago: University of Chicago Press, 2006.

Zifcak, Spencer. "The Responsibility to Protect After Libya and Syria." *Melbourne Journal of International Law* 13, no. 1 (2012): 9–93.

Index

About the Book

Even as human rights provide the most widely shared moral language of our time, they also spark highly contested debates among scholars and policymakers. When should states protect human rights? Does the global war on terrorism require restriction of rights? Are food, housing, and health care valid human rights? *Debating Human Rights* introduces the theory and practice of international human rights by examining fourteen controversies in the field.

Daniel Chong presents the major arguments on both sides of each debate, encouraging readers to think critically and form their own opinions. Designed for classroom use, the structure of the book makes it easy for students to become familiar with the major political and legal actors in the global human rights system and to understand the practical challenges of protecting civil, political, social, and economic rights.

Daniel P. L. Chong is associate professor of political science at Rollins College. He is author of *Freedom from Poverty: NGOs and Human Rights Praxis*.